Electra

AFTER FREUD

A volume in the series

Cornell Studies in the History of Psychiatry

edited by
Sander L. Gilman
George J. Makari

A full list of titles in the series appears at the end of the book.

Electra

AFTER FREUD

Myth and Culture

JILL SCOTT

CORNELL UNIVERSITY PRESS

ITHACA AND LONDON

Grateful acknowledgement is made to New Directions Publishing Corporation for permission to quote from H.D.'s *Collected Poems, 1912–1944* (© 1925 by Hilda Doolittle; © 1957, 1969 by Norman Holmes Pearson, © 1982 by the Estate of Hilda Doolittle; © 1983 by Perdita Schaffner); to Faber and Faber Limited Publishers and to HarperCollins Publishers Inc. for permission to quote from Sylvia Plath's *Collected Poems* (© 1960, 1965, 1971, 1981, 1989 by the Estate of Sylvia Plath; © 1981 by Faber and Faber Limited; editorial material copyright © 1981 by Ted Hughes); to Alfred A. Knopf, a division of Random House, Inc., for permission to quote from *The Colossus and Other Poems* by Sylvia Plath, copyright © 1962 by Sylvia Plath; to Calder Publications for permission to reprint the musical examples from Christopher Wintle's article "Elektra and the 'Electra-complex,'" in the *English National Opera Guide: Salome/Elektra* (copyright © Calder Publications / Riverrun Press 2004); and to the Office of Research Services, Queen's University, for financial assistance for the permissions fees.

First published 2005 by Cornell University Press

Printed in the United States of America

Design by Scott Levine

Library of Congress Cataloging-in-Publication Data
Scott, Jill, 1968–
    Electra after Freud : myth and culture / Jill Scott.
        p.   cm. — (Cornell studies in the history of psychiatry)
    Includes bibliographical references and index.
    ISBN 0-8014-4261-3 (alk. paper)
    1. German literature—19th century—History and criticism.   2. German literature—20th century—History and criticism.   3. Electra (Greek mythology) in literature.   4. Psychoanalysis in literature.   I. Title.   II. Series.
    PT345.S356 2005
    830.9'351—dc22

                                                                        2004023502

Cornell University Press strives to use environmentally responsible suppliers and materials to the fullest extent possible in the publishing of its books. Such materials include vegetable-based, low-VOC inks and acid-free papers that are recycled, totally chlorine-free, or partly composed of nonwood fibers. For further information, visit our website at www.cornellpress.cornell.edu.

Cloth printing   10 9 8 7 6 5 4 3 2 1

Contents

*Im Jahrhundert des Orest und der
Elektra, das heraufkommt,
wird Ödipus eine Komödie sein.*

HEINER MÜLLER

*Tu devrais savoir que tout homme
un peu lucide finit un jour
ou l'autre par n'aimer qu'Électre.*

MARGUERITE YOURCENAR

Acknowledgments

I owe a debt of gratitude to Electra for her enigmatic being that inspired me to explore her intricate contours over and over again, for being patient with my musings, for simply being in all her terrifying beauty. Electra is of course not the only one who has journeyed with me throughout the writing of this book. I have had the privilege of being guided by several gifted and extremely generous scholars: Inge Stephan, who sparked my mythic imagination during a seminar at the Humboldt University in Berlin; Linda Hutcheon, my mentor at the University of Toronto, who spurred me on with her undying enthusiasm, encouragement, wise counsel, and good humor; and Sander Gilman, my postdoctoral adviser at the University of Chicago, who helped me to take the project to a new level and who supported the book as editor of the History of Psychiatry series at Cornell University Press. My heartfelt thanks go to all of you. I would like to express my appreciation for the hard work and dedication of the editors at Cornell University Press and for the helpful comments of the anonymous reviewer. Financial aid for the research and writing of this book came from doctoral and postdoctoral fellowships from the Social Sciences and Humanities Council of Canada.

Intellectual companionship buoyed me along the way, and I would especially like to thank my friends and colleagues at the Centre for Comparative Literature at the University of Toronto, the German departments at the University of Toronto, Queen's University, and the University of Chicago, and "Team Tristan." For many inspiring conversations, critical insights and clerical help at various stages of the project, I thank Joanna Bottenberg, Marie Carrière, Caryl Clark, Taïna Tuhkunen-Couzic, Gus

Dierick, Petra Fachinger, Anita George, Shawna Kaufman, Heather Murray, Erika Reiman, Minoo Roshan, and Marc-Oliver Schuster.

My deepest gratitude goes to my family, who from day one encouraged me to pursue my passions as each one of them has pursued his or her own. Your love and support have helped me reach higher than I ever dreamed. Last and most important, I would like to dedicate *Electra after Freud* to Stephen Oikawa for making each day one in which miracles can happen.

* * *

I am grateful for permission to reprint two previously published articles. An earlier version of chapter 4 appeared as "Choreographing a Cure: Strauss's *Elektra*, the Waltz, and Modern Dance" in *Seminar* 38 (3) (September 2002): 226–40, and parts of chapter 5 were published as "Oedipus Endangered: Atrean Incest and Ethical Relations in Musil's *Der Mann ohne Eigenschaften*" in *Writing the Austrian Traditions: Relations between Philosophy and Literature*, ed. Wolfgang Huemer and Marc-Oliver Schuster (Edmonton: Wirth-Institute for Austrian and Central European Studies, University of Alberta, 2003), 160–180.

Unless otherwise indicated, all translations are my own.

Electra

AFTER FREUD

Introduction

WHOSE CENTURY? ELECTRA VERSUS OEDIPUS

Does the twentieth century belong to Oedipus or to Electra? Oedipus, it would seem, is the everyman of human psychological development, an archetype, an icon, a bastion of Western collective mythology. His story is so well known that it hardly requires repeating: The myth of Oedipus stages the son as hero who usurps power and privilege from the father and inherits the authority of the ancestral patriarchal lineage. Freud (1905) claims that the legend of King Oedipus from classical antiquity has universal validity and maintains that "every new arrival on this planet is faced by the task of mastering the Oedipus complex; anyone failing to do so falls victim to neurosis" (226).

Electra's story is equally compelling, essentially a tale of murder, revenge, and violence. In the ancient myth of Atreus, Agamemnon returns home from battle and receives no hero's welcome, no reward for his efforts on behalf of his nation. Instead, he is greeted with an ax, murdered in his bath by his wife, Clytemnestra, and her lover-accomplice, Aegisthus. Electra chooses anger over sorrow and stops at nothing to ensure that her mother pays. In revenge, Electra, with the help of her brother, orchestrates a brutal and bloody matricide, and her reward is the restitution of her father's good name. Amid all this chaos, Electra, Agamemnon's princess daughter, must bear the humiliation of being treated as a slave girl and labeled a madwoman.

Her blatant violence and aggression initiate a shift in gender relations, accroaching the role once reserved for male heroes alone. Unlike that of Oedipus, Electra's story is not obsessed with power—rather her part in the cruel murder throws the mythic cosmos off kilter, wreaking havoc on the ordered world of Mycenae. A powerful legend in antiquity, its relevance and resonance have not diminished over time.

Electra after Freud advances the thesis that Electra poses a threat to the primacy of Freud's oedipal model as a central trope of the modernist literary imagination. Though the stain of this master narrative appears to seep to the very core of cultural consciousness, the proliferation of Electra adaptations in twentieth-century drama, prose, and poetry undermines the privilege of the oedipal model. The readings of several pivotal Electra texts offered here demonstrate that the myth of the mourning princess daughter stages a narrative revolt against the psychological autocracy of Oedipus. The myth of Atreus is reevaluated in light of Freudian psychoanalysis with a focus on three central and recurring tropes: hysteria, death, and mourning. My concern is to highlight significant turning points in the production and reception of the myth in German and Anglo-American texts. To incorporate the close readings necessary for this type of analysis, the scope of this book has been limited to a few key works, each of which aptly demonstrates the trajectory of Electra's story in the course of a century saturated with the pervasive paradigm of Freudian psychoanalysis. Covering a wide range of genres and periods, the book devotes chapters to Hugo von Hofmannsthal's *Elektra* and Richard Strauss's operatic adaptation of this work, Robert Musil's *The Man without Qualities*, Heiner Müller's *Hamletmaschine*, and the poetry of H.D. and Sylvia Plath.

The choice of texts for this study, which, with the exception of the work of two women poets, consist of canonical works by male, Western writers, grew out of my interest in tracing a particular Germanic and Anglo-American reception of psychoanalysis in the myth of Electra. This focus means that important works from other traditions, for example Sartre's *Les Mouches* or Pérez Galdós's *Electra*, are not included. Nor have I been able to treat the distinct trajectory of the myth of Electra in film or the visual arts. The myth has been shown to have enduring relevance for times of revolt, and there are countless examples of adaptations of Electra's story mapped onto particular historical and political events, such as Athol Fugard's 1971 *Orestes*, which speaks to a specific event of racial conflict in apartheid South Africa. These are all fascinating aspects of the myth's reception, but it would require several book-length works to consider the plethora of texts and contexts.

To articulate my points about Electra and the narrative revolt against Oedipus, I engage with Freud's early works on hysteria and sexuality but also with the cultural theories of Johann Jacob Bachofen and Walter Benjamin, the philosophy of Ernst Mach, and the feminist psychoanalytic theories of Julia Kristeva and Melanie Klein. Few thinkers have had as lasting and significant an influence on our cultural consciousness as Freud—after all, have not terms such as the unconscious, repression, talking cure, slip of the tongue, and free association become part of our lexicon? In spite of or perhaps because of his contributions to culture and the history of ideas, Freud has been the subject of unprecedented controversy and debate. Freud brought this on himself, one might say, by deliberately staging his work in popular venues—he wrote introductions and summaries of his papers for a general audience and gave frequent public lectures. His legacy has caused no end of furor, perhaps best characterized by the postponement of the Freud exhibit, appropriately titled "Sigmund Freud: Conflict and Culture," scheduled to open at the Library of Congress in the fall of 1996.[1] In the 1980s and '90s, Freud received a great deal of negative criticism from scholars in many disciplines, but the media was equally skeptical—a 1992 *Time Magazine* article asked, "Is Freud Finished?"

Led by French feminists such as Luce Irigaray, Julia Kristeva, and Hélène Cixous and followed by Jane Gallop, Shoshana Felman, and Alice Jardine, among others, feminist theorists find psychoanalysis and specifically the arena of sexual difference important for their arguments, but they cannot accept Freud's discriminatory and ill-conceived theories of female sexuality. Other critics suggest that Freud never had any credence and was from the beginning nothing but a fraud. Frederick Crews (2003) is one of the most vocal critics in this camp: "Historians and philosophers have shown that Freud's 'findings' were coerced, muddled, and unsupported except by his own self-flattering anecdotes; that psychoanalytic inquiry, with its question-begging concepts, its open-ended rules of interpretation, and its inadequate precautions against suggestion, is always fatally circular" (615). Meanwhile, John Horgan's 1996 *Scientific American* article "Why Freud Isn't Dead" makes the argument that the persistence of psychoanalysis is a testimony to the failure of modern science to explain the mind.

My purpose in *Electra after Freud* is not to establish whether Freudian psychoanalysis has any merit as a clinical or theoretical paradigm but rather to acknowledge its influence in shaping a collective psyche in Western cultures and to track the enormous impact of psychoanalysis

1. For a full review of this debate, see Crews 1995.

on the cultural imagination of writers and theorists across continents and generations. Freud should not be excused for his shortcomings, nor should he be hailed as a hero; he should be read in context. David S. Luft (2003) suggests that "the principal problem with our understanding of Freud is that we remember virtually nothing else from the culture that produced him" (xi), a problem this book attempts to rectify by reading Freud against distinctly German and Austrian authors and thinkers. If nothing else, Freud was a revolutionary and a provocateur. We should not forget, for example, that the very act of inviting young women to speak openly about their experiences of mistreatment and abuse was radical in every way. He may have bungled the analysis, but Freud took risks merely by listening to women and taking seriously what they had to say as an integral component of their treatment. Freud shocked the medical establishment but also shook society as a whole by rethinking its most valued institution: the patriarchal family.

I seek neither to pass judgment—although I do adopt a critical standpoint—nor to heap praise but to treat Freud and psychoanalysis as a historical phenomenon worthy of close scrutiny. It is quite possible, after all, that without the backdrop of psychoanalysis and its focus on the myth of Oedipus, we would not have seen the renaissance of Electra adaptations in the twentieth century. Thus, it seems appropriate to consider the Greek myth of Atreus in its specific intersections with Freudian psychoanalysis and its aftermath.

With the aim of treating literature as cultural artifact, I consider the texts and authors included in this book in the specificity of a historical and cultural context, where reception is as important as production. Situating the Electra myth within a theoretical and cultural framework of psychoanalysis, medicine, and performance art (opera and dance), I investigate the mythological heroine's role at the intersections of history and the feminine, *eros* and *thanatos*, hysteria and melancholia.

"Oedipus will be a joke ..."

The Austrian novelist Robert Musil, best known for his voluminous masterpiece *The Man without Qualities*, jokingly remarks that the modern age has become dangerously dependent upon Oedipus: "One might indeed say that hardly anything is possible today without Oedipus, not family life and not architecture" (Musil 1998, 323).[2]

---

2. "Man darf wohl sagen, daß ohne Oedipus heute so gut wie nichts möglich ist, nicht das Familienleben und nicht die Baukunst" (Musil 1955c, 502).

With the wry humor that typifies his prose, Musil seeks in his 1931 essay "Oedipus Endangered" to undermine the cultlike status of Freud's mythical model. He is skeptical of the empirical methods of psychoanalysis, which he views as nothing more than a pseudoscience that promotes an extreme and socially debilitating narcissism. The respected novelist parts company with Freud over the fundamental issue of biology and refutes the somatic essentialism of the oedipal model. Musil provokes the ire of the psychoanalytical establishment with his bold prediction that despite his clout and current popularity, Oedipus will not last long: "As far as I know the previously mentioned Oedipus complex stands today more than ever at the center of theoretical thought. Almost all phenomena are adduced to it, and I am afraid that after another generation or two there will no longer be an Oedipus!" (325).[3] In the place once occupied by Freud's model son, Musil positions the myth of Electra and asks: "Will we get an Orestes instead of an Oedipus?" (325).[4]

Another prominent contemporary of Freud's, the Austrian writer Arthur Schnitzler, dared to criticize the Oedipus complex: "Precisely by generalizing its theories, for example, the Oedipus complex, psychoanalysis reduces their significance. If it is really the fate of every person to love his mother and hate his father, then this circumstance is a phenomenon of evolution, like all others, . . . and becomes uninteresting" (quoted in Luprecht 1991, 127). Schnitzler, like Freud, was a bourgeois intellectual, a Jew, and a trained physician. In fact, the two men had so much in common that in a letter commemorating Schnitzler's sixtieth birthday, Freud (2000b, 652) called him his double. Freud (2000a, 651) also expressed envy toward the writer who seemed to have "secret knowledge" of psychological phenomena that demanded "laborious research" on the part of the analyst. This is a rare acknowledgment from Freud that narrative is a suitable medium for the exploration of matters of the psyche—science it is not, but he does admit that fiction often gets it right.

Even Hofmannsthal sees more potential in Electra than in Oedipus when it comes to capturing the essence of "being,"[5] writing in his own notes: "The Alcestis and Oedipus theme sublimated in the

---

3. "Soviel ich weiß, steht heute der vorhin erwähnte Oedipuskomplex mehr denn je im Mittelpunkt der Theorie; fast alle Erscheinungen warden auf ihn zurückgeführt, und ich befürchte, daß es nach ein bis zwei Menschenfolgen keinen Oedipus mehr geben wird!" (Musil 1955c, 502).
4. "Werden wir statt des Oedipus einen Orestes bekommen?" (Musil 1955c, 504).
5. "das Sein."

'Elektra'" (1959b, 217).⁶ Hofmannsthal did write two Oedipus dramas, *Ödipus und die Sphinx* (1906) and *König Ödipus* (1907), but neither of these had the kind of impact that *Electra* had and were rarely produced. Electra, in Hofmannsthal's view, surpasses Oedipus when it comes to establishing what he calls "The Truth . . . , which is the source of all life" (217).⁷

These writers are not alone in questioning the primacy of Freud's archetypal son. Heiner Müller, the former East Germany's most outspoken playwright and poet, also suggests Oedipus's reign may be shortlived: "In the century of Orestes and Electra that is unfolding, Oedipus will be a comedy" (1996, 16). Müller objects to Freud's model of masculinity on the grounds that the Oedipus complex provides a simple framework for the passing down of power and property from one generation to another. This model perpetuates patriarchal regimes and ignores the crimes of history. Müller calls for the scrutiny of all fathers vis-à-vis their past actions: "A dead father might have been a better father. Best of all is a father born dead" (1992, 78). Oedipus, in Müller's view, was right to murder his own father, but his crime is the guilt he feels. Instead of wallowing in shame, he should stamp out the reign of fathers for good.

Aware that the vacuum created when one paradigm is toppled needs to be filled by another, Müller, like Musil, chooses Electra to succeed Oedipus. The playwright makes good on his promise to oust the incestuous son in his 1977 play *Hamletmaschine*, in which an insipid oedipal Hamlet abdicates in favor of a cruel and capable Elektra figure. His Elektra is a fresh alternative to the masculine model of modernity. Unlike Oedipus, who wanders like a sleepwalker into his fate and commits his acts unknowingly, this Elektra is conscious of her task and goes about murder with a will. This book presents the argument that it is no mere coincidence that both Musil and Müller plan to have Electra displace Oedipus from the mythic throne but rather that these authors' statements speak to a larger phenomenon.

Electra and the "Complex"

The ominous prediction that Oedipus will soon be extinct, coupled with the proliferation of Electra adaptations in twentieth-century narrative, prompts the question why this century is so obsessed with the

---

6. "Das Alkestis- und Ödipus-Thema sublimiert in der 'Elektra'"
7. "Die Treue . . . , die der Halt von allem Leben ist."

myth of Atreus. An extremely popular figure in Attic tragedy, Electra was largely ignored by authors in subsequent periods. And when she did make an appearance—for example in French classicism with the dramas of Corneille, Voltaire, and Crébillon—it was in the guise of Orestes' helper or Agamemnon's daughter rather than as a heroine in her own right. Like other vengeful women of antiquity such as Medea or Phaedra, the defiant and courageous mythological Electra seems to have been too controversial a figure for audiences and authors alike. And yet the twentieth century embraced her capacity for cruelty and her naked pain, perhaps in an effort to come to terms with the appalling violence in the world around us. But there is more to Electra's resurgence as a dominant trope in Western narrative than the mere fact of her signature characteristics of courage, cleverness, and cruelty. To answer this question more fully, we need to return to the role played by Oedipus.

Introduced in 1900 with Freud's first major publication, *The Interpretation of Dreams*, the Oedipus complex gained notoriety among enthusiasts of psychoanalysis, which was promoted as a revolutionary science of the soul. Oedipus became a paradigm for human sexual and psychological development and provided a universal model for the quintessential journey from infancy to adult masculinity. Oedipus is, however, wholly divorced from the context of Greek tragedy. Like Nietzsche and other modern thinkers, Freud strips the myth of its public and political emphasis and shifts the focus to a moral and intellectual struggle: "to escape a fate and acquire self-knowledge" (Schorske 1980, 199). Freud confines his discussion of Sophocles' *Oedipus Rex* to three scant pages, ending his remarks abruptly with the generalization that "it is the fate of all of us, perhaps, to direct our first sexual impulse towards our mother and our first hatred and our first murderous wish against our father" (1900, 4:262). The complexity of the myth is immediately reduced to a universal archetype, and a masculine one at that.

The Oedipus of Greek mythology is shattered to learn the full extent of his crisis when he discovers that he himself is the criminal he seeks—he is the murderer of Laius, his own father. So, too, Freud's own dreams and his self-analysis reveal him as Oedipus's double, albeit a metaphorical one. So strongly does he identify with Oedipus's plight that he posits it as the root of every family conflict, confiding in a letter to Wilhelm Fliess: "I have found, in my own case too falling in love with the mother and jealousy of the father, and I now regard it a universal event in early childhood. . . . If that is so, we can understand the riveting power of the *Oedipus Rex*" (Freud 1897, 265).

The Oedipus myth constitutes the basis for Freud's theories of taboo, though the legend is distilled to the key elements of patricide, incest, and their repression. Content with his male hero of Greek myth, Freud refuted C. G. Jung's concept of the Electra complex, introduced in 1913, and replaced it with his own term, the female Oedipus complex.[8] At its most basic level, the Electra complex refers to the phenomenon of the little girl's attraction to her father and hostility toward her mother, whom she now sees as her rival. The girl's desire to possess her father is linked to her desire to possess the penis, and the Electra complex is often described as penis envy. The threat of punishment from the mother results, according to Freud, in the repression of these id impulses. Freud even speculates that girls, because they must shift their original object choice, have a less fully developed superego, which regulates values and morality (1931, 230).[9] What is important for our purposes is that the Electra of literature takes on the dimensions of flesh and blood through her actions and interactions with others, offering rich opportunities not available within the pathology of a psychological complex.

The greatest cultural myth surrounding Electra is that there is no Electra complex per se. Jung made only fleeting reference to the complex without ever fully defining or describing it. The very existence of the term may have been an attempt on his part to distance himself from Freud, to stage a subtle critique of the Oedipus complex by suggesting there is a female counterpart. More interesting than the passing references to the Electra complex, whether by Jung or Freud, are the associations and assumptions connected with it and its manifestations as a trope in popular discourse and cultural production, for example Sylvia Plath's now famous statement that her poem "Daddy" is "about a girl with an Electra complex" (1981, 293).

8. Jung does not elaborate on the term Electra complex but simply writes: "The [oedipal] conflict takes on a more masculine and therefore more typical form in a son, whereas a daughter develops a specific liking for the father, with a correspondingly jealous attitude towards her mother. We would call this the Electra complex. As everyone knows, Electra took vengeance on her mother Clytemnestra for murdering her husband Agamemnon and thus robbing her—Electra—of her beloved father" (Jung and Kerényi 1961, 154). Jung makes the same generalizations as does Freud, concluding his discussion of the Oedipus complex with the following: "All of this is true also of the Electra complex" (155). One can see why Freud dismissed Jung's term, for it remains almost entirely undefined.

9. Julia Kristeva (1989) refutes this point by emphasizing the "tremendous psychic, intellectual, and affective effort a woman must make in order to find the other sex as erotic object," a fact that ultimately leads to a "psychic potential greater than what is demanded of the male sex" (30).

Perhaps the most telling aspect of the Electra complex is Freud's silence on the subject. This void in effect relegates female psychological development to a corollary, a mere afterthought to his primary project, and Freud writes in his essay "Female Sexuality" that "we are right in rejecting the term 'Electra complex' which seeks to emphasize the analogy between the attitude of the sexes. It is only in the male child that we find the fateful combination of love for the one parent and simultaneous hatred for the other as a rival" (1931, 229). Freud does not give any serious thought to the shortcomings of the Oedipus complex for female sexual development until the mid-1920s. His dissatisfaction with his female Oedipus complex stems from its failure to work as a convenient mirror image of the male process.

Freud seems puzzled by his own theories of female sexuality, declaring that sexual development in girls is much simpler because they do not experience castration anxiety (1924, 178–179), then later maintaining that the female oedipal stage is more complex because it involves a shift in sexual object, from female (maternal) to male (1925b, 251). Ultimately, this female complex, whether named after Electra or Oedipus, is a prepubescent sexuality and does not persist into adulthood. This means, according to Freud's view, that the appearance of the complex in a mature woman signals a regression. This psychoanalytic framework of Electra and femininity in general is highly problematic and ultimately limiting, and I have therefore chosen to focus my arguments not on the Electra complex but on the manifestations of the mythological character in literary adaptations.

The case Kaja Silverman (2000) makes for a rereading of Freud's Oedipus complex may be useful to illustrate the characteristics of the Electra myth I wish to highlight. She argues that the Oedipus complex constitutes a model for thinking about the self in relation to others. She sees the eroticizing of a particular familial axis as a positive step because "it makes room in our psyche for other people and things" (151). While I agree with Silverman in part, the Oedipus complex is still historically entrenched in a quest to discipline the family into a set of scientifically condoned structures. The Electra myth has all the positive elements Silverman speaks of—the eroticization of the familial axis, the opportunity for encounters with others—but without the normative objectives of the psychoanalytic structures. Kristeva (2000), too, takes sides with Oedipus, claiming that returning to the complex is "not only important but indispensable" (68). She argues that through Oedipus we begin to understand the logic of the desiring subject but adds sev-

eral important caveats that elaborate upon and further Freud's understanding of sexual difference. Unlike the boy, the girl has to shift the
original focus of her libidinal energies away from the mother: "She
must free herself from an 'inverse' desire for the mother before she can
bring her 'direct' incestuous desires to bear on the father (and men).
There is a notable difference" (79).

This "notable difference" that Kristeva and other feminist theorists
stumble over is precisely what Electra offers. The point is not that the
Oedipus complex is of no use from a psychoanalytic perspective but
rather that Electra as a mythological character presents a movement
away from the universal and the masculine, away from the *logic* of the
psyche to the realms of *imagination* and *fiction*. By emphasizing the
myth of Electra in narrative modes (drama, prose, poetry), where she is
free from the static mold of analysis, this book opens up new avenues
for thinking not just about one mythological character but about
human relations in general. Clearly, Electra does not fit easily into any
model, psychoanalytic or otherwise. Electra *is* complex, even if she
does not *have* a complex.

It is perhaps fortuitous that Freud spends little time discussing the
Electra complex. Because Freud deems her unfit to be a model of female development, Electra is spared from becoming an idée fixe. The
mythological heroine does not achieve the fame and independence of
her male counterpart, but Electra is never divorced from her story as is
Oedipus. Moreover, unlike Oedipus, she is not subjected to the analyst's gaze or made to wear the straitjacket of a universal archetype.

Despite the predominant theme of father-son conflict in modernist
narrative and specifically in German Expressionism, the Greek myth of
Oedipus itself does not inspire the writer's imagination in symbolism
and fin-de-siècle decadence. And while Oedipus claims the status of
cultural and psychological imperative, the myth itself is curiously absent as a major theme in literature. Gide, Montherlant, and Cocteau
and Stravinsky all breathe life into Oedipus, but the myth of the murderous, incestuous son does not seem to garner the same enthusiasm
among writers as the Atrean legend.[10] If Oedipus figures highly in the
abstract, theoretical realm of psychoanalysis, Electra is a strong presence in fictional narrative, figuring in many ways as Deleuze and Guattari's anti-Oedipus, other to Freud's complete model of subjectivity.
While his story is entrenched forever as a complex, her story opens up

10. André Gide, *Thésée et Oedipe* (1946), Henri de Montherlant, *La Reine morte* (1947),
Jean Cocteau and Igor Stravinsky, *Oedipus Rex* (1927).

to alternative avenues of discovery and adaptation. Electra is therefore an inviting blank slate.

An Electra for a New Century

Hugo von Hofmannsthal's groundbreaking reinterpretation of Sophocles' *Electra* serves as a platform for subsequent adaptations. This 1903 *Elektra* heralds the new century with a radical deviation from tradition, including the introduction of Freudian hysteria and the heroine's death in an ecstatic *Totentanz*.[11] Hofmannsthal's drama was lauded by audiences and critics alike and was given a promising start when it premiered under the direction of Germany's foremost director, Max Reinhardt, at the prestigious Kleines Theater in Berlin. With the flamboyant and provocative actress Gertrud Eysoldt in the title role, the play brought the house down. But Hofmannsthal's *Elektra* owes its fame mostly to the phenomenal success of Richard Strauss's 1909 operatic version. The influence of this seminal fin-de-siècle work on the subsequent reception of the myth cannot be underestimated. Its notoriety went well beyond the German-speaking world and arguably contributed to the phenomenal range of adaptations by European and North American authors that followed it in quick succession.[12]

The myth of Electra rapidly became a staple of European modernism with adaptations by such celebrated authors as Pérez Galdós

---

11. The full title of Hofmannsthal's play is *Electra. One Act Drama. Free Adaptation of Sophocles (Elektra. Drama in einem Aufzug. Frei nach Sophokles)*. The title alone makes clear that this is a radical deviation from the Greek version, first of all because it shatters the tragic imperative with a one-act play, and second by its indication that it is a free adaptation. Hofmannsthal is at pains to cue his audience not to expect the Greek drama they may know from their school education.

12. Many books document the vast array of modern versions of the myth and provide a survey of numerous examples including drama and prose. The best example of a broad, comprehensive account of the Electra myth is Pierre Brunel's *Le Mythe d'Électre* (1971), which provides a structuralist analysis of the myth with reference to more than twenty dramas from antiquity to the postwar period. Brunel is less concerned with the characterization of Electra than with tracing the formal evolution of the legend. Lois Mary Cech, in "Becoming a Heroine: A Study of the Electra Theme" (1984), considers a vast range of texts from all periods and genres and comes to the conclusion that Electra is limited to a helping role and that "she does not have the personal equipment for a fully heroic and human context" (513). Most recently, Batya Caspar Laks's *Electra: A Gender-Sensitive Study of the Plays Based on the Myth* (1995), drawing on nearly twenty plays to discuss how theater acts as a performance of "mythical deep structure," shows the continued resonance of ritual in dramatic form. She concludes that the myth is essentially about the masculine struggle for control over the maternal and laments "the voiceless nature of women throughout history" (179). The present volume does not aim to provide a survey but attempts instead to address the scholarly lacuna that exists in relation to the reception of Electra and the influence of psychoanalysis.

(1901), D'Annunzio (1927), O'Neill (1939), H.D. (1934), Giraudoux (1937), Eliot (1939), Sartre (1941), Hauptmann (1947), Yourcenar (1949), Pound (1949), Plath (1959), and Fugard (1979), to name only a few. Countless other works—Musil's *The Man without Qualities* (1930–1943) and Heiner Müller's *Hamletmaschine* (1977) are represented in this book—make covert allusions to the Electra myth, and, though not direct adaptations of Attic tragedies, they nonetheless make important contributions to the legend and its reception.

A figurative castration occurs in the late nineteenth and early twentieth centuries as male protagonists are sidelined in the literary and theatrical milieu. Powerful female protagonists eclipse their male counterparts and come to dominate the stages and pages of Europe. Electra is not alone but is one among many strong and formidable female figures. Salome, Lulu, Nora, and Hedda are all part of a new cultural fantasy of femininity and sexuality at the fin de siècle, challenging the status quo and playing havoc with traditional moral and social standards for women. Electra is part femme fatale and part "new woman" and places herself squarely within central debates surrounding gender, sexuality, and subjectivity. Freud was not the only one interested in the differences between the sexes. In fact, the changing roles of men and women were a topic of conversation in Vienna around 1900—in coffeehouses, literary salons, and the opera—everywhere people gathered in lively discussion and debate. Indeed, sexology was gaining notoriety as an acceptable scientific discipline and attracted the attention of scholars such as Krafft-Ebing, A. Moll, P. J. Moebius, Havelock Ellis, I. Bloch, M. Hirschfeld, and others, all of whom Freud cites generously in his early writings on sexual development.

The function of gender transcends the bounds of salons, lecture halls, and the theater to encompass the larger sphere of nationality. Austria itself is personified as the feminine other to Bismarck's masculine German empire with the image of Empress Maria Theresa as matriarch and patron saint of the nation's identity.[13] J. J. Bachofen's anthropological study of the rise and fall of matriarchy in ancient civilizations, *Mother Right* (1861), and Otto Weininger's *Sex and Character* (1901), which deplored the bisexualization and feminization of culture, contributed to the debates surrounding women's roles and the nature of femininity. Though separated historically by several decades, these two works constitute the cornerstones of the belief that femininity was on the rise and constituted a dangerous threat to modernization and the

---

13. Hofmannsthal posits Maria Theresa as the pillar of the Austrian psyche, feminine and powerfully so, while Franz Grillparzer describes Austria as "lying, a pink-cheeked youth, between the child Italy and the man Germany" (quoted in Le Rider 1993, 104).

forward march of civilization. The view that femininity was sapping the foundations of moral order and the faith in progress permeated the Vienna of Freud's and indeed Hofmannsthal's time.

Hofmannsthal's *Elektra* must be viewed within the context of a dual movement. On the one hand, misogyny was on the rise and women were mistrusted and blamed for social and moral decay. Rampant prostitution in Vienna, Paris, and London was the most cited result of uncontrolled female sexuality. On the other hand, the fascination and obsession with the powerful femme fatale was at an all-time high.[14] While science was busy trying to strap sexuality into a straitjacket, with Freud's Oedipus leading this race, the literary and theatrical arts were embracing an unprecedented irrationalism, working just as hard to loosen the buckles of that same straitjacket. Freud's theories of human psychological development were focused on masculine sexuality, a knowable and quantifiable entity. But feminine sexuality, an unknown and dangerous quantity, was left to the creative genius of authors such as Ibsen, Wilde, Wedekind, and Schnitzler.[15] These writers allowed feminine sexuality to blossom unbridled in an environment of experimentation and adventure, and *Elektra* was just part of that larger project. This phenomenon was perhaps most pronounced at the turn of the century, and yet traces of this polarity—misogyny versus fetish obsession with feminine sexuality—are arguably present throughout the twentieth century. After all, the race for modernization and technological advancement with its patriarchal and masculinist leanings does not end with the First World War. The proliferation of Electra texts in the twentieth century is in part a response to the constant pressure of science and the dominance of teleological paradigms in our world. Electras, as this book will show, have not been tamed over time by their authors or the science of the world we live in. More than ever, the Electras of recent times are cunning, cruel, and, yes, electric in their raw sexuality and in their refusal to conform.

Hofmannsthal's *Elektra*, because it is an important catalyst for the Freudian reception of the myth in subsequent adaptations, serves as the basis for three of the chapters in this book. With its bold deviations

14. This polarity is nowhere more apparent than at the university. By 1900, women were making inroads at the university, enrolling in great numbers. The majority of these women were Jewish because the Catholic Church actively discouraged women from pursuing higher education. The "Woman Question" is thus further complicated by the dual discrimination on the grounds of gender and religion (Hamann 2001, 16).

15. Henrik Ibsen, *The Doll's House* (1879) and *Hedda Gabler* (1890), Oscar Wilde, *Salomé* (1891), Frank Wedekind, *Earth Spirit* (1895) and *Pandora's Box* (1902) (the Lulu plays), Arthur Schnitzler, *Round Dance* (1900).

from the myth, the climate of hysteria, and Elektra's performance of raw sexuality in her famous *Totentanz*, this work is a testimony to the psychological turmoil of fin-de-siècle Vienna. The first chapter examines the impact of the heroine's death and the corpse as a memento mori, supplementary to the tragic unity of the drama. The crisis in representation spawned by Elektra's death and the resulting "thanatomania" recur in Heiner Müller's *Hamletmaschine*, discussed in chapter 2. In this violent and anarchic drama, the playwright seizes the power of myth to critique East Germany's corrupt socialist regime and its blindness to history's atrocities. Moreover, by replacing an oedipal Hamlet with an Elektra as a disabled destruction machine, Müller drills holes in several of the twentieth century's major narratives: the Name-of-the-Father, categories of gender, and teleology.

Chapter 3 constructs an interpretive dialogue between Hofmannsthal's *Elektra* and Freud's first famous case study in hysteria, "Fräulein Anna O." The similarities between the two women are remarkable, and it has been speculated that Hofmannsthal used Freud's patient as a model for his heroine. I intertwine Elektra's and Anna O.'s stories to expose the limits of the hysterical diagnosis and to show how each woman choreographs her madness as a theatrical production, turning pathology into performance. Continuing with the analysis of performance, chapter 3 engages with leitmotivs and metaphors of dance in Strauss's 1909 operatic adaptation of *Elektra*. The Viennese waltz recurs numerous times in the music and offers multiple and contradictory messages, arguing at times with and at times against the libretto. The composer employs the codified waltz motif to counter Hofmannsthal's biting irony but simultaneously appropriates Vienna's most sacred institution, the waltz, to parody fin-de-siècle hysteria and the nostalgia for the waning Habsburg Empire.

Chapter 4 shows how the myth of Atreus and its shadow of incest are imbedded in Robert Musil's *The Man without Qualities* as a subtle challenge to the psychological autocracy of the Oedipus complex in the cultural institutions of pre–World War I Vienna.[16] Musil invokes Ernst Mach's theories of the provisional ego and the sensation body as an alternative to the singular, masculine-gendered subject position of Freud's Oedipus. The novel's trajectory eventually transcends Vienna's narcissistic and clichéd crisis of identity to embark on a journey of discovery in which Agathe (Electra) and Ulrich (Orestes) create for themselves an alternative, imaginary world. The Atrean myth buttresses

---

16. Though set in the ominous year of 1913, Musil's masterpiece epic novel was written between 1924 and 1943 and not published in a complete volume until 1952.

Musil's quest to tease out the limits of utopia and anarchy and carve out a new ethics of social relations.

The final section of *Electra after Freud* initiates a shift in time, space, and genre. Electra comes to life as a poetic enactment in the works of the American poets H.D. and Sylvia Plath. Each author invokes the mythological heroine's story on a journey of healing, in which personal trauma becomes the raw material for a poetics of survival. Paralyzed and silenced by the atrocities of war, H.D. underwent analysis with Freud to confront her grief and end her writer's block. Through this analysis the poet adopts Electra as her muse in quest for spiritual and creative renewal. Her version of the legend banishes the hatred and violence of the male-dominated war machine in favor of a feminized politics of renewal, where beauty, *eros*, and fertility triumph toward an aesthetic of hope and peace.

Like that of H.D., Plath's rendering of Electra is a metaphoric one. She takes Agamemnon's mourning daughter as her poetic persona in her efforts to make sense of an experience of trauma that resists articulation in ordinary language: "Here is a poem," she writes in her famed "Daddy" verses, "spoken by a girl with an Electra complex." Plath not only uses a mythological character but also creates a mythology of the self in the process, in which Electra's story is scraped to the bare bones and consists of nothing more than a dead father and a hateful mother. Freud's, Klein's, and Kristeva's theories of mourning serve as a lens for my readings of Plath's efforts to resurrect metaphors of orality (a cannibalistic subject rhyme with the *Oresteia*) to enact the incorporation of the maternal body and negotiate a new relationship with her father's ghost. A shift in the mourning process leads to what I call a "reverse incorporation," whereby the introjection of the lost object is exchanged for enclosed, maternally connoted spaces. Ultimately, the speaker is nourished and healed by her own words.

The Power of Myth

From Dante and Shakespeare to James Joyce and Margaret Atwood, writers have been inspired by the transcendent power and archaic patterns of myth. These stories carry with them a certain unnamable and durable fascination, never going out of fashion. Rather, revival and repetition keep alive the cultural currency of myth. But what makes a myth mythic? Don Cupitt (1982) suggests that myth is paradigmatic but has no absolute paradigm: "Myth is typically a traditional sacred story of anonymous authorship and archetypal and universal significance" (29). These metanarratives are linked to ritual communal practices and often contain superhuman though anthropomorphic beings such as gods, heroes, spirits, and ghosts. George Steiner (1984) takes an even wider view of myth, claiming that it is tied to the origins of language: "The principal Greek myths are imprinted in the evolution of our language and on our grammars in particular. . . . We speak organic vestiges of myth when we speak" (303–304).[17] For Freud and more so for Jung, myth is part of our collective unconscious, imbedded at a very deep psychic level. These stories convey profound human truths not subject to the limitations of time, space, or cultural difference. Powerful as it is, myth is also a suspect medium, denigrated by Plato as seductive and inauthentic, a mere fiction carrying no more truth value than rumor itself. This may be so, but our fascination with myth rests in part upon this inherent dichotomy of truth and lies—the friction generated by this conflict sparks the magic of myth.

Every period has its own reasons for appropriating the power of these ancient legends. French classicism of the seventeenth century and Weimar classicism of the eighteenth century focus on the transcendent perfectibility of myth, its ability to render an ordered, harmonious cosmos. Goethe's conception of antiquity in collaboration with Johann Joachim Winckelmann is an obvious example—Winckelmann uses the anatomical perfection of the Greek statue as his model of the ancient world, which he describes as one of "noble simplicity and silent greatness," uniting the natural world with the plastic arts (quoted in Ward 2002, 135). The German romantics with their project of "New Mythology," however, advocate the regeneration of myth in language as a key to transcendence in a dialectical relationship between nature and the human spirit. Friedrich Schlegel's "Treatise on Mythology" introduces a system whereby the mythological aesthetic is turned into a transcendental philosophy (see Feldman and Richardson 1972, 307; Jamme 1991, 33). Thus myth becomes a kind of tautegorical absolute, to use Friedrich Schelling's terms, neither allegorical nor euhemeristic, but autonomous and devoid of all secondary meaning.[18] Another shift in the philosophy of myth begins with Richard Wagner, who consid-

17. Steiner (1969, 132) uses Heidegger's philosophy of *Lichtung*, the clearing or homecoming in which Being is made manifest, to posit Greek grammar and vocabulary as the markers of personal identity in the West. In these terms, Electra is permanently imbedded within the syntax of myth, but the character is also engaged in a diachronic dialogue with other Electras.

18. "Tautegorical" is a term specific to romantic philosophy, referring to the allegorical and self-reflexive character of myth. The *O.E.D.* cites for example a passage from Coleridge (1825): "This part of the *mythus* in which symbol fades away into allegory but . . . never ceases wholly to be a symbol or tautegory."

ered myth a fluid, organic medium not confined to the world of the Greeks. This view was considerably expanded upon by Friedrich Nietzsche, for whom myth is an essential component of all cultures, ensuring a healthy natural creativity and unifying artistic movements. Nietzsche's conception of myth is linked to a growing climate of irrationalism, and by 1900 myth had become part of a larger anti-Enlightenment project, rejuvenating the social sphere with terror, brutality, and the Dionysian spirit of wild intoxication.

It is easy to understand, then, why myth has seen such a strong revival in the twentieth century, a century that embraced with almost evangelical fervor the race for progress in science and technology as the savior of Western civilization. Countless writers have found themselves drawn to the mysterious aura of myth with its dark, supernatural underbelly. The return to myth can be seen in part as a backlash against the drive to rationalize and quantify the world around us.[19] These ancient legends insert an element of the unknown into a society ruled by logic; they are malleable and permeable and thereby offer up alternative and creative solutions to the larger problems of humanity that cannot be solved through technological advancement: war, violence, abuse, greed, and the vicious struggle for power and control. Writers throughout the ages have been inspired by myth's promise of social and cosmic order, of perfection, but more important for the century that has just ended, poets have been driven to explore myth's potential energy. For Paul Ricoeur (1991), such stories are never finished, in a perpetual state of motion; they present opportunities yet to be realized. He regards myth as "a disclosure of unprecedented worlds, an opening on to other *possible* worlds which transcend the established limits of our *actual* world" (490). The myth of Electra is no different—it, too, performs its potential energy in radical ways. The legend shape-shifts in the hands of the Greeks but also presents new horizons and challenges the status quo with continued resonance to the present day.

The Attic Tragedies

There is no mention of Agamemnon's second daughter in Homer—in the *Iliad*, Agamemnon offers up one of his three daughters (Chrysothemis,

---

19. Mythological adaptation also functions as an allegorical foil for sharp social criticism in the face of political oppression. Sartre's *Les Mouches*, for example, is a thinly veiled critique of the Vichy government's collaboration with the Nazis during the German occupation of France in World War II. Writers in the former East Germany often turned to myth to express their dissatisfaction with the socialist regime, most notably Christa Wolf in *Cassandra* (1983), but also Heiner Müller and Volker Braun.

Laodice, and Iphianassa) to Achilles as a reward to lure him back to war, but Electra is not among them. Although Homer does not mention her name (while the stories of Agamemnon, Clytemnestra, and Orestes are told in detail), after her introduction in Aeschylus's *Oresteia*, Electra plays an increasingly important role.[20] The *Oresteia* tells the story of Agamemnon's fateful homecoming from the Trojan War, where a trap awaits him and his concubine Cassandra. The scarlet tapestry of honor is exchanged for the sordid red of a bloody bath, and the war hero meets his end at the hands of his wife, Clytemnestra, and her lover-accomplice, Aegisthus. Electra appears in the second part of the trilogy, the *Choephori*, where she must wait patiently for her brother's return from exile. She finds the clues that confirm Orestes' arrival: the lock of hair left on their father's grave and the unexplained footprints. Together, the siblings plot the brutal matricide that will avenge their father's death. Aeschylus has Electra play the role of the confidante, not the accomplice; she is the sounding board for what is essentially Orestes' mission.

In his rendering of the myth, Aeschylus continues where Homer left off, portraying the struggle to free humanity from the hold of the gods in a shift away from supernatural forces toward the powers of reason. The Attic tragedian carries the ancient world from darkness to light and celebrates progress through the "civic marriage of men and gods" (Fagles and Stanford 1977, 93). The *Oresteia* creates a humanist tragedy out of myth, separating it from its barbaric past.[21] "Myth" originally meant both "speech" and "word," but the Greeks, starting with Plato, carefully separated and worked to suppress *muthos*, the mysterious, supernatural, and fictitious elements of myth deemed inferior to *logos*, the rational side of mythology (see Wunenberger 1994, 35; Nieden 1993, 12). All mythopoesis can be seen, therefore, as an attempt on the part of myth to transcend its own dark history, and it was to tragedy that the poets of antiquity turned to demythologize myth.[22] With its tightly

20. It is possible that Homer knew of Electra and the role she played in the matricide of Clytemnestra. In the *Odyssey* Orestes is set up as an example for Telemachus of a good son, an image that would have been considerably marred if he had been depicted as a murderer. Perhaps the legend is suppressed because the knowledge of the curse of Atreus would threaten the stability of Homer's mythological world.

21. Robert Fagles summarizes the relationship of Aeschylus to Homer as follows: "Adapting Homer more and more freely throughout the Oresteia, [Aeschylus] reverses the events and carries them from the darkness to the light—from the bloody return of Agamemnon to the triumphant return of Athena to Athens" (Fagles and Stanford 1977, 286).

22. "Mythopoesis" is the creation of new versions of already existing myths, whereas "mythopoetics" is the theory of the production of myth. And "mythology" refers to the general study of myth.

controlled structure, its emphasis upon the rise of conflict and cathartic resolution, tragedy enacts the civilizing influence of *logos* on the unwieldy nature of myth.

Aeschylus uses the structure of tragedy, but also its content, to achieve this demythologizing end. By the end of the trilogy, Athena has laid down the preliminary structures for a court of law, where justice prevails over the fancy of Zeus and his entourage. In the *Eumenides*, Orestes is acquitted of his crime, but Athena never declares his innocence. Instead, she justifies her decision by privileging civil institutions over divine law: "I honour the male, in all things but marriage. . . . / Even if the vote is equal, Orestes wins" (Aeschylus 1984, ll. 752,756). Athena places the union of man and woman above the blood relations of mother and child, thereby allowing civic, state law to triumph over the rule of the Olympian gods and the mythical powers of the earth.

In this new world order, it would appear that *logos* ascends as *muthos* is defeated. But appearances can be deceiving. As the new name in the Atrean family tree, Electra introduces an element of unpredictability into this dramatic ascent from darkness to light. In subsequent versions of the myth, Electra will become a thorn in the side of civilizing, justice-seeking tragedy. By the time Euripides writes his version of her story, Electra has come to play the title role.[23] In this most daring of the three Greek dramas devoted to the myth of Atreus, Electra is granted a depth and clarity of character suitable for the status of heroine. Euripides' Electra begins to assert her role and disturb the social hierarchy of the sexes. A humble farmer's wife dressed in rags, she delivers a harsh and unsubtle message: "I will be the one to plan my mother's death" (Euripides 1964, l. 647). She may not actually wield the weapon of her mother's fate, but her words are transformed into her brother's actions.[24] The daughter sets a trap for Clytemnestra, luring and deceiving her mother with the lie of a new grandson and the promise of a ritual sacrifice in his honor.

Euripides' Electra is wholeheartedly dynamic and forceful, with

23. There has been considerable dispute regarding the date of Euripides' and Sophocles' *Electra* plays, with some scholars insisting upon Sophocles' version as the earlier of the two (Brunel 1971, 17; Grant and Hazel 1993, 119; Graves 1955, 62; Laks 1995, 37; Eissen 1993, 245; Grene and Lattimore 1960b, 182), while other maintain that Euripides' *Electra* predates Sophocles' version (Klimpe 1970, 5; Batchelder 1995, 2; Kells 1973, 1). This controversy is largely attributable to the lack of a verifiable date for the Sophocles play, although recent scholarship tends to favor the position that Euripides' is the earlier of the two tragedies.

24. M. J. Cropp (1988) comments on Electra's newfound independence in Euripides: "The myth determined that Orestes should be the slayer of his mother. But Electra in this play 'grasped the sword' along with Orestes, virtually sharing the deed" (xxxvii).

little room for hesitation or self-reflection. Even tears of grief for the
deceased Agamemnon seem vengeful as she relishes her mother's ignorance: "How beautifully she marches straight into our net" (Euripides
1964, l. 961). Orestes is the reluctant one here—he is paralyzed with
trepidation, spurred on only by his sister's coaxing and prodding. Once
her revenge is complete, Electra is condemned to suffer shame and
guilt for her role in the matricide, but the conflict is resolved through a
nuptial union with Pylades.

Euripides ignores the Aeschylean precedent of a triumphant celebration of transcendence out of the dark world of god-ruled mythology. Instead, we are presented with a human, psychological conflict, in
which the starkness of the Oresteian oppositions is transformed into
the gray shadows of consciousness. In keeping with Euripides' more
human representation of characters, this Electra acts out of emotional
rage rather than a pure sense of *dike* (justice in the sense of Greek tragedy). She is concerned with action, not image, and through her actions
manages to eclipse Orestes' once dominant role, leaving her own indelible mark.

Sophocles' Electra forges ahead with the same unfailing ruthless-
ness as her Euripidean counterpart, although there are fewer signs of
psychological depth and self-reflection in this Atrean princess. Hardly
a character in Greek tragedy can compare with her for calculating determination, except perhaps Sophocles' Antigone.[25] Electra does not
command her brother to action, nor is she the mastermind of the plan,
but she is definitely the driving force behind the matricide. Of all the
Attic tragedians, Sophocles provides the most sensitive portrayal of
Electra, but her tears are soon replaced by an obsession with revenge.[26] She follows her mother's lead in her capacity for the cruel
hostility necessary for murder, though her impetuous idealism gives
way for a moment to a moving poignancy in the famous recognition
scene with Orestes.[27] We see here that Electra and Orestes are linked

25. George Steiner sees Sophocles' *Antigone* as the most perfect of all Greek tragedies
in its subtle but terrifying resolution with the heroine's death. Antigone is defiant, but
Electra is violent and for this reason perhaps a less appealing subject. See Steiner 1984,
145, 159; Sale 1973, 3–4, for comparisons of Electra and Antigone.

26. In her introduction to her translation of Sophocles' *Electra*, Anne Carson (2001,
41–48) goes to great lengths to demonstrate how Sophocles carefully manipulates Electra's
diction, especially the verb *lupê* meaning "pain of body" or "pain of mind," to paint a character full of strength and optimism rather than a sorrowful, weak girl.

27. J. H. Kells (1973) has suggested that Sophocles' Electra verges on madness, but
Michael Shaw (2001, 5, 38) takes the view that, given the erosion of her support system
throughout the play, her temporary irrationality is completely justified.

by common emotions of love and hate, and their primordial bond with life and death drives their mutual desire for revenge. They abandon their individuality and the siblings move collectively and single-mindedly toward matricide. Electra's satisfaction at the death of her mother is so powerful that one might assume she had wielded the murderous sword herself. In the last lines of Anne Carson's moving translation, the chorus confirms the successful partnership between sister and brother:

> O seed of Atreus:
> you suffered and broke free,
>
> you took aim and struck;
> you have won your way through
> to the finish.
> (SOPHOCLES 2001, LL. 2004–2008)

Electra and Orestes are credited with liberating themselves and their kin from the grip of the evil curse that has plagued the royal family for generations. The tragedy ends abruptly as if broken off in midstream, and the concise rhetoric of these last lines renders the shocking message all the more clearly: the siblings are free and their actions have been blessed.

While Euripides is applauded for his innovative dramatic technique and the daring psychological complexity of his characters, Sophocles is heralded for his insight into the perfection and sheer strength of the human spirit. Sophocles' drama has a transcendent quality that underscores humanity as a powerful agent of change, and it differs from Aeschylus's vision in the important sense that here the gods are faint figures of a forgotten mythical past. Neither Electra nor Orestes feels remorse for their cruel acts, but they instead embrace a newly restored harmonious state—justice has been enacted.

Sophocles's *Electra* might be called "matricide without tears," and the tragedian has been accused of being unconcerned with the morality of matricide (Denniston 1964, xxv; Kells 1973, 2–4). We can compare this attitude to that expressed in the opening scene of the *Odyssey*, in which Zeus warns Aegisthus against seducing Clytemnestra and murdering Agamemnon, not on moral grounds but because of the consequences he will face. The point here is that Sophocles is not merely showing his true colors of cruel insensitivity; rather, he is harking back in dramatic form to an earlier cultural paradigm, one that accepts violence as inherent to the mythological world. Sophocles expands on Electra's dramatic potential and uses the character to bring about a "re-mythification," a return to the *muthos* of Homer that Aeschylus seeks to transcend. Sophocles' return to the *muthos* of myth differs from the two earlier *Electra* tragedies in that the harsh brutality of retribution is not a fate imposed by the gods but surfaces from the darker myth-infested side of the human spirit itself.

As with the Electras of Aeschylus and Euripides, Sophocles' Electra, too, injects a wildcard into the tragic appropriation of myth and goes against the grain of the shift from the *muthos* of speech to the *logos* of tragedy. Though simultaneous with the movement away from the dark, supernatural elements of the mythical world, the introduction of Electra into the economy of the house of Atreus prohibits tragic transcendence. Be it by overstepping the bounds of gender or through her manic and violent behavior, Electra resists the efforts of the Attic tragedians to constrain her within *logos*. Mythology's mourning princess daughter prefers the larger *muthos* that looms within humanity itself.

In this brief overview of Electra's role in Greek tragedy, I have endeavored to show that the Atrean heroine resists and challenges the move from the irrational, destabilizing elements of myth to the structured, reasoned arguments of tragedy. We can thus link the Electras of antiquity to those of the twentieth century—in each case, the character serves to undermine masculinist rationalism and challenge the status quo of an ordered, static universe. The proliferation of Electra adaptations in the twentieth century presents an alternative to the Oedipus of psychoanalysis, ensconced in abstract and structured theories of human development. Where Freud attempts with Oedipus to create a science of the soul, Electra finds herself at home in the medium of fictional narrative, in which alternative and creative solutions are sought to the vexing problems of this world left unsolved by the *logos* of science and technology.

Gender also functions as a means to destabilize the project of de-mythologization, inserting disorder, irrationality, and even hysteria into the ordered world of tragedy. The Atrean myth may be about restoring the lost honor of the father, yet there is an equally significant shift from male to female as leader of the action. By participating in the matricide and exhibiting such "unfeminine" characteristics as anger, cruelty, and violence, Electra tests the limitations of her social sphere. Sue Blundell (1995) speaks to this trend in the classical world:

"Women in Greek myth can be seen more often than not as boundary-crossers: they are represented as anomalous creatures who, while they live in the ordered community and are vital to its continuance, do not belong there" (19). Blundell goes on to say that this disorderly behavior is seen by gods, warriors, and kings as highly dangerous, a threat to their patriarchal rule. This trend arguably extends right through the twentieth century, when the trope of Electra as threat to fixed limits applies to adaptations from Hofmannsthal to the post-1989 poetry of Barbara Köhler. It is not so much the deviant behavior of female characters such as Electra that strikes fear but rather the ambiguous liminality of such figures. Like myth itself, Electra is dangerous because she is unpredictable.

There is nothing static or dormant about myth, but rather it "unfolds the living chain which connects the recurrent recognition scenes of the human drama" (Slochower 1970, 14). In Aristotle's discussion of tragedy, recognition is always accompanied by the shock of reversal. We can imagine as integral to the tragic paradigm multiple and ongoing recognition scenes among existing and future Electras. Mythopoesis, then, is about imbedding in new adaptations of myth a catalyst for such a shock. Instead of viewing myth as having a hard kernel or mythologeme, we might envision it as a perpetually deferred signifier, never fully determined. Jacques Derrida reminds us that myth need not be a totality with a center and a fixed origin. The unity within myth is always tangential, a fleeting moment, virtual. Totalization within the myth is impossible owing to the rhythmic movement both away from and toward itself, oscillating between substitution and difference. Derrida (1994) calls this "a movement of *supplementarity*" and claims moreover that "one cannot determine the center, the sign which *supplements* it, which takes its place in its absence—because the sign adds itself, occurs in addition, over and above, comes as a *supplement*" (236–237). This theory suggests that the study of myth is more than a mere account of sources and influence but rather a perpetual textual deferral as well as a complex history of intertextuality, whether conscious or unconscious.

It is in this light—mythopoesis as supplementarity—that I will engage with the myth of Electra in the twentieth century. The character and the myth deny the distinction between *muthos* and *logos*, origin and invention, truth and lies and challenge the very form of tragedy and the fictional world itself. George Steiner (1984) emphasizes the magic of Greek myths as an existential idiom, keeping alive our "fragile moorings to Being" (133). He speaks of myth as a human grammar, a language capable of expressing immense concepts with great precision. *Electra after Freud* explores these aspects of myth in the syntax of twentieth-century adaptations. Electra may free herself and her family from the curse of Atreus, but she keeps on adding to the myth, further supplementing its grammar in a myth without end.

1

Beyond Tragic Catharsis

HUGO VON HOFMANNSTHAL'S *ELEKTRA*

Dancing Modernity

Dance in Western culture has often been associated with beauty, grace, and discipline. The stylized dances of the French court, established by Louis XIV, and ballet, which eventually gained its independence from its roots in opera, presented a highly civilized, regulated, and most important, legitimized form of dance. Ballet began to discipline the dancing body, which was increasingly subjected to the censorship of tight-fitting garments and rigorous training. By the mid-nineteenth century, the ballerina had become a synonym for ideal feminine beauty. In striving for such an unattainable standard, however, the perfect outward form has meant the pain of deformed muscles and bones and, in more recent times, has led to a range of eating disorders among female dancers.

While ballet disciplined the body onstage, ballroom dancing was an equally powerful regulator of class and conduct in society. Strict etiquette was enforced, women were traded as pawns, and the dance floor was a forum for educating young girls in their specific social roles. But dance has a long history of being labeled dangerous. Women's dancing in particular has been portrayed as the harbinger of madness, illness, and even death. In ancient Greece, King Solon issued a decree against women's maenadic dancing, singing, and tearing their hair as part of

elaborate mourning rituals. Women had become too powerful, and
their performances were seen as a threat to his rule (Blundell 1995, 75;
Holst-Warhaft 1992, 3). These emotional outbursts of grief were
among the only public activities carried out by women, and the spectacle brought them social prominence. By curtailing such practices, leg-
islators sought to discipline women and deprive them of their powerful
position as communicators with the dead (Holst-Warhaft 1992, 144).

In the sixth century, Boethius called the sirens "whores of the theatre" and had his Lady Philosophy banish these muses of poetry from
his sickbed, saying: "Get out, you Sirens; your sweetness leads to
death" (quoted in McCarren 1998, 1). Such choreographed rituals,
often invoked by poets to cure a mental block, here served as a metaphor of contagion. These associations of dance with morbidity
reemerged in the early fifteenth century as the Dance of Death motif
in mural paintings on the walls of churchyards and burial grounds. The
Dance of Death depicted in procession an alternating series of living
forms and cadavers or skeletons, the living figures generally presented
in the order of their social precedence on earth. Hans Holbein's famous woodcuts, dating from 1523, are a series of "memento mori,"
meant to remind mortals of human fragility, the fleeting nature of life,
and the omnipresence and universality of death.

The medieval and Renaissance tradition of the *Totentanz* does not
feature women specifically as harbingers of death. Yet the pairing of a
skeletal figure and a terrified human in a demonic frenzy bears some
similarity to the medieval Christian tradition of possession and dance
allied with female witchcraft. Such women were also accused of devilry
and illicit ecstasies. The undetermined mystical qualities of these so-
called demonic women elicited the same fears as the *danse macabre*.
Sarah Webster Goodwin (1988) characterizes these fears as "threshold
anxiety" (19), a liminal or in-between state of undecidability. One is
paralyzed by fear at a pivotal moment between the known and the unknown, between life and death. Because this moment harnesses great
power, it must be suppressed and regulated.

These two traditions, the Dance of Death and the possessed female,
merged into one powerful trope in the mid-nineteenth century, especially in France. Femininity, dance, madness, and morbidity were
rolled into one on the stages of French vaudeville theater and in the
cultural and literary imagination of the period. Coupled with the interest in alternative expressions of female sexuality, this made for a very
powerful potion. A new breed of solo dance artist, among them Loïe
Fuller, Isadora Duncan, Ruth St. Denis, and Maud Allan, took the

stage by storm and mesmerized European audiences. These so-called barefoot dancers sought to exchange the discipline of pointe shoes and the rigid gestures of ballet for loose-fitting garments and flowing movements. They liberated themselves from the corset and tutu alike. Seen as cultural icons of the new, these women were unapologetically brash. A woman dancing alone on stage posed a threat to the romanticized and heterosexual imperative of woman as wife and mother, narrated in the pas de deux. These new dancers controlled not only the gaze but the purse strings as well. They attained a high degree of economic freedom and the artistic autonomy it enabled. Maud Allan's *Vision of Salome*, for example, ran to over 250 performances at London's Palace Theatre (Koritz 1997, 133).

Among those taken with this new dance craze was Hofmannsthal (1874–1929). By 1900, at the age of twenty-six, the Austrian poet and dramatist had already gained a reputation as a gifted writer and had published volumes of poetry and lyric dramas in respected literary journals. With *Elektra*, Hofmannsthal made his mark, this time with a dynamic drama written specifically for the stage. In keeping with the dominant tropes of dance, disease, morbidity and sexuality at the fin de siècle, the poet introduced a strikingly daring innovation with Elektra's magnificent exit from the stage. The heroine's role here is not eclipsed by the shocking matricide committed by Orestes, as it is in the Greek tragedies. In fact, Elektra upstages her brother's actions by performing an ecstatic Dance of Death, with which she mesmerizes her audience and destroys the tragic unity of the drama all at once. Indeed, the example of her triumphant *Totentanz* ushers in a new century of Electras.

Despite the finality of Elektra's dance, it does not signal the death of the character for twentieth-century literature. On the contrary, playwrights and poets ever since have been inspired by the force of her end. Elektra's death in the Hofmannsthal play has become so important in the context of the myth that some critics have all but forgotten that this was not part of the Attic tradition.[1] Matthias Braun's *Elektra's Death* (1970),[2] for example, makes Elektra's death the central element in the drama. Braun distills the action down to its essence, and the first scene begins after the murders of Klytämnestra and Ägisth, resembling the course of events in Euripides' *Orestes*. Here, Elektra does not die of natural causes, nor does her life end in an ecstatic rapture. Rather, she

---

1. George Steiner (1984, 145) speaks of Electra's death in the myth while referring to the Sophoclean Electra.
2. *Elektras Tod*

dies as part of the harsh new reality Braun creates for his characters. The stage directions provide an uncanny echo of Hofmannsthal's own, cited later in this chapter:

> Elektra remains standing for a long time. Then she walks slowly forward. Directly in front of her we see an outstretched arm with a knife coming swiftly toward her out of the dark. Elektra takes a few more arduous steps and falls dead to the ground. (Braun 1970, 66)[3]

Braun's dramatic use of Elektra's death bears the mark of Hofmannsthal's innovations in the sheer brutality of the scene. The significance of her departure would not be the same without the example of the fin-de-siècle Elektra. Indeed, so potent is the addition of Hofmannsthal's epilogue to Elektra's story that it permanently alters the form of tragedy. Elektra's death constitutes an irreducible supplement to the fixed structure of the Attic tragedies and ignores the Aristotelian laws calling for cathartic transcendence. This additional element or plot innovation renders Hofmannsthal's drama in defiance of strictly defined tragic requirements. All tragedies end with the resolution of the central conflict, in this case the revenge of Agamemnon's death with the murder of Klytämnestra. Elektra's dead body lying inert upon the stage is a corollary to the tidy conclusion of matricide and introduces an element of uncertainty. The corpse constitutes a memento mori that disrupts the peace and destroys tragic unity. Hofmannsthal's unprecedented move is a radical anti-Sophoclean shift in the myth and amounts to a crisis in representation, the consequences of which reverberate throughout the century.[4] Elektra's death is not a sacrifice or a failure; rather it must be read as a *danse macabre*, a maenad's ecstatic frenzy, and ultimately as a moment of triumphant liberation

Hofmannsthal was influenced by several writers popular in fin-de-siècle Vienna, including J. J. Bachofen, Erwin Rohde, Nietzsche, and Freud, all of whom were fascinated by the new reception of myth. With research on artifacts from new archeological digs making its way into Europe, the classical world took on new meaning, no longer resembling the enlightened perfection of Goethe and Winckelmann. In-

---

3. "Elektra bleibt lange stehen. Dann geht sie langsam vor. Dicht vor ihr sieht man einen erhobenen Arm mit einem Messer aus dem Dunkel gegen sie hervorschnellen. Elektra geht mühsam noch einige Schritte und fällt tot zu Boden."
4. Malcolm Davies (1999, 55) argues that Elektra's death can be viewed as a "regression to the world of earlier Sophoclean tragedy" and suggests that Elektra represents a shift to an archaic form of tragedy in which death is not a normal component.

stead, myth became the subject of historical, sociological and psychological debate, with a renewed interest in the rough, unpolished nature
of Aeschylean tragedy. Hofmannsthal's *Elektra* reflects these new concerns.

Elektra and Its Literary Milieu

Elektra's fateful end marks the commencement of a new era in the
myth, one intimately linked to the site of its inception. The young
Hofmannsthal was highly influenced by his milieu, where decadence
and death, *eros* and *thanatos* were unequivocal partners. Vienna, at the
center of the Austro-Hungarian Empire, was living in the frenzy of its
penultimate moment, alternately indulging itself in forbidden fruits
and repressing its desires beneath a veneer of refinement. Freud was
the rising star of this neurotic, death-obsessed society, preparing himself for the diagnosis of the century. Hofmannsthal's *Elektra* was born
out of this diseased ambiance, and Elektra finds her exit in much the
same way. Sophocles' play of the same name is Hofmannsthal's direct
intertext, though Hofmannsthal's play is by no means a simple translation of the original Greek.[5] While he worked with the Greek text, the
poet's understanding of Attic tragedy was influenced by contemporary
thinkers and standard translations.[6]

Far from the elevated rhetorical style used by Sophocles, Hofmannsthal's poetic language conveys an atmosphere of dread and mystery. He cues his audience that the suffering in his drama is not cathartic
but a strange and awful experience, bordering on the subhuman. The
author calls for the stage to be lit in lines of black with spots of deep
blood-red. A deformed fig tree dominates the stage, crooked and bent
on the roof of the palace like a crouching animal (Hofmannsthal 1951c,
82). Already the spectator has a clear sense of the sick and crippled world
where the action takes place. Not only does the stage reflect Elektra's
diseased milieu but it conveys the terror of being lost in an endless
labyrinth of horror. The set is narrow and inescapable, a description
conjuring up claustrophobic anxieties even through the printed page.

Hofmannsthal's directions are in deliberate contrast to Goethe's

---

5. For a detailed comparison of the Sophoclean source text and Hofmannsthal's *Elektra*,
see Davies (1999).

6. Hofmannsthal used Georg Thudichum's 1838 translation of Sophocles' Elektra, from
which he frequently took words and phrases for his new version (Bohnenkamp 1976, 198).
We know that Hofmannsthal was already reading parts of Sophocles' *Electra* in 1892 in the
original Greek in order to prepare himself to write a renaissance drama (König 2001, 427).

Iphigenia in Tauris, which Hofmannsthal considered a cold and pristine drama, purged of all remnants of sexuality or human instinct. *Iphigenia* offers space and light, and most of all a humanist optimism, which Hofmannsthal regarded as naïve: "This Hellenized product seemed to me upon rereading it to be devilishly humane" (1959a, 131).[7] Despite his pointed concerns about creating an *Elektra* manifesting a wholly different image of Greekness, Hofmannsthal remains faithful to the Sophocles tragedy to a certain degree. As in the Attic version, the dramatic tension in Hofmannsthal's play escalates throughout the action. But Sophocles builds the energy and suspense throughout five acts, whereas Hofmannsthal squeezes his into a compact one-act drama. Sophocles' chorus, crucial for the classical *Electra*, takes sides with Electra and Orestes, almost condoning the siblings' actions, whereas Hofmannsthal eliminates the chorus altogether. The closest we come to a chorus in the later play is the opening scene, when the maids speak about Elektra to prepare the spectator for her first dramatic monologue. There are other considerable omissions as well, including the famous speech of the messenger, who tells in epic fashion of Orestes' death in a chariot race at the Olympic Games. This lengthy speech was much appreciated by audiences, contributing toward the immense popularity of this play with the Athenians. Hofmannsthal, however, distills the action to its very essence, his economy of style adding to the intensity of the play's foreboding mood.[8] In fact, Richard Strauss remarks in a letter to Hofmannsthal regarding the libretto for the operatic version that the already distilled text would gain in strength and conviction if Orest and Ägisth were entirely absent, leaving the action to the dynamic triad of women: Elektra, Klytämnestra, and Chrysothemis (Forsyth 1989, 26). He even suggested that *Elektra* would be a "purer work of art"[9] if Orest did not appear at all (quoted in Ward 2002, 133). This suggestion aside, the fact remains that Hofmannsthal hands over the dramatic tension to his heroine.

Not surprisingly, Hofmannsthal chose the Sophoclean version of the myth to stage his anti-Goethean polemic and to showcase his demonic

7. "Dieses gräcisierende Produkt erschien mir beim erneuten Lesen verteufelt human."
8. We find an illustration of this economy in Hofmannsthal's choice of words for Elektra's famous line, where he reduces a whole sentence to three powerful words: "Strike again!" ("Triff noch einmal!"). Sophocles' version in the translation Hofmannsthal used reads: "Strike again, / If you have the strength for a second time!" ("Schlage zu, / Wenn du die Kraft hast, zum zweiten Mal!") (quoted in Schadewaldt 1960, 581).
9. "reineres Kunstwerk"

Elektra and her equally dysfunctional family. After all, this Greek tragedy is known as matricide without tears, and one could argue that Hofmannsthal is likewise unconcerned with the morality of the drama. Instead, the emphasis is placed upon Elektra's violent anger, hatred, and her determination to enact revenge.[10] Like the Sophocles play, this version hinges on the recognition scene between Elektra and Orest, though the scene is considerably condensed and lacks the finality conveyed by the Greek tragedy. The dialogue achieves the important goal of restoring Elektra's resolution to act, and after Chrysothemis's blatant rejection of the murder plan, the heroine motivates Orest to perform the dreadful deed. Her failure to present her brother with her chosen murder weapon demonstrates the tension between action and contemplation: "I couldn't give him the axe!" (Hofmannsthal 1954, 68).[11] But this turns out to be a mere hesitation on Elektra's part, and in the final analysis her determination to carry out the murders drives the plot.

While action is an important theme in the Sophoclean source text, Hofmannsthal goes further and creates an existential crisis to foreground his heroine's demise. Elektra's earlier inaction is counterbalanced by her harsh command to her murdering brother, perhaps the most famous line in the play: "Strike again!" (Hofmannsthal 1954, 68).[12] Elektra's self-reproach for having failed to provide the ideal weapon is followed directly by the brutal demand that Klytämnestra be spared no punishment. She thus condones the cold-blooded violence of matricide, a moment that acts as preparation for her own imminent end. Commenting on Sophocles' version, Wolfgang Schadewaldt (1960, 581) suggests that Elektra's daring order that the axe be drawn one more time is virtually her own death cry and goes on to suggest that Electra's death is implicit in the Greek play. Similarly, Martin Mueller (1986) contends that Hofmannsthal merely stages what is the logical end of the heroine in the first place: "One may well argue that Elektra's death is the most 'Sophoclean' feature of Hofmannsthal's version" (86). And yet such an interpretation ignores one significant difference—the tragic transcendence of Sophocles' drama indeed depends on the fact that both Electra and Orestes are living

10. Hermann Bahr had this to say of Elektra after the premiere: "Eating hate, drinking hate, spitting hate. Wounded because of hate, lecherous because of hate, wild because of hate: No longer a being that hates, but hate itself." ("Haß essend, Haß trinkend, Haß speiend. Wund vor Haß, geil vor Haß, toll vor Haß: Nicht mehr irgend ein Wesen, das haßt, sondern der Haß selbst.") Quoted in Kronberger 2002, 202.
11. "Ich habe ihm das Beil nicht geben können."
12. "Triff noch einmal!"

and free at the end of the action. The chorus clearly illustrates this fact:

> Children of Atreus, from great suffering
> You have won freedom at last
> By what has been done here, today.
> (SOPHOCLES 1990, LL. 508–510)

Consequently, Elektra's death is the most un-Sophoclean element we can find. In the Hellenic *Electra*, the dark curse of Atreus has at last been lifted and the siblings are elevated to a higher level of being, the violence of their collective act forgotten in the beauty of the moment. It would have been unthinkable for Sophocles to supplement this triumphant conclusion with the death of the heroine. The perfection of the tragic catharsis is wholly a function of the symbolic union of brother and sister in freedom and in life. The Sophoclean Electra is no Antigone, who must die in order to complete her defiance of Creon's rule and to meet her brother Polyneices on an equal plane. Hofmannsthal's *Elektra* is a striking departure from this Aristotelian tragic form, challenging the genre with a radical reform. The heroine's exit is a poetic act, relieving her of the horrific, almost possessed state that plagues her throughout most of the drama. Hofmannsthal's stage directions tell the story of Elektra's silent dance: "*She flings her knees up high, she stretches out her arms, it is a nameless dance in which she strides forward. . . . She takes a few more steps of the most suspenseful triumph and collapses*" (1954, 74–75).[13]

In a later address, the author describes Elektra's *Totentanz* as that of the drone after depositing his seed inside the queen bee. He expires from exhaustion once he has made his potent strike:

> Even the end was immediately clear: that she can no longer go on living, that when the deed is done her life and innards must gush from her, just as life and innards along with the fertilizing sting must gush from the drone when the queen has been fertilized. (Hofmannsthal 1959a, 131)[14]

---

13. "*Sie wirft die Kniee, sie reckt die Arme aus, es ist ein namenloser Tanz, in welchem sie nach vorwärts schreitet. . . . Sie tut noch einige Schritte des angespanntesten Triumphes und stürzt zusammen.*"

14. "*Auch das Ende stand sogleich daß: da sie nicht mehr weiterleben kann, daß, wenn der Streich gefallen ist, ihr Leben und ihr Eingeweide ihr entstürzen muß, wie der Drohne, wenn sie die Königin befruchtet hat, mit dem befruchtenden Stachel zugleich Eingeweide und Leben entstürzen.*"

The question remains, if Elektra is the drone, who is the queen bee? It is telling that Hofmannsthal uses the metaphor of a copulating male insect to capture the essence of his heroine. This has important ramifications with respect to the representation of gender in the drama. Hofmannsthal refers at least twice to Elektra's inability to hand over the murder weapon to her brother as a sign of her feminine weakness: "The deed goes contrary to a woman's nature" (1952, 354).[15] The contradiction is striking—the first example paints the image of the drone, the equivalent of a slave in the insect realm, using its last resources to fertilize the queen bee toward a new birth. The second example paints Elektra as a stereotypically passive and incapable female. The author's contradictory statements are a reflection of the struggle surrounding new social roles for women. Elektra epitomizes the paradox of a search for alternative modern models and a simultaneous nostalgia for lost traditions.

Vienna did not embrace modernism with the vehemence and enthusiasm of rival European cities such as London, Paris, or Berlin. The Austrian capital showed none of Berlin's optimism about its future position in European politics but rather found itself in the midst of a crumbling empire. Instead of attempting to bring about social change with the pseudo-science of extreme realism as did the naturalists, Vienna turned to the psyche, focusing on inner suffering and ignoring political reality. This fin-de-siècle society turned to art to aestheticize its own death scene. Carl Schorske (1980, 19) argues that for the young Hofmannsthal, the beauty of art was the key to instinct and irrationality. These qualities, though presenting obvious dangers, were the only true means of engagement with life in the form of action. Deeds alone could change the world for the better. In this form of aestheticism action takes on meaning in Hofmannsthal's *Elektra*.

Though Hofmannsthal carefully avoided referring directly to matters of Viennese politics, he was intensely aware of the crisis at hand. Within a framework of Old World decay and sociopolitical transition, Viennese moderns looked to tradition to ease the pain of change. Fears of spiraling technological advances fueled a general feeling of malaise in the apocalyptic fin-de-siècle period. In the midst of the ensuing cultural chaos, the moderns turned to the enduring universality of myth as a stabilizing factor. Instead of embracing the social as an arena for change as did the naturalists, Hofmannsthal and his contemporaries viewed modernity in aesthetic, psychological, but mostly individualistic

15. "Die Tat ist für die Frau das Widernatürliche."

terms. Jacques Le Rider conceives of Viennese cultural life circa 1900 in terms of a crisis of this newfound individualism. The genius artist with fragile nerves and a marked obsession with his own personal aesthetic became the mark of this newfound subjectivity (Le Rider 1993, 3). Given the crisis of individualism, which escalated to include ontological doubt, it is hardly surprising that a certain "thanatomania" came to reign over the Viennese literary scene in the works of Hofmannsthal and others.[16] Viennese authors and artists had no control over the real or perceived political, social, or moral decay of empire, but they could influence the cultural representations of mourning for a lost identity, personal and national. They chose to do so through the aestheticization of this individualism and its crisis of self-destruction.

Hofmannsthal's *Elektra* is caught in this web of cultural ambivalence, which culminates in the oscillation of *eros* and *thanatos*. At first glance the story of the Atrean princess would appear to have little to do with its social milieu of fin-de-siècle Vienna. And yet, despite its removal in time and space from Hofmannsthal's Austria, the Electra myth responds to the desire on the part of its audiences to escape their social reality. Set in antiquity, the play maintains a comfortable distance from everyday problems, all the while evoking moral stability and fixed cultural codes. Hofmannsthal exploited the false sense of security created by the classical setting to question representations of gender, sexuality, and subjectivity; hence the liberties he took with his source material.

Elektra's *Totentanz* is not Hofmannsthal's first or last brush with dramatic death—this theme preoccupies him throughout his lifetime. His early dramatic works *Der Tod des Tizian* (*The Death of Tizian*) (1892) and *Der Tor und der Tod* (*Death and the Fool*) (1894) deal explicitly with death. In the latter, Death appears in personified form to Claudio, whose shortcoming is his failure to act—he prefers to be a spectator in life and never ventures into action. When Death comes to Claudio he is ill prepared but pleads for a second chance at life. All is not lost, how-

16. The general obsession with death and decay did not emerge from nowhere at the turn of the century. The fixation is grounded in romanticism, with contributions from Blake, Shelley, Wordsworth, Hugo, Novalis, Schlegel, and Schopenhauer, among others. These writers and philosophers among others were responsible for giving death a special status that was linked to transcendent and mythical qualities. Death was no longer to be feared, but embraced for its imaginative and spiritual potential. Hofmannsthal was no doubt familiar with this tradition (as well as with the death-inspired work of later authors such as Baudelaire, Mallarmé, Verlaine, and Rimbaud) and had his roots firmly anchored in this strong literary history. Vienna was not alone in embracing morbid decadence—this sensibility permeated European culture.

ever, as his final tragic speech implies: "Only as I die do I feel that I am" (Hofmannsthal 1946, 292).[17] Claudio does not truly die but instead gains a heightened sense of awareness, a new and ready state that was not available to him in his waking life.[18]

Hofmannsthal's last and perhaps most important work, *Der Turm* (*The Tower*), returns to these same considerations. The play is a loose adaptation of Pedro Calderón de la Barca's *La vida es sueño* (*Life Is a Dream*), which Hofmannsthal began translating just prior to his work on the Elektra material (Curtius 1950, 184). The protagonist, Sigismund, is a dreamer like Claudio, though his problem is not that he has remained a spectator in life but rather that he cannot distinguish clearly between the real world and the dream. He hesitates between the outside world and his self-contained existence of the tower, to which he has been confined most of his life. His death shows that the dreamer is doomed to perish in the chaos of the modern world, but this death also foretells that those who do not dare to dream are destined to commit terrible acts. Here again, death does not indicate a radical finality but hints rather at a return to the unstable state in an extra-earthly realm where the dream still offers hope.[19] Hofmannsthal's Elektra is caught in a similar battle between the urges to dream, mourn her lost father, and enact revenge on his behalf. On the one hand, she resembles Claudio and Sigismund in her fixation with anger and pain. On the other hand, Elektra goes beyond her male counterparts to shake off the hypnotic dream state and move the action forward to its cruel end.

Elektra's Mythological Sisters

Perhaps there is more at work in Elektra's death than the question to dream or not to dream. While Electra's life is spared in the Attic tragedies, Hofmannsthal makes her part of a tradition of female sacrifice. Her *Totentanz* harks back to the fates suffered by women in her

17. "Erst da ich sterbe, spür ich, daß ich bin."
18. Critics have often viewed Hofmannsthal's early work as an obsession with aestheticism as a "disease of the spirit" ("Krankheit des Geistes") (Mauser 1977, 45), but *Der Tor und der Tod* in fact illustrates an attempt to find a way out of aestheticism and into life. The lyric drama is not so much an adolescent retreat from identity as an attempt to ground identity in action, and acts as a prelude to similar concerns in *Elektra*.
19. Hofmannsthal is not the sole author in his literary circle with a fixation on death as a literary metaphor. The central character in Arthur Schnitzler's novel *Sterben* asks for the works of Schopenhauer and Nietzsche to be brought to his deathbed. Schnitzler's narrator leads the reader to understand that while these philosophers may provide a deeper understanding of the divine nature of death, the dying man can find solace in the aesthetic realm of literature alone.

36 CHAPTER I

mythological lineage who paid for their strength with death. Though Electra has only a minor part to play in Aeschylus's *Oresteia*, the character inherits the legacy of incest and parricide. She takes on the curse handed down to her, thereby granting her twentieth-century death more significance than can be gathered from Hofmannsthal's play alone. In the legend of Atreus, a cycle of sacrifice and terror becomes a way of life for generation after generation. The most traumatic example is Iphigenia's slaughter at Aulis, where her life is offered up as a gift to appease Artemis. In Aeschylus's version, the goddess demands she be sacrificed as recompense for Agamemnon's killing of her prized stag. Iphigenia becomes a "bride of death," and Artemis restores the wind so the ships can make haste to their Trojan destination.

In this world of cruel justice, two wrongs do not make a right but inevitably lead to further bloodshed, this time in the form of Agamemnon's concubine, Cassandra. Aeschylus's *Agamemnon* tells of Clytemnestra and Aegisthus's ironic welcome of the adulterous couple, whereby the purple robes of victory are bestowed upon Agamemnon, only to be traded for his own red blood when he is murdered. But the war hero is not the only victim of this fateful homecoming. As she is sacrificed, Cassandra lets out a bloodcurdling scream, the kind that echoes throughout the memories and imaginations of future generations. Her terrifying cry is a purging akin—in function though not mood—to that of Elektra's ecstatic dance. Both reveal the intensity of emotion these women can muster.[20]

A third maiden of death is Persephone, daughter of Demeter. She is involved by implication since her tale is told at the outset of Aeschylus's *Eumenides* for its relevance to Athena's triumph over Apollo at the end of this drama. Persephone was abducted to the underworld by Hades, causing her mother grief and prompting her to inflict blight on the earth. Zeus finally relented so that mother and daughter were at last reunited, though the agreement required Persephone to descend to the bowels of the earth as bride of death each year thereafter. This ritual enactment of death grants her strength, and she rises each spring bearing the harvest grain as her mother's thanksgiving.

It is not coincidental that all three sacrificed women are found in

20. Eden Liddelow (2001) comments on the vital connection between Cassandra and Electra, united by their common love for the murdered Agamemnon: "In a sense [Cassandra] takes the disaster into herself, carries it like a child but cannot be delivered of it. Upon her death . . . Electra must take it over, feel it and express it, unceasingly trying seeking resolution in her dramatic exchanges with others" (7).

Aeschylus's *Oresteia*. It is not certain whether Hofmannsthal read the *Oresteia* in the original; however, he was likely influenced by Nietzsche's and especially Bachofen's response to Aeschylus. The young poet wrote enthusiastically about Bachofen's *Mother Right*: "I can hardly say what this book meant to me. Since then, I do indeed count this man among my teachers and benefactors and to this day I have yet to finish my readings of his books" (Hofmannsthal 1955, 477–478).[21] In *Mother Right* (1861), Bachofen attempts to prove a universal law of history through a systematic reading of mythology. His evolutionary argument proposes that as a society advances it liberates the human spirit "from the paralyzing fetters of a cosmic-physical view of life" (Bachofen 1967, 236).[22] For Bachofen, death is unequivocally linked with life as a play of opposing forces in a single process of transformation. Aeschylus's *Oresteia* is used to illustrate the transition from matriarchal law to the rule of patriarchy.

Bachofen links matriarchal law to the material-corporeal and the maternal-tellurian fecund earth, where the darkness of death opposes the luminosity of growth. The only light amid this darkness is the ethical relationship between mother and child, which fosters moral development according to the mysterious powers of the maternal. Matriarchy thus manifests itself through "the reciprocal relation between perishing and coming into being, disclosing death as the indispensable forerunner of higher rebirth as prerequisite to the 'higher good of consecration'" (Bachofen 1967, 87–88).[23] There are strong parallels between Hofmannsthal's characterization of Elektra and Bachofen's description of matriarchy. The feminine is very much connected to the chthonian materiality of human nature in Hofmannsthal's drama, illustrated, for example, in the numerous associations between Elektra and wild animals. We also witness the enraged heroine literally digging her way into the earth in search of the murder weapon. Moreover, an atmosphere of dark mystery prevails throughout the action. For Bachofen, darkness and matriarchy are intimately linked: "The night is identified with the earth and interpreted as a maternal-chthonian

21. "Was das Buch mir bedeutete, läßt sich kaum sagen. Ich rechne diesen Mann seit damals wahrhaft zu meinen Lehrern und Wohltätern, und ausgelesen habe ich seine Bücher bis heute nicht."
22. "aus dem lähmenden Fesseln einer kosmisch-physischen Lebensbetrachtung" (Bachofen 1984, 286).
23. "Das Wechselverhältnis von Tod und Leben den Untergang als die Vorbedingung höherer Wiedergeburt, als die Verwirklichung des 'höheren Erwerbs der Weihe'" (Bachofen 1984, 100).

power; here the night is the oldest of deities and stands in a special relation to woman" (114).[24]

Hofmannsthal's play differs from Bachofen's description of matriarchy in the relationship between mother and daughter. Elektra's relationship to Klytämnestra in no way resembles the loving connection
between Demeter and Persephone, but is fraught with hatred and ill
will. Bachofen illustrates the transition from matriarchy to patriarchy
through Aeschylus's example: Clytemnestra avenges Iphigenia's murder (her offspring alone according to matriarchal law) by killing
Agamemnon, but the ensuing matricide upholds the rights of the father through the institution of marriage. When Athena acquits
Orestes, the primacy of patriarchal law is confirmed. Apollo is behind
this new social hierarchy as he declares:

> The mother is no parent of that which is called her child, but only nurse
> of the new-planted seed that grows. The parent is he who mounts.
> (Quoted in Bachofen 1967, 159.)[25]

Bachofen concludes that the institution of marriage attains its full
height in the shift from matriarchal to patriarchal law and represents a
teleological advancement in which rational civic hierarchies prevail.

Though Bachofen's argument is appealing, Elektra's death in Hofmannsthal's rendition contradicts this easy conclusion. She appears to
stand on the side of the father, but the presence of her corpse at the end of
the tragedy forestalls the neat transition from the subterranean, material
right of the mother to the celestial, Olympian right of the father. Elektra's
dying is in a suspended state—it represents a coming into being through
perishing but simultaneously a movement toward a higher rebirth.

Nietzsche's philosophy affirms this exhilarating power of death. He
develops a theory in *The Birth of Tragedy* based on the polar opposition
of Apollo, the god of higher civilization, who sponsors the rise of the
individual, and Dionysus, the god of fertility, intoxication, and orgiastic worship, who promotes the dissolution of subject boundaries.
Nietzsche, too, turns to Aeschylus to illustrate his theory of tragedy
born out of the Dionysian chorus as the archetypal drama. The ritualistic aspect of myth is transposed to tragedy via the chorus and unveils

---

24. "Mit der Erde identifiziert sich die Nacht, welche als chthonische Macht aufgefaßt,
mütterlich gedacht, zu dem Weibe in besondere Beziehung gesetzt und mit dem ältesten
Zepter ausgestattet wird" (Bachofen 1984, 135).
25. "Nicht ist die Mutter ihres Kindes Zeugerin, / Sie hegt und trägt das auferweckte
Leben nur; / Es zeugt der Vater" (quoted in Bachofen 1984, 191).

the power that lies below the surface of humanity, buried under layers of individuation. Tragedy must arrest the decay of myth, not attempt to transcend it as did Euripides, whom Nietzsche accuses of squeezing the last drops of myth from his dramas. Aeschylus and Sophocles provide tragic models that retain strong mystical elements and foster a Dionysian truth.

Hofmannsthal was inspired by Nietzsche's defense of the mythic elements of tragedy and transposed this sensibility onto his Elektra figure. The Atrean princess ushers in the *muthos* of tragedy like a warrior endowed with the calm wisdom of dying, be it from the perspective of Bachofen's material-chthonian matriarchal law or in the sense of Nietzsche's Dionysian tragedy. Elektra's death is an affirmation and a celebration, and yet in the ecstatic moment of her dance she is forced to relinquish her earthly existence.[26] Elektra's *Totentanz* is a metaphorical recapitulation of Persephone's descent into the underworld, her life not ended but rather apprehended in a state of ontological ambiguity. Hofmannsthal plants this seed in his text by omission—nowhere does the text state that Elektra actually dies. The stage directions tell us that she collapses, and yet her unburied body confirms the lack of finality in her exit by contradicting the terms of Aristotelian tragedy.

The corporeal is thematized throughout Hofmannsthal's drama. Prior to her final moment, Elektra recoils at the strangeness of her own body. Chrysothemis, attempting to involve her sister in the celebrations, reports that the ground is littered with dead bodies and asks if Elektra hears the joyful cries of the citizens of Argos. Elektra is incensed at such a question and retorts that the music comes from inside of her. The crowd is gathered and awaits her dance, but Elektra hesitates:

> I know very well that they are waiting, because I must lead the round dance, and I cannot, the ocean, the enormous, the twentyfold ocean buries my every limb with its weight, I cannot lift myself up! (Hofmannsthal 1954, 74)[27]

Elektra has metaphorically internalized the dead bodies, and her own flesh now resounds with the cries of the dead. She acknowledges her

---

26. Christoph König (2001) argues that Hofmannsthal's principal concern is the relationship between life and death within Elektra's character, a relationship that is sublimated to become mythic: "He privileges death and wants to elevate it to the level of myth" ("Den Tod privilegiert er und will ihn zum Mythos erheben") (437).

27. "Ich weiß doch, daß sie alle warten, / weil ich den Reigen führen muss, und ich / kann nicht, der Ozean, der ungeheure, / der zwanzigfache Ozean begräbt / mir jedes Glied mit seiner Wucht, ich kann mich / nicht heben!"

duty to fulfill the promise she made to Agamemnon in her first monologue: to dance in celebration of his restored honor. But she is held back
by a terrible weight and embodies the heaviness of Bachofen's chthon-
ian-maternal imagery. Elektra carries the shadow of death throughout
the play, becoming more and more burdened until she can barely lift
her limbs: "I bear the burden of happiness, and I dance before you"
(75).[28] Her dance is a metaphorical *Reigen*, a round dance initiating the
community into her ceremony to help her. And yet it is not—it is in fact
a maenad's dance of Dionysian ecstasy. Elektra twirls alone, oblivious to
those around her, though she sacrifices herself for them. Her movements are not to be compared to Salomé's nimble steps, shedding her
veils and relieving herself of earthly cloaks. Elektra's maenadic frenzy is
hardly graceful—it more closely resembles a death march than the first
waltz at a debutante's ball.[29] Her dead fall is perhaps the very moment
when Elektra is truly relieved of the weight she has been carrying.
Nietzsche praises dance above all other arts in *Thus Spoke Zarathustra*,
where the tightrope dancer becomes a metaphor for humanity's potential for transcendence. In his defiance of gravity and his acceptance of
the imminent danger, he liberates himself from the confines of the
earth. Just as Nietzsche's tightrope dancer must risk falling to his death,
so too Elektra dares to dance her way to her end.

Hofmannsthal's decision to choreograph Elektra's last fateful steps
was likely also influenced by the innovations in dance at the time by
such figures as Loïe Fuller, Ruth St. Denis, and Isadora Duncan. Duncan's idiosyncratic dance style of maenadic gestures swept through Europe at the turn of the century and Hofmannsthal likely witnessed one
of the performances of her Austrian debut in 1903, the same year he
wrote his *Elektra*. The poet was also enamored with Sarah Bernhardt
and Eleonora Duse, whose dramatic dance performance captured his
imagination (Hofmannsthal 1951b, 71). The cultural currency of deadly
dancing women in Ibsen's *The Doll's House*, Strindberg's *The Dance of
Death*, Wilde's *Salomé*, Wedekind's Lulu plays, and Stravinsky's *The Rite
of Spring* whetted the appetites of fin-de-siècle audiences for such mor-

28. "Ich trag die Last / des Glückes, und ich tanze vor euch her."
29. Reinhold Schlötterer (1987, 48) points out the contradiction in Hofmannsthal's understanding of Elektra's dance as both a *Reigen* and a maenadic solo. The former is a round
dance, indicated by the Greek *choréuo*, a slow and methodic dance performed by the chorus, hand in hand and often accompanied by song. In contrast, the *orchéomai* is the solo
mimetic dance of the maenads, the women who followed Dionysus and celebrated his rites
in ecstatic frenzy. Hofmannsthal had seen the images of Greek maenads in Thomas Taylor's book on the Elysian mysteries and had read descriptions of Bacchants in Rohde's 1893
Psyche, Seelenkult und Unsterblichkeitsglaube bei den Griechen (Meister 2000, 85).

bid performances. Hofmannsthal's drama is part of this larger dialogue of dance played out in literature and performance.

Innovations in the arena of dance were not the only important influence for Hofmannsthal. New trends in the theater also had an important effect on the outcome of *Elektra*. Bernhard Greiner sees Elektra's death in the context of Hofmannsthal's engagement with the modernist theater of Max Reinhardt (which anticipates many elements of expressionist theater and early German cinema) and suggests that when Elektra is sacrificed the drama itself dies for a moment.[30] So extreme are the dramatic elements of this theater that Elektra cannot live on without it. Elektra, when herself taken as a dramatic symbol, is extinguished when the action comes to a conclusion (Greiner 1996, 265–266). Elektra's death presents an interesting riddle precisely because of the intersection of various influences, be they from philosophy, literature, or the pragmatics of the stage.

Allegories of Death

Walter Benjamin's concept of allegory proves a useful tool for an analysis of Elektra's death dance as an ongoing process of mourning, indeed as a memento mori. Benjamin turns to baroque tragic drama, with its tensions between destruction and hope, catastrophe and rescue, to illustrate fundamental shifts in the culture of modernity: "Allegory," asserts Benjamin in *The Origin of German Tragic Drama*, "established itself most permanently where transitoriness and eternity confronted each other most closely" (1977, 224).[31] Precisely these contradictions and tensions are echoed in the final scene of Hofmannsthal's drama.

---

30. Through Reinhardt's influence, Hofmannsthal began to see drama as a medium of potential energy. In an essay on Reinhardt he cites the director's most important innovation: "The key to understanding this phenomenon is this: the dramatic text is something incomplete" ("Der Schlüssel, dieses Phänomen zu verstehen, liegt hierin: der dramatische Text ist etwas inkomplettes") (Hofmannsthal 1959c, 328). Hofmannsthal's encounter with Reinhardt had a lasting impression on his dramas, which constitute what Benjamin Bennett (2002) calls a "theater of adaptation" (102).

31. "Die Allegorie ist am bleibendsden dort angesiedelt, wo Vergänglichkeit und Ewigkeit am nächsten zusammenstoßen" (Benjamin 1972c, 397). Benjamin relies on compounded, often contradictory, keywords and layered images to convey his sense of baroque allegory—fragment, ruin, transience, incompletion, undefined terms piled upon each other in a shapeless heap. Not really a model, theory, or system, allegory for Benjamin is more a mode, trope, conceptual tool, or lens through which to view modernity's contradictions. *The Origin of German Tragic Drama* is itself an example of baroque allegory with its ornate, highly decorative, and not so demonstrative language, endlessly winding its way into a maze to which there is no exit. Absurdity and ludic whimsy intermingle with a grotesquely abstract prose as Benjamin avoids anything approaching the clarity and harmonious completeness of Enlightenment classicism.

This unique theory of allegory rests on the assumption that the baroque era lacked the certainty of redemption present in the Middle Ages, and yet *Trauerspiel* (literally, a mourning play) is determined not to give up hope of salvation in some form. Unlike Greek tragedy, the allegorical aesthetic of tragic drama does not pay homage to a cosmic order that issues decrees of fate, but rather illustrates the horrid, corrupt, and transitory condition of those who inhabit the earth. There is no direct route to a heavenly realm—instead mortals are destined to exist between realms in a perpetual state of uncertainty.

The allegorical is the material residue of suffering that cannot be sublimated into an abstract ideal. Elektra's corpse highlights the transient nature of organic matter and the inevitability of decay, and yet it is precisely destruction itself that makes redemption possible in Benjamin's system; hence the celebration of death as a dance. Elektra must literally bear the burden of happiness, using it to fuel her dance. Throughout Hofmannsthal's work, hope and optimism reside in alternative states of being, be it the dream, the unconscious, or the unreality of the stage. At the end of *Der Turm*, for example, when all appears lost and Sigismund is about to die, two small boys cry: "Let him die!—Rejoice!" (Hofmannsthal 1958, 207).[32] Sigismund dies because of his inability to distinguish between the real world and his interior world within the tower, and yet his death, like Elektra's, is imbued with a sense of optimism that borders on the utopian.

For Benjamin, the melancholy nature of allegory is joined with the joy it promises. It is sorrow that affirms one's relationship to the source of all creation, and this force rescues the lost from their abyss of suffering. And yet there can be no rejoicing without the destruction of the material world. Allegory redeems by holding onto the ruins, represented in *Elektra* by the corpses strewn in front of the palace, including her own. For Benjamin, the corpse is the ultimate allegorical residue: "Seen from the point of view of death, the product of the corpse is life. . . . There is in the physis, in the memory itself, a *memento mori*" (1977, 218).[33] Elektra, who has been plagued with haunting memories of her father, now embodies memory itself. Her body is the physical evidence of that memory, that which is at once present and absent, fragmenting human experience for all time.

It is impossible to read Hofmannsthal's *Elektra* as an example of

---

32. "Lasset ihn sterben!—Freude!"
33. "Produktion der Leiche ist, vom Tode her betrachtet, das Leben. . . . Ein 'Memento mori' wacht in der Physis, der Mneme selber" (Benjamin 1972c, 392).

tragedy in the sense that Sophocles' drama deploys the genre, precisely because the body of the Atrean princess remains behind as a memento mori. Hofmannsthal violates important formal traditions since, as Aristotle makes clear in the *Poetics*, the success of tragedy depends on the resolution of conflict. All deaths must be accounted for when the action comes to a close—only then can order be restored. In Hofmannsthal's *Elektra*, the entire tragic peripeteia is thrown off balance by the heroine's death in all its decaying beauty as a supplemental coda to the drama. Elektra's *Totentanz* unveils the fundamental ambiguity of fate in the modern world, the same radical incommensurability of hope and mourning, dream and waking, truth and fiction that characterizes Benjamin's allegorical mode. The decaying corpse forestalls any cathartic finality: "The characters of the *Trauerspiel* die because it is only thus, as corpses, that they enter into the homeland of allegory" (Benjamin 1977, 217).[34] Even if destruction is a necessary component of allegory, as Benjamin tells us, the somatic ecstasy of the death dance results in newfound freedom. Through Elektra's unburied body, tragic form and the character are left in a permanent state of unresolve that will haunt future Electras for more than a century to come.

34. "Die Personen des Trauerspiels sterben, weil sie nur so, als Leichen, in die allegorische Heimat eingehn" (Benjamin 1972c, 391–392).

2

Shakespeare's Electra

HEINER MÜLLER'S *HAMLETMASCHINE*

Hamlet has been an obsession for German audiences and intellectuals and has played a crucial role in shaping the German psyche and national consciousness since the nineteenth century, when Goethe read Shakespeare's Danish prince as a young man ill prepared for the task that awaits him: "Astonishment and melancholy overcome the lonely [Hamlet]. . . . A great deed rests on a soul that is not ready for the deed" (quoted in Loquai 1993, 3).[1] Clearly, the metaphor here is Germany as an immature nation, not yet a state in the proper sense and not equal to its European rivals.

Goethe was not alone in his equation: "Hamlet has no way, no direction, no manner," wrote Ludwig Börne in 1829; "I would not be surprised if a German had written *Hamlet*" (quoted in Stern 1992, 301). Ferdinand Freiligrath was even more blatant in his 1844 poetic depiction: "Germany is Hamlet! Serious and silent" (quoted in Loquai 1993, 5).[2] And if there is any room for doubt, Heinrich Heine dispels it when he claims: "We [Germans] know this Hamlet as well as we know our own face" (quoted in Loquai, 5).[3] Hamlet's story and his guilt were

---

1. "Staunen und Trübsinn überfällt den Einsamen [Hamlet]. . . . Eine große That auf eine Seele gelegt, die der That nicht gewachsen ist."
2. "Deutschland ist Hamlet! Ernst und stumm."
3. "Wir kennen diesen Hamlet, wie wir unser eignes Gesicht kennen."

never more appropriate than during the immediate postwar discussions of Nazi Germany, when German adaptations of Hamlet proliferated.[4]

Hamlet's hesitations and vacillations, which have often caused him and not Oedipus to be selected as the ideal German archetype, are no longer considered ideal by Heiner Müller (1929–1995).[5] In his own "Oedipus commentary," the dramatist writes of the murdering son of Thebes: "He lives, his own grave, and is chewing his dead" (Müller 2001, 92). As with Oedipus, Hamlet's weaknesses have become a liability. Freud's comparison of the two heroes focuses on Hamlet's neurosis: "In the *Oedipus* the child's wishful phantasy that underlies it is brought into the open and realized as it would be in a dream. In *Hamlet* it remains repressed" (1900, 4:264). Hamlet is understandably more compelling for Freud than Oedipus given the German tradition of Hamlet reception. Jean Starobinski (1989, 156) argues that Hamlet is a more likely case study for Freud because he has depth and context, born in a time when subjectivity is a concept, whereas Oedipus is mythic and immutable. If the modern Oedipus is characterized by *desire*, desire to love his mother and murder his father, then Hamlet, viewed through the lens of psychoanalysis, is characterized by *neurotic desire*. Müller sees no reason to cure his Hamlet of his neurosis. Instead of prescribing hours on the couch with talk therapy, he declares him a hopeless case and simply kills him off.[6]

Like Oedipus, Müller's Hamlet is tainted by his failed attempt at attaining a complete and stable subjectivity, calling it his "undivided self" (Müller 1978, 19).[7] Hamlet and Oedipus alike are hampered by their narcissistic obsession with the selfsame subject. Electra, a fresh alternative to the masculine model of modernity, has never had the same agenda as her oedipal Other. Electra is a negotiator, a manipulator, clever in attaining consensus among the Atrean tribe. She is Hamlet's opposite: a woman of action, decisive and sure in her goals.

Müller, the former East Germany's famously outspoken playwright and poet, wages war on Freud's master myth of the incestuous son:[8] "In

---

4. Hamlet was the theme of adaptations by Ernst Weiss, Günter Grass, Martin Walser, and Wolfgang Hildesheimer. See Franz Loquai's *Hamlet und Deutschland* (1993).

5. In describing his reasons for choosing Hamlet as a dramatic subject, Müller says it is probably because *Hamlet* was the first Shakespeare play he read but also because it reflected his own concerns and those of Germany (Hauschild 2001, 346).

6. In *After Oedipus*, Julia Reinhard Lupton and Kenneth Reinhard (1993) conclude that Hamlet is the " 'model object' of neurotic desire" (5).

7. "ungeteilter Selbst"

8. "Famous" and "Heiner Müller" are words that don't often go together in the English language. This is not so in Germany, where he is a folk hero, revered as the most signifi-

the century of Orestes and Electra that is unfolding, Oedipus will be a comedy" (1996, 16).[9] Müller puts ammunition behind his words and exposes the fissures and holes in Freud's oedipal model in his 1977 play *Hamletmaschine* by fashioning a feeble Oedipus in the form of an insipid Shakespearean Hamlet. The leading male gladly cedes his role to his female counterpart, the suicidal Ophelia, who is then transformed into an assertive and vengeful Elektra. Müller's Elektra threatens to take her own life and eventually enacts her rage in a violent destruction of her own body. In the end, Oedipus/Hamlet is eclipsed by an Ophelia/Elektra who annihilates all creatures in her path and is left a cadaverous, if living, shell.[10] In antiquity, Electra's opposite is always Orestes, but it is clear that this Hamlet is a stand-in for Oedipus. It is telling that while Ophelia morphs into Elektra, Müller's oedipal Hamlet simply disappears from the stage—Freud's everyman is erased from history.

Müller's Elektra is undaunted by the horrors of death and presides over scenes of cruelty with elegant poise. Nonetheless, she takes full responsibility for a community and its history. Like Hofmannsthal's *Elektra*, Müller's anarchic *Hamletmaschine* parallels Benjamin's allegorical mode. The playwright began reading Benjamin in the 1950s (though most of his works were banned in the former German Democratic Republic), and his thought runs throughout Müller's work with the constancy of a musical leitmotiv. He embraces Benjamin's conception of history as an endless chain of catastrophes that incessantly heaps ruins upon ruins, a theme very much evident in *Hamletmaschine*.[11] Müller's play is much more a *Trauerspiel* than a tragedy, following Benjamin's formula in *The Origin of German Tragic Drama*: "The

---

cant playwright since Brecht. Upon his death in 1995, thousands marched through the streets of Berlin. In North America, his death was marked by a brief Reuter's obituary. The reason for his obscurity in the English-speaking world may be what Jonathan Kalb (1998) calls "an intellectually ambitious theater that undermines the insidious contract between complacent audiences and the dominant bourgeois dramatic tradition" (2).

9. "Im Jahrhundert des Orest und der Elektra, das heraufkommt, wird Ödipus eine Komödie sein."

10. Elektra's revolt against the production machine is mirrored in the form of Müller's work. It has been described as a "theatrically impossible text" (Wirth 1995, 215) because it rejects all dramatic conventions. Often there is no indication of who is speaking. Even the radical deconstructionist director Robert Wilson expressed helplessness when first confronted with the enigmatic text (Wirth 1995, 215). Yet Wilson further fragmented the text by staging it in a highly choreographed manner, separating audio and visual tracks, thus stretching the shrunken eight-page text to a two-and-a-half-hour production. Müller's text and Wilson's self-conscious production escalate the machine metaphor to the point of dysfunction.

11. "die unablässig Trümmer auf Trümmer häuft" (Benjamin 1972b, 697).

Trauerspiel, it was believed, could be directly grasped in the events of history itself" (1977, 63).[12] Benjamin's allegorical thinking flickers at the edges of Müller's text, which is careful to unravel the smooth lines of the beautiful, the truthful, and the imminent that Benjamin so vehemently rejected. The playwright sutures these allegorical musings to the myth of Hamlet and Electra to articulate and problematize in a bald and undistorted manner the contradictions of history as a cycle of destructive redemption. Paradoxically, for Müller the play is about history but brings history to an end.[13] The playwright claims that after *Hamletmaschine*, "no substance for dialogue exists anymore because there is no more history" (quoted in Kalb 1998, 107). *Hamletmaschine* is Müller's thinly veiled critique of the GDR's ahistoric and simplistic approach to *Vergangenheitsbewältigung*, its problematic antifascist rhetoric, and its totalizing politics.[14]

The drama is deeply rooted in its sociohistorical context: the GDR at the height of the Cold War. To call the work a play is to stretch the definition of the dramatic genre to its limits, for here we encounter a blatant revolt against plot, character development, tragic resolution, or any other theatrical convention. Even the Shakespearean division into five acts is a sarcastic reminder of tragic form.[15] The author demonstrates his irreverence for this canonical work in Hamlet's first self-negating lines: "I was Hamlet. I stood on the coast and spoke with the surf BLABLA" (Müller 1978, 11).[16] In what appears at first glance to be a nonsensical, almost anarchic text, Müller presents his audience with a rich conglomeration of historical and literary citations, a deliberately constructed puzzle with no simple solution. Müller quotes in a figurative way from the tortured legacy of European history in the twentieth century, at once refusing temporal coherence and jostling his audience out of complacency and forgetting. The text also quotes literally from Shakespeare's *Richard III*, Hölderlin, T.S. Eliot, Andy Warhol, Sartre,

---

12. "Man glaubte, im geschichtlichen Ablauf, selbst das Trauerspiel mit Händen zu greifen" (Benjamin 1972c, 243).

13. David Ravit (1999/2000, 172) situates Müller squarely between the two (conflicting) influences of Benjamin and Brecht. While Müller takes from Benjamin the interest in history the aesthetic distance or aura that gives a work its cultic and ritualistic value, he is also faithful to Brecht's concern for the future and distancing as a radical refusal of history.

14. *Vergangenheitsbewältigung* literally means "coming to terms with the past" and refers specifically to attempts to understand Germany's troubled history of National Socialism and the Holocaust.

15. The five sections present a multiplicity of images in a complex web of intertextual and self-reflexive associations. The richness of the text lies in the layering of Müller's finely tuned tableaus.

16. "Ich war Hamlet. Ich stand an der Küste und redete mit der Brandung BLABLA."

E. E. Cummings, tabloid journalism, common proverbs, and of course
Müller himself.[17] The richness of this intertextual network further
destabilizes his already fragmented text, which functions as a form of
Brechtian *Verfremdungseffekt*, albeit firmly rooted in a strong literary
tradition.[18] Müller's use of citation is also his way of paying homage to
Benjamin's interpretation of history as anything but a continuum of
progress. Benjamin advocates that history be interrupted by a stand-
still, which demands engaged reflection (Maier-Schaeffer 1995, 23).

Elektra is injected into this intertextual labyrinth, a character without a plot and seemingly out of context, in a play that takes its title
from one of Shakespeare's greatest works rather than from antiquity's
tragedians—this is a *Hamlet* like no other. Müller's disturbed protagonist carries out a brutal act of violence against his mother—Hamlet
rapes Gertrude to punish her crimes. This effectively places him in the
role of the father, the upholder of traditional authority, and renders
him guilty by association. But Hamlet also revolts against his father,
here portrayed as a tyrant fully deserving of the murderous homecoming he receives. Müller models his Hamlet around several historical
characters, including the son of the Hungarian dictator Rajk. This
Hamlet must return to Budapest in 1956, knowing full well that he is
the son of a tyrant—hence the reference in the play to "Pest in Buda"
(Müller 1978, 17). Müller also includes allusions to Gustaf Gründen, an
important GDR stage actor, who played Hamlet in 1936 and was later
arrested and imprisoned for involvement with the Nazis during the
Third Reich. Furthermore, the author writes his own past onto his
character, providing his Hamlet with autobiographical elements. Like
his protagonist, Müller too was deprived of his father, who was sent to
war and died in a prisoner-of-war camp. But Müller allows himself no
self-pity. He brands himself with the guilt of a respected intellectual
and a writer in the GDR with privileges and rights denied to others.
This self-blame is evident when he states in the stage directions that a
picture of the author is to be torn apart by the actor playing Hamlet. It
can be no coincidence that Müller's initials, H. M., mirror those of his
play, *Hamletmaschine*.

This play is essentially about socialism gone awry, about Stalinism
and a politics devoid of dialogue. Many critics have viewed the work as

---

17. For a full account of these references, see Arlene Akiko Teraoka's *The Silence of Entropy or Universal Discourse: The Postmodern Poetics of Heiner Müller* (1985).
18. *Verfremdungseffekt* literally means "making strange" and refers to Brecht's theory of
distancing in epic theater. Brecht invites the audience to assume a critical distance from
the action onstage to achieve a didactic effect.

a highly pessimistic piece: " 'Hamletmaschine' is by far Müller's most negative play" (quoted in Raddatz 1991, 193).[19] Müller had translated *Hamlet* in the early 1950s and also composed a poem on the subject, projects out of which *Hamletmaschine* emerged. The silence of Budapest's Stalinist politics in 1956 and state corruption following the Rote Armee Faktion terrorist crisis motivated the playwright to distill the canonical work down to a few scant pages. In fact, the original text numbered some two hundred pages, which *Müller* condensed into a dense handful that he called a "shrunken head" (Girshausen, Schmiester, and Weber 1978, 26).[20] He confesses his fascination with the Shakespearean archetype: "For thirty years, Hamlet was an obsession for me, so I wrote a short text, 'Hamletmaschine,' with which I tried to destroy Hamlet" (quoted in Wieghaus 1984, 268–269).[21] Under Müller's hand, there is no hope for Hamlet.[22]

If Hamlet is doomed, it is up to Elektra to preside over the destruction scene—hers is the task of aiding in Hamlet's defeat and finding hope in the ruins left behind. Hamlet admits that he literally turned his back on the devastation surrounding him: "my back to the ruins of Europe" (Müller 1978, 11).[23] But Elektra embraces the challenge, not flinching at the naked pain she witnesses, and sets her stage with Conrad-inspired imagery: "In the heart of darkness. Under the sun of torture" (23).[24] Elektra is not alone in upstaging Hamlet but is joined by women in general. Using his mythological heroine's courage as a metaphor, Müller illustrates his conviction that women have a crucial role to play in taking over the revolution where men have failed: "When the men can't do anything more, the women have to think of something. . . . Lenin always said the movement comes from the provinces, and woman is the province of man" (1992, 295).[25] Müller confirms that Elektra is not merely an afterthought in a play mostly about the decline

---

19. "Die 'Hamletmaschine' ist das mit Abstand negativste Stück Müllers."
20. "Schrumpfkopf"
21. "Dreissig Jahre lang war Hamlet eine Obsession für mich, also schrieb ich einen kurzen Text, 'Hamletmaschine,' mit dem ich versuchte Hamlet zu zerstören."
22. If Müller shrinks Shakespeare's drama down to a few pages, performance presents another opportunity further to question the relationship of words and actions. In one Argentinian production called *Máquina Hamlet*, performed at the Brooklyn Academy of Music, the text was projected as supertitles above the stage. The actors made sounds that had no obvious bearing on the text. Brian Walsh (2001) reads this performance as a means to confront the "cultural revision of literary authority" (25).
23. "im Rücken die Ruinen von Europa"
24. "Im Herzen der Finsternis. Unter der Sonne der Folter."
25. "Wenn auf der Männerebene nichts weitergeht, muss den Frauen etwas einfallen. . . . Lenin hat immer gesagt, die Bewegung kommt aus den Provinzen, und die Frau ist die Provinz des Mannes."

and fall of yet another male hero. On the contrary, she is just the woman to lead the way to the anarchic revolution.

Müller's literary marriage of Hamlet and Elektra is not arbitrary. Indeed, there is a long history of incestuous textuality linking Shakespeare's play to the Atrean myth. These principal characters often find themselves overlapping in terms of both plot and psychological development. Even within the Attic tragedies, Electra's character undergoes a significant shift. She assumes increasing responsibility for the Apollonian oracle and with it the ensuing psychological turmoil. Shakespeare's Hamlet, full of melancholic despair and bordering on hysteria, resembles the Electra of later antiquity. Schadewaldt (1960) observes: "It should be noted how the *one* character from Shakespeare's *Hamlet* dramatically corresponds to the sibling *pair* in Sophocles" (591).[26] And yet what of Ophelia? Is she to be relegated to an insignificant role? Schadewaldt claims of the Shakespearean Ophelia: "Ophelia's suffering is femininely dull, simple, naive, uncritical, and unspeakably sweet in its appearance" (594).[27] The Shakespearean Ophelia is at the opposite pole from Müller's heroine, about whom the author says: "The main character here could rather be Ophelia than Hamlet." He even goes so far as to call his leading lady "a criticism of Hamlet" (Müller 1984, 50). Given that Oedipus is implicit within Müller's Hamlet, the character can equally be read as a critique of Freud's model son.

If Elektra's and Hamlet's subjectivities are blurred, we witness an equal conflation of Elektra and Ophelia. In fact, this play could be said to have just one character, albeit with many faces. Just when we begin to understand Ophelia, she introduces herself as someone else: "This is Elektra speaking" (Müller 1978, 23).[28] Throughout this most condensed of *Hamlets* we are bombarded with conflicting images of the two principal characters' gender and identity. Ophelia/Elektra reveals in the *Scherzo* that she is prepared to sacrifice a vital organ as a cannibalistic offering, asking, "Do you want to eat my heart, Hamlet."[29] Her partner seems not to hear the rhetorical question, instead responding: "I want to be a woman" (15).[30] Hamlet does not want to eat her—he wants to *be* her. This desire is reinforced when he appears dressed in

---

26. "Sei hier bemerkt, wie die *eine* Gestalt von Shakespeares *Hamlet* dramatisch dem Geschwister*paar* von Elektra und Orest bei Sophocles entspricht."
27. "Das Leid der Ophelia ist weiblich dumpf, elementar, naiv, unreflektiert und in seiner Erscheinung von unsagbarer Süßigkeit."
28. "Hier spricht Elektra."
29. "Willst du mein Herz essen, Hamlet."
30. "Ich will eine Frau sein."

the clothes Ophelia/Elektra has already shed in her "Striptease," which
acts as a prelude to their role reversal.[31] The play has been read as a Christological allegory, whereby the
corporeal son, Hamlet, is sent by the ghostly (spiritual) father to com-
plete a mission of redemption for the world, a vision that emphasizes
the divine teleology of the Judeo-Christian view of history (Teraoka
1985, 116–117). In offering up her heart, however, Ophelia/Elektra arguably usurps Hamlet's role as sacred martyr, which the prince willingly abdicates by declaring his desire to be a woman. Ophelia/Elektra
takes over where Hamlet leaves off, but she does not consent to the
teleological mission. Instead she engages in a different reading of history, as illustrated by her stripping off her old clothes and stepping out
in naked freshness. This third act, labeled a *Scherzo*, is an enigmatic
void, not a middle but a muddle. It is the only time Hamlet and Ophe-
lia/Elektra appear onstage together, but the moving recognition scene
we have come to expect is missing; instead, the two characters do not
even acknowledge each other's presence. In Müller's version of the
myth there is no anagnorisis; rather, the stiff structure of tragedy im-
plodes when Hamlet is erased by the female lead, who literally makes
him up as a whore.[32] Finally, he resigns from his duties altogether:[33]

> I'm not Hamlet. I'm not playing a role anymore. . . . I go home and kill
> time, at one/with my undivided self. . . . I want to be a machine. Arms
> for grabbing legs for walking, no pain no thought. (17–21)[34]

This last line is yet another of Müller's thinly veiled allusions, this time
to Andy Warhol's famous line: "I want to be a machine." While Hamlet wants to be a machine, Elektra vehemently refuses this role, prefer-
ring to flirt with self-destruction rather than to be caught up in the

---

31. Luc Lamberechts (2000, 63) points to the *Scherzo* as evidence of Müller's postmodern resistances, citing the carnivalesque promiscuity of the strip-tease dance as a parody of
German intellectualism.
32. Wilson's production captures the virtual atmosphere of the scene by inserting it as a
film segment, replacing linguistic acoustic with the emotional sonority of opera music.
33. In having his Hamlet cede his power and his hero status, Müller follows Benjamin's
prescription for a proper *Trauerspiel*: "The subject of fate cannot be determined. The
Trauerspiel therefore has no individual hero, only constellations of heroes" (Benjamin 1977,
132) ("Das Subjekt des Schicksals ist unbestimmbar. Daher kennt das Trauerspiel keinen
Helden sondern nur Konstellationen" [Benjamin 1972c, 310–311]). The singularity of the
hero is tragic, whereas plurality is symptomatic of Benjamin's allegorical *Trauerspiel*.
34. "Ich bin nicht Hamlet. Ich spiele keine Rolle mehr. . . . Ich gehe nach Hause und
schlage die Zeit tot, einig/mit meinem ungeteilten Selbst. . . . Ich will eine Maschine sein.
Arme zu greifen Beine zu gehn kein Schmerz kein Gedanke."

endless cycle of production. The particular motivation for the machine metaphor, Müller tells us, is that during his stay in Bulgaria in 1956, when he first engaged with the Hamlet material, there was a nuclear power plant directly across from the building where he was living (Müller 1992, 293). This impetus, coupled with his first trip to the United States, where he was confronted with television-obsessed and theatrically ignorant American audiences, left Müller in a rage against the tyranny of the machine. The machine metaphor is further emphasized by Robert Wilson's 1986 production, in which all movements are exaggerated, robotlike gestures. When Hamlet definitively abdicates his role as male hero for that of mindless automaton, Ophelia/Elektra willingly takes on the responsibility for their drama. She replaces Hamlet's lack of conviction with the angry determination and sheer violence that permeate her every word.

Unlike her mythological predecessor, Müller's Ophelia/Elektra shows no interest in revenging the brutal murder of Agamemnon. This rebellious woman shows none of the self-pitying sorrow of the young maiden mourning her dead father but instead toys with her own mortality. She relates her own suicide attempt with sullen coldness. And, unlike the weak-willed Hamlet, she is unafraid to assert her own ontology:

> I am Ophelia. Whom the river didn't keep. The woman hanging by a rope The woman with the slashed arteries. The woman with the overdose SNOW ON THE LIPS The woman with her head in the gas oven. Yesterday I stopped killing myself. I'm alone with my breasts, my thighs, my womb. (15)[35]

This is a matter-of-fact account of self-destructive behavior, the kind that leads to the original Ophelia's death. With Müller's character, however, we never know whether she ends up dead or alive. This Ophelia is no benign appropriation of her Shakespearean namesake; rather the character serves as a palimpsest of three powerful historical women. The first is the revered socialist leader Rosa Luxemburg, "Whom the river didn't keep," murdered but not forgotten.[36] The sec-

35. "Ich bin Ophelia. Die der Fluss nicht behalten hat. Die Frau am Strick Die Frau mit den aufgeschnittenen Pulsadern. Die Frau mit dem Überdosis AUF DEN LIPPEN SCHNEE Die Frau mit dem Kopf im Gasherd. Gestern habe ich aufgehört mich zu töten. Ich bin allein mit meinen Brüsten, meinen Schenkeln, meinem Schoß."
36. Rosa Luxemburg, assassinated on January 15, 1919, was thrown into the Landwehr Canal in Berlin, where her body remained uncovered until May of that year.

ond is the haunting figure of Ulrike Meinhof, "The woman hanging by a rope," a prominent member of the radical terrorist organization, the Red Army Faction, which threatened the authority of the Bonn government.[37] And the last is the author's own wife, Inge Müller, "The woman with the slashed arteries. The woman with the overdose . . . The woman with her head in the gas oven." The horror of their respective demises grants credence to collective memory. The very fact that this Ophelia/Elektra is modeled on a proliferation of private and public losses contributes to the ambiguity of the character, whose constantly shifting identity hovers on the cusp between life and death. The image echoes the author's conviction that "it is a mistake [to believe] that the dead are dead" (quoted in Kluge 1996, 145).[38]

Müller thus emphasizes the ability of collective cultural memory to transgress and destabilize boundaries when he transforms his suicidal Ophelia into the aggressively violent Elektra. She (Elektra) stopped killing herself (Ophelia) to live her dying in a more visceral way, as her words testify: "I set fire to my prison. I throw my clothes in the fire. I dig the clock that was my heart out of my breast. I go into the street dressed in blood" (Müller 1978, 15).[39] The new Elektra does not hide the intensity of her rage but uses her own body in a theater of cruelty. She is unafraid of the pain and danger of writing a new form of history, one that involves wrenching out one's own pacemaker device.

Ophelia/Elektra may have stopped killing herself, but her body shows obvious signs of abuse and degeneration. She is disabled to the point that she remains confined to a wheelchair from beginning to end. Just before her last lines the stage directions read: "*Deep sea. Ophelia in a wheelchair. Fish ruins corpses and dead limbs hurry past . . . while two men in white smocks wrap bandages around her and the wheelchair, from bottom to top*" (23).[40] The proliferating dead bodies surrounding this Ophelia-cum-Elektra drag her down with them. Unlike Hofmannsthal's Elektra, who feels burdened by the weight of happiness, Müller's Elektra is initiated into the world of allegorical ruin, rescued (in Benjamin's terms) only though the power of decay. If Ophelia/Elektra has halted or postponed her own death, she is unequivocal in her own destructive

37. It is suspected that Meinhof like Ophelia took her own life in prison.
38. "Es ist ein Irrtum, daß die Toten tot sind."
39. "Ich lege Feuer an mein Gefängnis. Ich werfe meine Kleider in das Feuer. Ich grabe die Uhr aus meiner Brust, die mein Herz war. Ich gehe auf die Straße, gekleidet in Blut."
40. "*Tiefsee. Ophelia im Rollstuhl. Fische Trümmer Leichen und Leichenteile treiben vorbei . . . während zwei Männer in Arztkitteln sie und den Rollstuhl von unten nach oben in Mullbinden schnüren.*"

conviction. Instead of pitying herself as the victim of the cruel world, enslaved within a chthonian realm, she reappropriates her body, not as a baby-machine but rather as an organism intent upon annihilating all life-forms. She prophesies an apocalyptic end, ironically transforming her nourishing womb into a death-cave of its own:

> In the name of victims. I eject all the sperm I have received. I turn the milk of my breasts into deadly poison. I take back the world I gave birth to. I choke between my thighs the world I gave birth to. I bury it in my shame. Down with the happiness of subjugation. Long live hate, contempt, rebellion, death. When she walks through your bedrooms carrying butcher knives you'll know the truth. (23)[41]

The last line is another of Müller's citations, not from Shakespeare or Eliot but from the testimony made by Susan Atkins, a member of the Charles Manson "family" responsible for the Tate-LaBianca murders in 1969 (Müller 1992, 294). We can almost hear the author's ironic laughter as he puts such violent words into the mouth of a corpselike invalid physically incapable of carrying out her promise of destruction. In this morbid scene, a metaphor for the unbearable weight of the ruin of history, Müller's inconspicuous use of a tabloid quote from *Time* magazine instantly reminds us that history is made with kitchen knives. The author lightens his heroine's load by using a playful juxtaposition of cultural frames—American television kitsch versus German history—to confront her own maimed status and the collective ruin over which she presides.

Even though Ophelia/Elektra willfully sabotages her own body in order to squelch the possibility of producing future generations, Müller's dark humor keeps morbidity at bay. The author even legislates the reception of his works as comedy: "If you don't understand 'Hamletmaschine' as a comedy, the play will be a failure" (Müller 1982, 3).[42] History with a capital *H* suffocates between Ophelia/Elektra's clenched thighs, and yet the invisible ruinous heaps are the raw material for new histories. If Hamlet expresses a desire to become the machine, Shake-

41. "Im Namen der Opfer. Ich stoße alle Samen aus, den ich empfangen habe. Ich verwandle die Milch meiner Brüste in tödliches Gift. Ich nehme die Welt zurück, die ich geboren habe. Ich ersticke die Welt, die ich geboren habe, zwischen meinen Schenkeln. Ich begrabe sie in meiner Scham. Nieder mit dem Glück der Unterwerfung. Es lebe der Haß, die Verachtung, der Aufstand, der Tod. Wenn sie mit Fleischmessern durch eure Schlafzimmer geht, werdet ihr die Wahrheit wissen."
42. "Wenn man die 'Hamletmaschine' nicht als Komödie begreift, muss man mit dem Stück scheitern."

speare's Elektra distorts the purposes of the machine and produces alternative versions of history with her body as antibaby-making machine. The portrait of Elektra in *Hamletmaschine* initiates an alliance with other female mythological figures such as Medea and Phaedra, who take control of their circumstances through violent acts and refuse to give in to their fate. Müller is at pains to show that mythology is not the idyllic origin of humanity but a truly imperfect world permeated with horror and destruction. Unlike Bachofen, who views the transition from matriarchy to patriarchy as a smooth evolutionary process, Müller reminds us of the proximity of myth's brutality to the quotidian by infusing his drama with references to contemporary political circumstances.[43] Here, myth is an infinite process and our female protagonist is destined to repeat her suicide/nonsuicide indefinitely in a cycle of destruction without end. For Müller, death is never a reason for sentimentality or nostalgia, for this is precisely the sleep-inducing reaction that stifles any opportunity for reflective redemption. The author warns: "These charnel houses, this museum, the attempt to honor the dead through monumentalization . . . : This is death-kitsch" (quoted in Kluge 1996, 146).[44] Müller disallows the kitschification of the dead by refusing his Elektra a glorified and sanitized death. Instead, she remains in a semimutilated state, mummified in bandages.[45]

In leaving his Hamlet-cum-Elektra maimed but not dead, Müller pays homage to Benjamin's insistence upon death as the important link between materiality and truth: "Death buries the jagged line of demarcation between physical nature and meaning" (Benjamin 1972c, 343).[46] Elektra's undead state, hovering between realms, represents the ruins of history, the unfinished edges, where baroque allegory lives. As in Hofmannsthal's *Elektra*, here again the decaying body is the ultimate expression of the allegorical. Left forever in an indeterminate realm, Müller's Elektra represents the double articulation of hope and de-

43. Müller was not alone among writers of the GDR in his appropriations of mythological subject matter. Christa Wolf, Anna Seghers, Volker Braun, and Peter Hacks also turned to myth as a means of illustrating what could not be said in plain terms under the socialist regime.

44. "Diese Beinhäuser, dieses Museum, der Versuch, Tote zu ehren durch Monumentalisierung . . . : Das ist Totenkitsch."

45. Müller also portrays the mythological Electra in the small vignette simply entitled "Elektratext." This is an even more severely condensed version of the Atrean myth, consisting of a sequential list of violent acts beginning with Tantalus and ending with the murder of Clytemnestra and Aegisthus.

46. "Der Tod [gräbt] die zackige Demarkationslinie zwischen Physis und Bedeutung ein."

struction, the allegorical refusal of a reduction to one or the other. As Hamlet's other, she epitomizes Benjamin's allegorical idea as an inevitable backward glance, a return to history and the scene of ruinous disintegration. Elektra is thus an embodiment of what Benjamin calls "allegorical people,"[47] which he characterizes as "apparitions from the realm of mourning" (370).[48] She is forever of the flesh, permanently allied with chthonian materiality and ruin. But Müller's Elektra is also master of her own self-willed death, figured as both a productive decay and a politically motivated disruption.[49]

By replacing his oedipal Hamlet with an Ophelial Elektra as a disabled destruction machine, Müller drills holes in several of the twentieth century's major narratives: Oedipus as universal psychological model, the name of the father, categories of gender, and teleology, to name a few. More important, by insisting on the transitoriness and unfinished nature of Benjamin's allegorical project, Müller questions his own and his nation's engagement with the past. The incompleteness of allegory undermines the former GDR's forward-looking, constructivist approach to *Vergangenheitsbewältigung* as an uncomplicated process of renewal. By placing his Hamlet/Elektra at the crossroads of history, looking backward at the ruins of history like Benjamin's prophetic angel, Müller critiques the naïvete of an antifascist politics that places blame squarely in the territory of the other. His anti-Hamlet confesses his own guilt at having ignored his responsibility to look history in the face: "I was Hamlet. . . . my back to the ruins of Europe" (Müller 1978, 11).[50] The rhetoric of antifascism is here exposed as nothing more than shallow propaganda.

Hamletmaschine is Müller's manifesto and his promise of historical vigilance, a terrorist approach to memory and forgetting. He employs his literary efforts to take German history to task and to castrate for eternity the nation's hero and the hero as nation. And yet Müller's mission extends far beyond Germany and indeed focuses not merely on the limits or aspirations of any one nation. His concern is with humanity as a whole and the oedipal subject as a dispensable, outdated, and problematic ideal for his allegorical project.

---

47. "die allegorischen Personen"
48. "Erscheinungen aus dem Reiche der Trauer"
49. Dagmar Jaeger (2001, 51) demonstrates that Müller often uses the half-dead, halfalive state to problematize the history of German fascism and the drowsy subject of history.
50. "Ich war Hamlet. . . . im Rücken die Ruinen von Europa."

3

From Pathology to
Performance

HUGO VON HOFMANNSTHAL'S *ELEKTRA* AND
SIGMUND FREUD'S "FRÄULEIN ANNA O."

Hysteria has a long and controversial history. The first documented
cases of the infamous disease of the "wandering womb" date back to
classical antiquity. The perception that Hippocrates was the first to discover this ailment was popularized in the nineteenth century and became part of the accepted lore on the subject, though this view has for
some time been called into question.[1] The nineteenth century also witnessed a period of extraordinary increase in the treatment and study of
hysterics, and this proliferation of knowledge precipitated the interest
in the unconscious and psychoanalysis. No clinical diagnosis or scholarly analysis of hysteria can be viewed without a full consideration of
the cultural and ideological implications surrounding the pathologization of human behavior.

Hysteria is a loaded term for many reasons, not the least of which is
recent investigations into the power dynamic of the doctor-patient re-

1. Despite its indisputable etymology linking it to the female womb, hysteria was not
the invention of Hippocrates but that of late practitioners who were responsible for this
interpretation. Indeed, it was not until the Middle Ages and Renaissance that hysteria appears as a recorded illness with symptoms and suggested treatments (King 1993, 4–5).

lationship. This dynamic has most recently gained notoriety through the media debates of the early nineties surrounding "false memory syndrome," in which accusations of childhood sexual abuse led to ruined families and outrageous legal battles.[2] Interestingly, there are considerable similarities between false memory syndrome and Freud and Josef Breuer's early case studies of young women in *Studies in Hysteria*. In both instances, the (almost exclusively female) patient is posited as victim. At stake here is not just the reduction of the afflicted person to the role of "patient," subjected to the probing clinical gaze, but also the larger debate surrounding the gendering of hysteria as a condition specific to women.

Freudian psychoanalysis has been taken to task on this issue by feminist theorists and historians (Luce Irigaray, Elaine Showalter, Jane Gallop, and Shoshana Felman, for example). Some advocate a wholesale dismissal of Freud's misogynist monopoly on female psychosexual disorders, while many others promote a rereading and reevaluation of these theories, with the view that one must first appropriate and reclaim this previously patriarchal territory in order to subvert its means and methods. My own position is that hysteria is best understood within the larger context of feminist and psychoanalytic criticism. In this chapter on Anna O. and Elektra and the one that follows it on Strauss's opera, I argue that Elektra is not a hysteric and show how she undermines any diagnosis by appropriating and indeed performing the medical discourse and disease as a defensive strategy. But I also show how Elektra's hysteria is perhaps intrinsic to her femininity and that it is like a language not understood by the dominant discourse of the Symbolic Order. Hysteria in this instance represents the radical otherness of Elektra as woman.

This twofold approach reflects the properties of two distinct feminist methodologies: *identity politics* and *sexual difference*. When I argue that Elektra is not a hysteric but that she uses "performance" to construct a positive identity for herself, I am relying on the constructivist arguments first made by Judith Butler in *Gender Trouble*. Butler (1996) proposes that feminist politics can do without a subject, that "there need not be a 'doer behind the deed,' but that the 'doer' is invariably constructed in and through the deed" (367). Identity for Butler becomes a *signifying practice* or a *strategic deployment* of language and be-

2. Elizabeth Loftus (1995, 20) compares false memory syndrome to the witch hunts of the sixteenth and seventeenth centuries; in all such cases potentially innocent people are tried and convicted without a shred of evidence save for the accusations of the self-acclaimed victim.

havior, which through repetition establishes agency outside the boundaries of ontology. Parody plays a central role here, used to undermine
predetermined roles. Where Butler's main concern is to disentangle
gender from sex, I will show how Elektra and Anna O. parody the discourse of hysteria through performance, all the while developing an alternative and powerful agency.

When I show how hysteria is allied with Elektra's radical femininity
and that these behaviors destabilize the Symbolic Order, I align myself
with the position of sexual difference associated with the theories of
French feminists, most notably Luce Irigaray.[3] Irigaray locates feminine strength within women's bodies and the specificity of women's
pleasure. Women should not aspire to be men's equals or rivals, claims
Irigaray, nor should they pretend to be either subject or object of a discourse. Instead, she advises "jamming the theoretical machinery itself"
and exiting the economy of logos entirely by implementing a *disruptive
excess* of the feminine, not as a mimesis reinforcing sameness but in the
form of mimicry (Irigaray 1996, 318). This is exactly what we witness in
Elektra and Anna O. as they adopt an aggressively hysterical stance.
They speak a language all their own, and their mimicry challenges the
hierarchical structures and the phallocentrism of Argos.[4]

Given this twofold approach to hysteria, the question might well be
put: Is Elektra a hysteric or is she not? My response would have to be
that it depends on positionality. If my position appears ambivalent, it is
because I believe that both of the above-mentioned approaches have a
valid place in feminist criticism and that one character, in this case
Elektra, can arguably play both roles, the hysteric and the antihysteric,

---

3. For Irigaray (1993a, 12), sexual difference is a thing of great beauty, modeled on
Descartes's first passion: *wonder*. Sexual difference does not mean a war between the sexes
but rather constitutes the opportunity for a new *ethics*. This new ethics develops precisely
out of and within the relations between the sexes, with the Other.

4. The proponents of sexual difference have been taken to task for perpetuating *essentialism* and therefore limiting woman to biological determinism. Monique Wittig (1996)
suggests that "the concept of difference between the sexes ontologically constitutes
women into different/others" (408), but Teresa de Lauretis (1996) counters this argument
by asking: "If there are no women as such, then the very issue of women's oppression
would appear to be obsolete and feminism itself would have no reason to exist" (383).
Other feminists have attempted to bridge the divide, for example Rosi Braidotti (1994),
who proposes a "nomadic consciousness" as an "oasis of nonbelonging" (19) for women at
the intersection of identity politics and sexual difference, but very clearly speaking as
woman. My own position takes into account the strengths of both arguments and uses
both to construct a positive *positionality* for Elektra that might even be characterized as nomadic. I read her as both performing hysteria and mimicking an excessive hysteria that explodes the logos of the phallocentric. My point is that the divisiveness within feminism is
of no use and that the two camps are not as much at odds as some would have it.

performing femininity and accentuating the difference of the feminine, with successful outcomes. This issue of gender construction ties in with the larger question of whether Hofmannsthal's *Elektra* is a misogynist play. In *Elektra and Her Sisters*, Nancy Michael argues that the drama and its author are essentially misogynist because, following Otto Weininger's argument, it portrays women and the feminine at the root of social decay in fin-de-siècle Vienna.[5] With matricide, the patriarchal order is restored. This is perhaps true, but it is also the case that Elektra is the strongest character in the drama—aggressive, rebellious, sexually liberated, and independent. It is a question not of either/or but of both/and. That is to say that misogyny and emancipation exist simultaneously in this drama. Ambivalence characterizes gender relations in general at the turn of the century, both culturally and historically, and this ambivalence is reflected in Hofmannsthal's portrayal of Elektra. Elektra cannot be reduced or distilled down to a single archetype but must be viewed from different angles and allowed to play several roles: the aggressor, the victim, the mourner, the survivor. In order to respect the plurivocality of the character, I also invoke various approaches to feminist criticism in my analysis of Elektra and her negotiations with the discourse of hysteria.

Written a mere three years after the publication of Freud's seminal work *The Interpretation of Dreams*, Hofmannsthal's *Elektra* spoke to the general public fascination with these new theories claiming to unravel the mysteries of the human psyche. In fact, the Austrian dramatist is said to have modeled his heroine after Freud's first famous case study, "Fräulein Anna O.," published in *Studies in Hysteria* (1895), and indeed there are many uncanny similarities between the two. The ideas of Freud's circle and the work of other psychiatrists were such an integral part of intellectual discussion that it is safe to say that the unconscious was an essential thread in the fabric of the cultural psyche.

Elektra and Anna O. each stage madness as a theatrical production and thereby demonstrate the limitations of the hysterical diagnosis and the established institution of the "female malady." The fictional character in the case study of Anna O. transforms the mania of her real life

---

5. Michael (2001) writes: "To see Elektra as an example of the 'emancipated woman' . . . is a misperception. Hofmannsthal was neither a bourgeois liberal nor a feminist. . . . Hofmannsthal's Elektra is instead the creature of a biological-determinist view of woman as a subspecies of man" (84). She concludes that Hofmannsthal's *Elektra* reflects his classical conservative humanism and that the drama reflects the "punitive strategies imposed by the dominant male order" (97).

counterpart, Bertha Pappenheim, into a rage against the injustices endured by women. Freud's quintessential lunatic undergoes a metamorphosis and emerges as a feminist revolutionary and social activist. Elektra, too, despite her initial portrayal as a hysteric, manipulates the drama into a carefully choreographed performance, in which she restores her father's lost honor, plays analyst to her mother, and symbolically cures her author's writer's block. She uses her hysterical diagnosis strategically to foil her enemies in the Atrean court, who mistake her violent actions for a disease.[6] Her triumphant exit as the wild maenad in the Dionysian *Totentanz* that ends Hofmannsthal's drama is symbolic of Elektra's larger project of transforming pathology into performance.

An important distinction must be made between clinical hysteria and madness. When referring to Anna O.'s hysteria, I invoke the medical pathologization of behavior and the discourse of psychoanalysis. With Elektra's hysteria, I address the character's specific maenadic traits as well as a more generalized cultural neurosis that inhabits the *Zeitgeist* of fin-de-siècle Viennese life. This chapter explores the interstice between such a cultural discourse of hysteria and the actual clinical case studies conducted by Freud and Breuer.

Our collective cultural imagination perpetuates the view that Freud was the founder, father, and sole inventor of hysteria. While this is clearly not the case, a set of circumstances, a social climate, and a charismatic personality came together in Vienna around 1900 to allow the ambitious physician to claim full paternity rights. One might say that Freud benefited from a milieu of burgeoning change on the cusp between a decaying empire and the novelty of modernism. Mark S. Micale (1995) argues that the accumulation of meanings of hysteria peaked at this time: "Hysteria during the European *fin de siècle* came to mean so many different things that by around 1900 it ceased to mean anything at all" (220). Hysteria was no longer a mere moniker for a set of symptoms and behaviors; it had become a cultural syndrome.[7]

6. Elektra's hysteria is imbedded in the subtext of Hofmannsthal's drama. The author uses his stage directions more than her speech to indicate the heroine's maniacal behavior. We are told repeatedly that Elektra is like a caged animal, wild with intoxication, and that she cackles uncontrollably at the cowardice of her mother and sister. As the drama progresses, however, her actions become more controlled and calculated, and her victory dance appears almost rehearsed.

7. If historians have disproved the myth that hysteria sprang forth from Freud's own imagination, it is also true that the debates surrounding hysteria have hardly diminished. A resurgence of interest in hysteria began in the 1980s, specifically in feminist reinterpretations. Almost twenty years later, hysteria is still creating scandals. The publication of Elaine Showalter's *Hystories: Hysterical Epidemics and Modern Culture* (1997) prompted a public outcry from many of the groups examined in the book. Showalter turns her atten-

Whatever the conditions that led to Freud's rise to power as the exclusive authority on matters of the psyche, the fact remains that he
barely acknowledged his sources.[8] Though he had an avid interest in
antiquity and was a serious collector of artifacts unearthed through recent archeological discoveries, the physician seemed strangely uninter-
ested in the Greek tradition of hysteria. The Oedipus of psychoanalysis is wholly divorced from his Hellenic family and mythic context.
Freud makes no more than a passing reference to his greatest teacher,
the pioneer of French psychiatry, Jean-Martin Charcot, with whom he
studied extensively in Paris. Moreover, he distances himself in an altogether hostile manner from his most faithful mentor, Josef Breuer, the
coauthor of *Studies in Hysteria*, without whose careful documentation
of early case studies Freud would have had no basis to prove that his
were the very first experiments in the particular methods of psychoanalysis. Mikkel Borch-Jacobsen provides us with evidence that Freud
spread malicious rumors about his friend and colleague Breuer in order
to discredit his reputation.[9] This break between the two doctors is of
significance because it makes it all the more difficult to establish the ve-
racity of events in the case study of Anna O.

Hofmannsthal's Elektra displays many of the same characteristics as
Freud and Breuer's seminal hysterical patient Anna O.[10] Hofmannsthal
was an extraordinarily well-read man with a baroque erudition and was
conversant in nearly all European literatures and languages. It is hardly
surprising that he was amply familiar with Freud's theories of psychoanalysis. While Hofmannsthal was not a convinced disciple of Freud,

tion to hysteria as a social disease, manifested in such phenomena as the fascination with
alien abduction, false memory syndrome, and satanic ritual abuse. She claims this kind of
hysteria is alive and well, an infectious disease more contagious than ever before. This
field, that is, mass culture as hysteria, promises to be a continuing trend, witness Elisabeth
Bronfen's equally novel approach in *The Knotted Subject: Hysteria and Its Discontents* (1998).
Bronfen demonstrates that hysteria is more than a condition or a disease, that it is indeed
a manifestation of psychic discontent and anguish at the level of culture at large. Hysteria
is thus not limited to the "patient" but is a magnetic vortex that attracts all those in its
midst, an enigma that afflicts the patient and clinician alike; indeed, all onlookers become
afflicted with its manipulative power.

8. Freud's claim of having "discovered" the unconscious is wholly unfounded, as
Lancelot Whyte (1960) writes: "The general conception of unconscious mental processes . . . was *conceivable* . . . around 1700, *topical* around 1800, and *fashionable* around
1870–80" (266).

9. Borch-Jacobsen (1996, 110) quotes a letter from Breuer's daughter-in-law, Hanna
Breuer, stating that after the rupture of the working relationship between the two men,
Freud refused to acknowledge Breuer when they met in the street.

10. Lorna Martens (1987), Bernd Urban (1978), Michael Worbs (1983), and Silvia Kronberger (2002) all comment upon the tradition of Elektra as the hysteric.

he was intrigued with the notion of the unconscious and incorporated these ideas into his literary works.[11] Shortly before beginning work on his *Elektra*, Hofmannsthal wrote to Hermann Bahr asking to borrow Freud's first book on hysteria: "Can you perhaps lend me (send me?) Freud and Breuer's book on the healing of hysteria through the revealing of a repressed memory for a few days?"[12] (Hofmannsthal 1937, 142).[13] Bahr wrote about the connection between *Elektra* and Freud's *Studies in Hysteria* in his 1904 *Dialog vom Tragischen*, and it is possible that Hofmannsthal was responsible for popularizing the case studies, which were largely unknown. Between 1895 and 1902 the eight hundred copies of Freud and Breuer's hysteria book had still not been sold (Worbs 1999, 7). My own concern is not whether it can be proved without doubt that Anna O. served as the model for Hofmannsthal's heroine. Rather it is my aim to compare the manifestations of hysteria in each case and examine their separate attempts to manipulate the imposed pathologies into a performance, be it theatrical, somatic, or psychological.

There are indeed some correspondences of a very concrete nature between this new Elektra and Anna O., for example, the untimely death of their fathers. Anna's illness began after her father, "of whom

11. Hofmannsthal states in a letter some years after he wrote his *Elektra*: "I hold Freud, whose writings I know somewhat, apart from professional meticulousness (the clever Jewish doctor), for an absolute mediocrity full of bigoted, narrow-minded arrogance" ("Freud, dessen Schriften ich sämtlich kenne, halte ich abgesehen von fachlicher Akribie [der scharfsinnige jüdische Artzt] für eine absolute Mediocrität voll bornierten, provinzmäßigen Eigendunkels") (quoted in Hirsch 1971, 74). Vanity was one of Hofmannsthal's major traits, and it was not uncommon for him to make disparaging remarks about his contemporaries, regardless of their social and professional rank. It is possible, however, that his scathing remarks are somewhat colored by the fact that both men shared a Jewish heritage. Hofmannsthal's grandfather had converted to Christianity, and the author did everything in his power to distance himself from his family history. There is no evidence that he was an anti-Semite, but he may have resented Freud's ambitions and stereotyped them as Jewish. For more on Hofmannsthal's Jewish influence, see Kovach (2002, 9–11) and Seeba (2002, 35–41).

12. "Können Sie mir eventuell nur für einige Tage das Buch von Freud und Breuer über die Heilung der Hysterie durch Freimachen einer unterdrückten Erinnerung leihen (schicken?)"

13. Opinion is in fact divided on the subject of Hofmannsthal's reception of Freud. In *Hofmannsthal, Freud und die Psychoanalyse* (1978), Bernd Urban quotes Adorno's observation that Hofmannsthal used psychoanalysis without ever letting it invade his literary works. On the other hand, Walter Jens (1955) maintains that it cannot be proven that this 1903 *Elektra* was modeled after Anna O. because "certain psychological categories . . . 'were simply in the air'" ("gewisse psychologische Kategorien . . . 'gleichsam in der Luft lagen'") (7). Moreover, Heinz Politzer (1973, 7) claims that Hofmannsthal did not need Freud to explain to him psychological phenomena and that he invented his characters solely on the basis of his own observations.

she was passionately fond" (Freud 1895, 22), fell ill.[14] Similarly, in her
first monologue, Elektra finds herself alienated and isolated from the
world without her father: "Alone! Oh! all alone. Father is gone, driven
down into the cold pit" (Hofmannsthal 1954, 14).[15]

Also, both women grieve in the twilight hours. At the opening of
Hofmannsthal's drama, the maids announce Elektra's agonizing
mourning: "It is indeed her hour, the hour when she cries for her father. . . . Always when the sun lies low, she lies and groans" (Hofmannsthal 1954, 9).[16] This reference to the evening hours echoes the
indication in Breuer's notes of Anna O.'s sharp change of tempera-
ment according to the time of day: "The regular order of things was:
the somnolent state in the afternoon, followed after sunset by the
deep hypnosis. . . . After the deep sleep had lasted about an hour she
grew restless, tossed to and fro and kept repeating 'tormenting, tormenting'" (Freud 1895, 27–28). It seems the shadows of the evening
hours allow for the expression of pain, whereas the daytime with its
bright light holds too many associations of the doctor's probing
gaze. This interpretation is reinforced by Hofmannsthal's stage directions for *Elektra*, which specify dark and ominous lighting in
shades of red.

Anna and Elektra also have in common the somatic manifestations
of inner psychological disturbances. Throughout her treatment Anna
develops ever more physical symptoms of her mental condition. The
doctor is originally summoned because of a cough, which he immediately diagnoses as a "hysterical cough," a *tussis nervosa*. Her symptoms
include headache, squint, disturbances of vision, and paralysis of the
right upper arm that migrates to the lower extremity, eventually en-
compassing the entire left side of her body. Subsequently, Anna begins
to suffer from hallucinations and aphasia. There are physical repercussions from Elektra's ordeal as well. She complains to Orestes that she
has been robbed of her beauty and reduced to a mere shadow of her

14. Anna's father died after the treatment of her disorder had already begun and the
hysteria was considerably advanced. When she learned of his death, Anna's condition
worsened and she could no longer recognize people around her, even close family members: "All the people she saw seemed like wax figures without any connection with her"
(Freud 1895, 26).

15. "Allein! Weh, ganz allein, Der Vater fort, / hinabgescheucht in die kalten Klüfte."
Silvia Kronberger (2002, 235) points out that the two women also have similar relations to
their mothers. Bertha Pappenheim was apparently oppressed by her mother and did not
begin to travel or publish until after her death.

16. "Ist doch ihre Stunde, / die Stunde wo sie um den Vater heult. . . . Immer, wenn die
Sonne tief steht, / liegt sie und stönt."

former self: "I am only the corpse of your sister, my poor child. I know I make you shudder" (Hofmannsthal 1954, 62).[17]

Moreover, the two hysterics are said to be passionate and clever[18] and are also both virgins.[19] Yet each woman is sexualized to some degree by her role. Anna O. employs the theatrical arts to stage a false pregnancy near the end of her treatment, naming Breuer as the father. Perhaps she is merely responding to the doctor's own repressed fantasies about his patient.[20] Elektra is portrayed in a highly eroticized manner, mirrored in the stage directions, which indicate her scant dress: "Elektra wears a despicable awful garb, which is too short for her. Her legs are naked, as are her arms" (Hofmannsthal 1951c, 84).[21] The mythological heroine has been compared to Wedekind's Lulu and Wilde's Salomé, two of the most seductive characters to grace the European stage. Together with these sexual icons, Elektra epitomizes the

17. "Ich bin nur mehr der Leichnam deiner Schwester, / mein armes Kind. Ich weiß, es schaudert dich / vor mir."

18. Breuer's initial description of Anna emphasizes her powers of intellect: "She was markedly intelligent, with an astonishingly quick grasp of things and penetrating intuition. She possessed a powerful intellect which would have been capable of digesting solid mental pablum and which stood in need of it." However, his description of her during her illness shows a considerable deterioration in these talents and a general progression whereby emotions dominate thought processes: "Her states of feeling always tended to a slight exaggeration, alike of cheerfulness and gloom; hence she was sometimes subject to moods" (Freud 1895, 21). Similarly, Hofmannsthal's Elektra is given to emotional extremes, and yet she has qualities of strength and intelligence, as Klytämnestra observes: "If only you wanted to, you could say something to help me. . . . you are clever. In your head, all is strong" ("Wenn du nur wolltest, / du könntest etwas sagen, das mir nützt. . . . du bist klug. / In deinem Kopf ist alles stark") (Hofmannsthal 1954, 30). However, the maids who mock Elektra at the beginning of her drama present her in negative terms and label her a cat and a demon. They suggest she be kept under lock and key. It becomes apparent that both Anna and Elektra are understimulated, causing each to resort to performance as a means of amusing herself.

19. Breuer makes this explicit when he comments: "The element of sexuality was astonishingly undeveloped in her" (Freud 1895, 21). It is curious that this statement is inserted for no apparent reason. Perhaps it was in Breuer's interest to emphasize Anna's asexuality, thus deflecting any suspicion about his intentions toward his patient. Similarly, Hofmannsthal's Elektra is a virgin. This is a significant detail, for her status as virgin makes it possible for her to participate in the matricide. Marriage would have restricted her movements severely. Though Elektra is a virgin, Hofmannsthal sexualizes her character by using animal imagery (see McMullen 1985, 649). Such erotic overtones imply that Elektra has figuratively lost her virginity, that she has been robbed of her chastity by Agamemnon's ghost. Elektra tells Orest that her father is to blame for her lost beauty: "this sweet shiver I have had to sacrifice to my father. . . . Jealous are the dead" ("diese süssen Schauder / hab ich dem Vater opfern müssen. . . . Eifersüchtig sind / die Toten") (Hofmannsthal 1954, 63). We might say that Anna O. loses her youthful innocence, violated by Breuer's treatment.

20. See Borch-Jakobsen (1996) and Kronberger (2002) for a full account of this episode.

21. "Elektra trägt ein verächtliches elendes Gewand, das zu kurz für sie ist. Ihre Beine sind nackt, ebenso ihre Arme."

archetype of the "femme fatale" so prevalent in the artistic productions of the fin-de-siècle period.[22]

The introductory notes to *Studies in Hysteria* do not mention sexuality but concentrate rather on the element of repressed memories and their subsequent articulation in language via the associative method. And yet as early as 1896, one year after the publication of the first case studies, Freud delivered his lecture "The Aetiology of Hysteria," in which he amended his earlier theory, adding a significant corollary on sexuality. He claimed: "I have been able to discover this connection [between hysteria and sexuality] in every single symptom, and, where the circumstances allowed, to confirm it by therapeutic success" (1896, 199). Thus, although these underlying sexual forces are nowhere mentioned in Anna O.'s case study, Freud included it retroactively. This proclamation also provided the basis for his "seduction theory" made famous in the case of Dora, where Freud interpreted her claim of unwanted sexual attention as a sign of her repressed desires. His thesis was that "at the bottom of every case of hysteria there *are one or more occurrences of premature sexual experience*" (Freud 1895, 203). We might consider the consequences of this statement for Anna O. Would Freud have speculated that Anna was traumatized by an early sexual experience? Such a view obviously contradicts Breuer's claim that Anna's sexuality was "astonishingly undeveloped" (Freud 1895, 21). Hofmannsthal's erotic depiction of his hysterical Elektra anticipates Freud's later representation of the hysteric in sexual terms.

Freud subsequently added yet another dimension to his thought on hysteria, obviously following from his treatment of oedipal conflict in "Three Essays on the Theory of Sexuality." He concluded that hysterical symptoms were the somatic representation of a repressed bisexual conflict, an unconscious refusal to accept a single and defined subject position in the oedipal structures of desire and identity. Resolution of sexual fantasy is impossible because there are "*two* sexual phantasies, of which one has a masculine and the other a feminine character," from

22. The femme fatale is a ubiquitous figure at the turn of the century. Young women were deemed prone to prostitution, as they were considered by nature promiscuous. In *Difference and Pathology*, Gilman (1985, 54) argues that the explosion in child prostitution is concomitant with the general fascination with female sexuality in all its polymorphous forms. In a typically determinist fashion, Otto Weininger states in *Geschlecht und Charakter* (*1903*): "The longer I think about it, the more prostitution *appears to be a possibility for all women*" ("Je länger ich über sie nachdenke, desto mehr die Prostitution eine *Möglichkeit für alle Frauen zu sein scheint*") (Weininger 1980, 313). While Elektra is by no means a prostitute, Weininger's theory reflects the cultural climate of the time, which upheld the belief that all women were liable to give in to their base erotic instincts.

which Freud concluded that "one of these phantasies springs from a homosexual impulse" (1908, 164). "Bisexuality" here refers to ambiguity with respect to the hysteric's sexual identification, portrayed for example in Elektra's masculine-gendered traits.[23] She was an anomaly in her time in that she was solely responsible for her actions, with no man around her to restrict her movements—her father dead, her brother exiled, and no husband.

Elektra is not alone in her refusal to embrace femininity entirely. Sarah Kofman explains that this is indeed the case for all women because becoming woman is an endless process. By Freud's own definition, then, this implies a certain degree of masculinity in every woman. When a girl relinquishes her original bisexuality, she has three choices: "the path of 'normal' femininity, the path of the neurotic (hysterical) woman, and the path of masculine overcompensation (that of the woman who is never able to accept her 'feminine destiny')" (Kofman 1985, 123). Kofman argues that hysteria is merely a manifestation of the trauma of undecidability. Becoming fully "feminine" or "masculine" is a choice that no woman should have to make. As we have seen, Elektra has difficulty allying herself definitively with either the masculine principle or the feminine principle. She wants to revenge her father's death, thus following the masculine ideal, and yet her decision to take matters into her own hands and enact a bloody murder simultaneously allies her with Klytämnestra's feminine principle.

There are many reasons why the case study of Anna O. was crucial for Freud and Breuer. First of all, the original therapy, beginning with Anna's father's illness in July 1880 and ending with Breuer's abrupt departure in April 1881, was contemporaneous with key discoveries documented by Charcot and Pierre Janet, two of the foremost French psychiatrists. Freud and Breuer wanted to claim the rights to this new field, and their description of Anna O.'s therapy provided them that opportunity. In their introduction to *Studies in Hysteria*, they state that this case was the first instance where a truly psychoanalytic method was used to treat the patient, although it is plain that Anna herself was to some extent instrumental in guiding her physician. After all, it was she who labeled their discussions the "talking cure" (Freud 1895, 30), creat-

23. We might consider Elektra's overtly sexualized behavior toward her sister as an instance of such bisexual ambivalence and her inability to resolve it as one of the causes of her hysteria. Freud maintains that hysterical symptoms result from a person's inability to accept a particular subject position and object choice. However, Elektra's polymorphous sexuality can also be read as a rebellion against fixed oedipal structures. Her unbridled sexual energy seems to fuel her struggle for revenge.

ing a lasting epithet for Freud's cathartic or associative method. Breuer reports that Anna also gave this process another term, "chimney-sweeping," a word that may be read as an ironic statement on her part, drawing attention to the invasive nature of therapy. It all depends on who is doing the sweeping, of course, but perhaps Anna was making fun of Breuer's method of probing and prodding her for the kind of information (memories) that would best serve his project.[24]

One of the most radical reevaluations of this striking case is Mikkel Borch-Jacobsen's *Remembering Anna O.: A Century of Mystification*. This is both a scholarly work and a cross between a paper chase and a murder mystery, in which Borch-Jacobsen unveils a tale of fabrication and deceit behind the façade of the case study. For example, he reveals that the cathartic method was first in use in 1889 (Borch-Jacobsen 1996, 26) and maintains that Freud and Breuer could not have known of this method at the time of Anna O.'s treatment: "Clearly, then, the theme of pathogenic memory was introduced into the Bertha Pappenheim case only later on, to make it fit the theory of traumatic hysteria put forward by Charcot and the Salpêtrière school" (55).[25]

Borch-Jacobsen questions Freud and Breuer's methods of analysis and many subsequent assumptions made on the basis of this one case study, and he demonstrates that it was a complete failure: "It may be true that the cure of Anna O. consisted—*partly*—in her relating 'memories' to Breuer, but it is just plain untrue that this treatment ever got rid of her symptoms" (9).[26] We learn that when Breuer abandoned

---

24. Fritz Schweighofer (1987) puts it another way, arguing that Anna O. had her own carefully constructed package of lies that she was selling to Breuer for the price of his attentions. He hypothesizes that Pappenheim, a very intelligent yet bored young woman, transforms herself into Anna O. of her own volition so as to escape her restrictive role as her father's nurse: "This means that in the given situation: Bertha betrays Breuer, he betrays Freud, and Freud betrays the public" ("Das heißt in der gegebenden Situation: Bertha betrügt Breuer, dieser betrügt Freud, und Freud betrügt das Publikum") (7–8). Each has valid reasons for constructing a web of lies, but no one of them is single-handedly responsible for the resulting betrayal. What is important in Schweighofer's version is the shift in perspective from Anna as victim to her active and manipulative performance.

25. Jeffrey Masson (1984, 51–54) also confirms that Freud concealed a number of important details about his Parisian education under men such as Antonin Delcasse, Paul Brouardel, and Ambroise Tardieu. He returned to Vienna with books by them dealing with the subject that would become his obsession for the next decade, but nowhere does he cite them as sources for his theories.

26. Breuer states optimistically in the case study that when the treatment had ended "her condition was bearable, both physically and mentally" (Freud 1895, 32). In short, the case study paints the therapy as "a successful cure" (Freud 1916a, 15:257). Borch-Jacobsen (1996) uses letters from the doctors who treated Bertha Pappenheim subsequently to show that Pappenheim was not well after her analysis and that it was quite some time before she was able to carry on with her life.

Pappenheim's treatment, she was sent to a sanitarium. In a letter to his fiancée, Martha Bernays, Freud mentioned Breuer's distress at the situation: "Breuer is constantly talking about her, says he wishes she were dead so that the poor woman could be free of her suffering. He says she will never be well again, that she is completely shattered" (quoted in Borch-Jacobsen 1996, 25). This death wish raises the question of how the story should end. The doctor appears to be distressed that there has been no neat closure to the analysis such as her death would have provided. Hofmannsthal could not have known about this detail, though when he finishes off his drama with Elektra's death Breuer's secret wish is metaphorically fulfilled. Unlike the mythological character, however, the heroine of this case study survives in the end as a reminder of Breuer's failed project.[27]

Perhaps more interesting than the similarities between Elektra and Anna O. are the markers that divide the mythological character from her clinical counterpart. For instance, each has discrepancies in her memory, one of the key elements in Freud and Breuer's initial discussion of hysteria. The physicians claim that once the repressed memory of an original trauma has been "put into words," the patient ceases to suffer from the afflicting symptoms: "*Each individual hysterical symptom immediately and permanently disappeared when we had succeeded in bringing clearly to light the memory of the event by which it was provoked*" (Freud 1895, viii–xix). This may be true in Breuer's account of Anna O.'s progress (if not in reality), but Hofmannsthal's Elektra does not suffer because she is unable to remember the cause of her discomfort. On the contrary, the root of her disturbance is precisely her inability to *forget* Agamemnon's murder. Memory haunts her, not repression.

In the second scene of the play, Elektra attempts to enlist her sister's help in carrying out the matricide, but Chrysothemis will have none of it, claiming that it is inappropriate for women to concern themselves with such matters and that she is not prepared to sacrifice her life for the cause: "No, I am a woman and want a woman's fate" (Hofmannsthal 1954, 19).[28] She urges Elektra to forget about their father's awful death, provoking this outraged response: "Forget? What! Am I

---

27. Two very different interpretations of Anna O. have been proposed. The first, put forward by Showalter (1985) in *The Female Malady*, shows the patient as an innocent and unwilling participant: "Evening after evening, like the sultan with Scheherazade, Breuer made Anna tell him stories" (156). Borch-Jacobsen (1996) takes the opposite view, which corresponds with my own reading, in which Anna appears as the stage manager of her own treatment.

28. "Nein, ich bin / ein Weib und will ein Weiberschicksal."

an animal? forget? . . . I'm no animal, I *cannot forget!*" (20–21).[29] Elektra
has become the embodiment of memory itself, and her sister's suggestion disgusts her. She may not be a civilized woman in her present state
as slave girl of Argos, but she knows that her honor and her family's
name depend on her memory of Agamemnon's murder.

If Elektra suffers from memory, her mother is plagued by her efforts
to repress the memory of her role in her husband's murder. Klytämnestra can find no peace and must repeatedly relive her own fear and dread
through terrifying dreams. Exasperated by these nightmares, she im-
plores her daughter: "Have you no remedy for dreams?"[30] to which
Elektra responds with false innocence, barely concealing her pleasure at
her mother's distress: "Do you dream, Mother?" (Hofmannsthal 1954,
29).[31] In the long conversation following this exchange, Elektra takes on
the role of the analyst to the troubled Klytämnestra, who has already
chosen to play the helpless patient. She describes her discomfort:[32]

> It is nothing, not even a nightmare, and yet it is so terrible that my soul
> wishes to be hanged and every limb yearns for death, and yet I live and
> am not even sick: you can see for yourself: do I look sick? Is it then pos-
> sible to perish, alive, like a rotting carcass? (Hofmannsthal 1954, 31)[33]

Klytämnestra's complaints bear an uncanny resemblance to the classic
symptoms of hysteria and to a case study in Freud's work closest in date
to Hofmannsthal's play: *The Interpretation of Dreams*. Though few
people had actually read the entire work, the controversial book was
the talk of Viennese society at the time when Hofmannsthal was writing his *Elektra*. The dramatist does not make immediate reference to
the concept of wish fulfillment, but dreams here are clearly a porthole
to the troubled psyche.

In their passionate exchange, Elektra and her mother both suffer
from the poison of memory in ways that are complementary and yet

---

29. "Vergessen? Was! Bin ich ein Tier? vergessen? / . . . ich bin kein Vieh, ich *kann
nicht / vergessen!*"
30. "Weißt du / kein Mittel gegen Träume?"
31. "Träumst du, Mutter?"
32. This idea was first put forward by E. M. Butler (1938–39, 169) in an influential article, though the text is clear enough on this point; Klytämnestra openly acknowledges her
daughter's special healing talents.
33. "[N]ichts ist es, nicht einmal ein Alp, und dennoch, / es ist so fürchterlich, daß
meine Seele / sich wünscht, erhängt zu sein, und jedes Glied / an mir lechzt nach dem Tod,
und dabei leb ich / und bin nicht einmal krank: du siehst mich doch: / seh ich wie eine
Kranke? Kann man denn / vergehen, lebend, wie ein faules Aas?"

equally destructive. As observed by Lorna Martens (1987): "Each woman represents a part of the other's psyche" (43). Their codependency can be described as symbiotic or even mutually parasitic: The analyst requires the disturbed patient and the patient requires the therapist to explain the mystery of the disorder. Elektra cleverly adopts the role of the doctor, as Klytämnestra herself observes: "She speaks like a physician" (Hofmannsthal 1954, 26).[34] The analytic session takes place in the middle of the one-act play and constitutes the tragic anagnorisis. The rising tension is finally broken when Klytämnestra's maidservants inform her that Orestes is dead. She is overjoyed with relief that her son will never be able to threaten her rule over Argos. But, as it turns out, this is merely another in a long line of tricks to which the murderous mother falls victim.

Underlying the intense atmosphere of loathing, fear, and deceit in Hofmannsthal's drama is another narrative thread: the problem of language. The tension-fraught dialogue between Elektra and her mother is littered with references to speech and words, to silence and the failure of language. The exchange between the two women clearly mirrors the larger language crisis that preoccupied many thinkers such as Fritz Mauthner, Ernst Mach, and Ludwig Wittgenstein during the fin-de-siècle period. The connection between the perceived decay of written and oral communication and diseases of the mind is inevitable. After all, disorders of speech were cited as common symptoms of hysteria, and words and their associations are at the root of Freud's "talking cure."

Klytämnestra turns to her daughter for help with her crippled tongue. She confesses her growing frustration with the ambiguities surrounding her: "What the truth is no one will know. No one on earth knows the truth about hidden things" (Hofmannsthal 1954, 28).[35] While she ostensibly refers to the whereabouts of her son, her skepticism can be read symbolically to refer to the psychoanalytic method, casting doubt on the ability of any therapist to shed light upon the hidden recesses of the mind. Nevertheless, she puts faith in her daughter's ability and urges her to use the power of words as a healing agent: "How a word or a sentence is pronounced, much depends on this" (29).[36] She demands that Elektra use her talent for language: "But you have words. You could say much to help me. Even though a word is

34. "Sie redet wie ein Artzt."
35. "Was die Wahrheit ist, / das bringt kein Mensch heraus. Niemand auf Erden / weiß über ein verborgnes Ding / die Wahrheit."
36. "Wie man ein Wort und einen Satz ausspricht, / darauf kommt vieles an."

nothing more than that!" (30–31).[37] Klytämnestra contradicts herself, first claiming that language can make all the difference and then negating the material power of the word altogether. Finally, in her anger and frustration, she threatens her daughter with her own words: "one way or another, I will get the right word out of you into the daylight" (38).[38] Half crazed, the mother seems sure that there is a "right word," absolute and perfect in its expressive capabilities. Ironically, the more faith Klytämnestra puts in the authority and healing power of words, the deeper she falls into the trap. Playing upon her mother's desperation and vulnerability, Elektra fabricates a riddle, telling her patient that when the right blood flows, her haunting nightmares will subside, and she will be free at last to sleep in peace. Elektra carefully doles out one clue after another: A woman must die and a strange man must do the killing. And yet, incapable of comprehending any but the most literal use of language, Klytämnestra is deaf to Elektra's subtle ironies. The mother thus descends further into her hysterical tirade.

Is it purely coincidental that this interpretation of clues resembles the method Freud and Breuer claim to have discovered through their analysis of Anna O.? Whether or not Hofmannsthal consciously appropriated the practices of psychoanalysis, it seems that the associative method does not work for everyone. Klytämnestra is too naïve to benefit from the subtlety of her analyst's language. Ultimately, Klytämnestra confirms that words leave behind the indelible trace of her actions:

> and our deeds! Deeds! We and deeds!
> What strange words these are! For am I still
> the one who did this? And what if! done, done!
> Done! what a word you throw
> in my teeth!
> (HOFMANNSTHAL 1954, 35)[39]

The patient now begins to see she will have to eat her words—and her deeds for that matter. Indeed, as is only fitting for a doctor, Elektra has the last word when she helps to silence her mother for good and usurps what little voice she has left. She spits out the answer to the riddle and

---

37. "Aber du hast Worte. / Du könntest vieles sagen, was mir nützt. / Wenn auch ein Wort nichts weiter ist!"

38. "aus dir / bring ich so oder so das rechte Wort / schon an den Tag"

39. "und unsre Taten! Taten! Wir und Taten! / Was das für Worte sind. Bin ich denn noch, / die es getan? Und wenn! getan, getan! / Getan! was wirfst du mir da für ein Wort / in meine Zähne!"

exclaims that Klytämnestra is the one who must bleed for amends to be made. Elektra is done playing and now uses the whole signifying force of language, sparing her mother no horrors as she describes her future death:

> You want to scream, but the air stifles the unborn cry and lets it drop silently to the ground. . . . Your venom dribbles bitterly into your heart, perishing you want to remember one word, to utter just any one word once more, just one word, instead of the bloody tears not even denied the animal in death: I stand here before you, and now with a frozen gaze you read the terrible word that is written on my face: for my face is made up of a mix of my father's features and yours, and so by standing here in silence I have destroyed your last word; your soul is hanged inside your-self—(Hofmannsthal 1954, 39–41)[40]

With this violent speech, Elektra performs a kind of linguistic hypnosis upon her mother, diagnosing a very strange form of speech impedi-ment. Like the hysterical patient Anna O., Klytämnestra has developed an acute aphasic disorder. Not only has her voice been destroyed, but Elektra predicts her mother's end. When justice comes in the form of an axe, words have no bearing. At the moment of truth, Klytämnestra will finally see language for what it is—a shifting set of signs that her daughter employs to fabricate a mother's most dreaded nightmare. This important scene revises the oedipal story in that the son no longer usurps the authority of the father, but rather the daughter appropriates her mother's position of power and prestige in the court of Atreus. Where Oedipus is an unwilling participant in patricide, immediately regrets his actions, and suffers tremendous guilt, Elektra is the sole agent of change. The steadfastness of her resolve becomes a poignant motif for women in the twentieth century.

Hofmannsthal as Hysteric

Elektra is not the bona fide hysteric she at first appears to be. Klytämnes-tra is at least as mad as her daughter. Yet we should perhaps consider to

---

40. "Du möchtest schreien, doch die Luft erwürgt / den ungebornen Schrei und lässt ihn lautlos / zu Boden fallen. . . . Die Galle träufelt / dir bitter auf das Herz, verendend willst du / dich auf ein Wort besinnen, irgend eines / noch von dir geben, nur ein Wort, anstatt / der blutgen Träne, die dem Tier sogar / im Sterben nicht versagt ist: da steh ich / von dir, und nun liest du mit starrem Aug / das ungeheure Wort, das mir in mein / Gesicht geschrieben ist: denn mein Gesicht / ist aus des Vaters und aus deinen Zügen / gemischt, und da hab ich mit meinen stummen / Dastehn dein letztes Wort zunicht gemacht, / er-hängt ist dir die Seele in dir selbst—"

what extent the author, too, suffers from a nervous disorder of his own. Hofmannsthal seems to have been afflicted with a rare form of linguistic aphasia similar to the speech disorder Anna O. develops during her treatment with Breuer. The doctor describes Anna's symptoms as follows:

> Alongside of the development of the contractures there appeared a deep-going functional disorganization of her speech. It first became noticeable that she was at a loss to find words, and this difficulty increased. Later she lost her command of grammar and syntax; she no longer conjugated verbs, and eventually she used only infinitives. . . . In the process of time she became almost completely deprived of words. (Freud 1895, 25)

Breuer observes that the hysteric's symptoms dissipated entirely once he was able to cull from her the inhibitions that lay at the root of her disorder. And yet Anna's own label, "talking cure," is layered with ironies, since this method resulted in her loss of speech and not in renewed expressive abilities. Anna finds herself incapable of speaking German and must resort to using her schoolgirl English.

Although Hofmannsthal never lost the capacity for speech entirely, his ailment had potentially severe consequences, since the loss of faith in language can be devastating to a writer. In response to this profound doubt, he adopted a fictional narrative persona, through which he disguised his true identity and yet nonetheless expressed his innermost feelings. This is the famous Lord Chandos, the younger son of the earl of Bath, whom Hofmannsthal had write a letter to Francis Bacon "apologizing for his complete abandonment of literary activity" (Hofmannsthal 1951a, 7).[41] Chandos claims that he is in need of medicine to heal the ailments of his inner self, describing this condition as a "disease of my mind" (8).[42] He laments that language has lost its authenticity, that it is contaminated and decayed. He sums up his doubts in a frank manner:

> In short, my case is this: I have completely lost the ability to think or to speak of anything coherently. . . . I experienced an inexplicable unease in speaking the words "mind," "soul," or "body." . . . The abstract terms the tongue must naturally use to voice a judgment crumbled in my mouth like moldy fungus. (Hofmannsthal 1951a, 12–13)[43]

---

41. "wegen des gänzlichen Verzichtes auf literarische Betätigung zu entschuldigen"
42. "Krankheit meines Geistes."
43. "Mein Fall ist, in Kürze, dieser: Es ist mir völlig die Fähigkeit abhanden gekommen, über irgend etwas zusammenhängend zu denken oder zu sprechen. . . . Ich empfand

"Unease" (*Unbehagen*), the word Chandos uses to describe the sensation of pronouncing these abstract concepts, can be read as a synonym for Freud's famous term "uncanny" (*unheimlich*), which denotes both a feeling of strange familiarity and one of terrifying fright (Freud 1919, 220–221). This same duplicity inhabits Chandos's relationship to language. He relies upon words to express his innermost self, but language has also become his enemy and fails him in his desire to articulate abstractions. As with Freud's "uncanny," Chandos's distress results from the slippery quality of language, which signifies something and nothing at the same time. Abstract terms present the greatest difficulty for him, and he craves a tangible element to save him from the emptiness he endures:

> I experience in and around me a simply delightful endless refraction, and among the materials playing against one another there is not one into which I cannot flow. (Hofmannsthal 1951a, 18)[44]

The paradox of Chandos's misery is that while his doubt leaves him in a helpless aphasic crisis, he is nevertheless intoxicated with the ecstasy of linguistic confusion.

Hofmannsthal uses the famous "Chandos Brief" (1901) to expose his phobia regarding the failure of language, and *Elektra* is his first major work published after his literary breakdown. The play has been seen as a turning point for Hofmannsthal, in which he leaves the inner world of poetry and rises to new expressive heights in his dramas of action. He abandons his former lyrical obsession with expressing the loneliness of the artist, isolated in his own consciousness, a state that Lord Chandos mourns as "the whole of existence as one great unit" (Hofmannsthal 1951a, 10).[45] This ideal collapses and is now reduced to mere fragments: "For me everything disintegrated into parts, the parts again into parts" (14).[46] It seems clear that Hofmannsthal hoped to replace the emptiness of the written page with the interaction of the real bodies onstage.

---

ein unerklärliches Unbehagen, die Worte 'Geiste,' 'Seele' oder 'Körper' nur auszusprechen. . . . Die abstrakten Worte, deren sich doch die Zunge naturgemäß bedienen muß, um irgendwelches Urteil an den Tag zu geben, zerfielen mir im Munde wie modrige Pilze."

44. "Ich fühle ein entzückendes, schlechthin unendliches Widerspiel in mir und um mich, und es gibt unter den gegeneinanderspielenden Materien keine, in die ich nicht hinüberzufliessen vermöchte."

45. "das ganze Dasein als eine große Einheit"

46. "Es zerfiel mir alles in Teile, die Teile wieder in Teile."

Elektra's role as analyst expands to encompass various members of her family—Klytämnestra, and to a certain extent Chrysothemis and Orestes—but she also symbolically treats her author as a patient, nursing him through his aphasic crisis. Hofmannsthal writes on the raw edges of language in *Elektra*, and the sheer dynamism of the heroine along with the horror of the action is just the therapy required to cure him of his linguistic skepticism. As many critics have noted, "the deed" (*die Tat*) becomes the driving force behind the plot, sending the royal family of Argos to their collective fate (see Jens 1955; Nehrung 1966; Rey 1962). As he dons the mask of the courageous princess, Hofmannsthal is able to trade the decadent and overused language that Lord Chandos despises for his own character's faith in action. In her strength and resolve to avenge her father's lost honor, and in her second role as healing agent, Elektra overturns her reputation as hysteric. Instead of accepting the diagnosis and resigning herself to the psychoanalytic couch, Elektra invents clever ways of using her madness to subvert the rules of the game and triumph over her circumstances.

Performing Hysteria

Performance is the key to Elektra's triumph. Following her convincing act in the medical theater, where she displays her talents in the healing arts with her mother and her author, she dances her own death in a powerful display of bacchanalian celebration. As Terpsichore, she again displays her gift for the sake of others: "I bear the burden of happiness, and I dance before you" (Hofmannsthal 1954, 75).[47] In her opening monologue, Elektra promises her dead father that once justice has been brought to bear, she will dance the *Reigen*. Hofmannsthal's stage directions indicate the explosive nature of her death dance: "She flings her knees up high, she throws out her arms" (74).[48] Elektra's body convulses in mute spasms before she tumbles limp to the ground. She dies in a magnificent and consciously willed exit. Her maenadic twirls of Dionysian ecstasy confirm the restoration of her father's lost honor but perhaps more important allow her to shed her hysterical diagnosis in a deliberate performance that exceeds the bounds of language and thought.

47. "Ich trag die Last / des Glückes, und ich tanze vor euch her."
48. "Sie wirft die Kniee, sie reckt die Arme aus."

Such a "dance," with its jerky and spasmodic steps, is not dissimilar to the behavior and somatic contortions documented by early practitioners of psychiatry, such as Freud's Parisian mentor, Jean-Martin Charcot.[49] In medical theaters, doctors were choreographing the performances of their patients, carefully documenting their behaviors as symptoms, literally a somatic code of movement and gesture. Charcot and Paul Richer's publication *Démoniaques dans l'art* reestablished the link between hysteria and demonic possession largely through iconography that underlined their resemblance to dancing. Felicia McCarren (1998) points out that "the significance of dance representing madness, hysteria, or possession changes with the medical climate of the nineteenth century" (3). Nineteenth-century medicine develops new ways of reading the body, making a semiology of signs, symptoms, and behaviors. In fact, various forms of hysteria continued to be called "choreas" because they looked like dance (McCarren 1998, 14). Moreover, Sander Gilman (1993, 345) has pointed out that hysteria has been largely characterized by the visual and the theatrical, which facilitates the association between dance and madness. McCarren builds on this link and argues that "dance's visuality must be read in relation to its silence. . . . The dancer's willful withholding of speech makes her art enigmatic, multivalent and ultimately, powerful. . . . Dance expresses nonhysterically what only hysteria has been able to express" (17). Hence, the power of Elektra's final words: "Be silent and dance" (Hofmannsthal 1954, 75).[50]

There may be obvious parallels between Elektra's *Totentanz* and the classic case of the hysteric. Still, she manages to hold her spectators in an emotionally charged moment of rapt, even hypnotic, attention, controlling the gaze and turning voyeurism on itself. We might compare this performance to McCarren's description (1995) of Loïe Fuller's dance as making "an art of madness" (753). If hysteria can be viewed as dance, Elektra appropriates this somatic vocabulary and makes it her own. She uses the clinical apparatus to great effect to mesmerize her audience. Rather than a manifestation of demonic possession, Elektra's death performance is a violent purging of the mad curse that has plagued her family and the nation of Argos for generations.

---

49. Charcot was famous for exhibiting his patients' hysterical symptoms in front of large audiences in a surgical theater. He documented their movements as a form of choreography and transformed their spasmodic gestures into an entertaining performance spectacle. See Gilman (1993) for a full discussion.

50. "Schweig und tanze."

Just as Bertha Pappenheim must be seen as an active agent in shaping Anna O., so too is Gertrud Eysoldt a real-life driving force behind Hofmannsthal's conception of Elektra.[51] About 1900 the talented actress was quickly gaining notoriety for her intensely dramatic performances of such figures as Salome and Lulu and was the inspiration behind Elektra. Mastering the Expressionist techniques of Max Reinhardt, the avant-garde director of the Kleines Theater in Berlin who commissioned *Elektra*, she could encompass a whole range of emotions in a single gesture or word. Eysoldt's response to the first draft of *Elektra* illustrates the passion behind her performance:

> Tonight I brought the *Elektra* home with me and just read it. I'm lying here shattered by it—I'm suffering—I'm suffering—I'm screeching from the immensity of the violence—I'm afraid of my own strength—I'm afraid of the anguish that awaits me. (Eysoldt 1996, 9)[52]

The broken syntax mirrors Eysoldt's intense engagement with the role she would play. It also reflects her conviction that language pales in comparison to the communicative capacity of the corporeal. If she performed the part with the same emotional outburst demonstrated here, it is not hard to see why the premiere provoked such uproar from the critics, one of whom called the play "a sadistic orgy" (quoted in Ward 2002, 135).[53] It is difficult to say whether the hysteria pinned on Elektra emanated more from the drama itself or from Eysoldt's striking performance, which Hermann Bahr claimed put an end to "the world as we know it" and knocked the wind out of audiences (Meister 2001, 195).[54] What emerges is a powerful evocation of feminine strength in the actress's ability to manipulate her audience. It is

---

51. Hofmannsthal first thought of Adele Sandrock for the title role, but in May 1903, as he was just beginning work on the *Elektra* manuscript, he saw Eysoldt play Nastja in Max Reinhardt's production of Gorki's *Nachtasyl*. It was immediately clear that she was the right woman to play Elektra.

52. "Heut Nacht habe ich die *Elektra* nun mit nach Hause genommen und eben gelesen. Ich liege zerbrochen davon—ich leide—ich leide—ich schreie auf unter dieser Gewalttätigkeit—ich fürchte mich vor meinen eigenen Kräften—vor dieser Qual, die auf mich wartet."

53. "Orgie des Sadismus."

54. Monika Meister (2001) compares Eysoldt's performance to that of Sarah Bernhardt as Salome, Cleopatra, and Theodora and argues convincingly that these actresses played fantastic, unreal characters onstage because the real issues of emancipation were too threatening to their male authors.

moreover evident that for Eysoldt hysteria is much more performance than pathology.[55]

If Elektra (with the help of Eysoldt) undermines her pathological diagnosis and even transforms her death into a powerful expression of the strength of human will through her performance of hysteria, it is from Anna O. that she takes her lead. Anna stages her own show and is *not* the helpless patient that Breuer presents to us. In order to gain a full understanding of the patient's theatrical talents, the case study needs to be reexamined within the larger context of her historic persona of Bertha Pappenheim. Breuer and Freud's account is just the beginning. It seems Bertha was at least as good an actress as the legendary Eysoldt. The clever patient had, after all, feigned pregnancy toward the end of her treatment and pinned the paternity upon Breuer. The incident resulted in the doctor's breaking off the analysis, perhaps the effect Pappenheim desired to bring about through her theatrics. At any rate, this embarrassing detail is an important lacuna in the published version of the treatment. Could it be that Pappenheim fabricated this and the other wonderful stories to entertain her analyst and fooled him into believing that she was a hysteric in order to escape the rigid restrictions of her father's house? After all, we are told that she was a highly intelligent and imaginative girl, though bored and understimulated, and that she led "an extremely monotonous existence in her puritanically-minded family" (Freud 1895, 22).[56] Like Elektra, she learns to exploit the resources at her disposal, using her "private theater" (22) to undo the logic of her opponent.[57]

Following the abrupt end of her treatment with Breuer, Pappenheim was sent to convalesce at the Burghölzi clinic in Zurich, where she regained her health, mental and physical. She went on to devote

55. The performance of hysteria is not limited to the theater and Freud's and Breuer's case studies. Franziska Lamott (2001, 52) documents the case of an actual turn-of-the-century hysteric, Hedwig Müller, and shows how this woman performed hysteria in a murder trial, manipulating the outcome through her own self-representation.

56. Anna O. does not receive the kind of stimulation she deserves and needs. In fact Breuer admits that during the course of her treatment she became less imaginative: "It became plain from her evening stories that her imaginative and poetic vein was drying up" (Freud 1895, 31). Perhaps he was responsible for dulling her creative inspiration by using her as a muse to fabricate his own inventive stories for his brilliant case study.

57. Dianne Hunter (1983) concludes that "Pappenheim actually treated herself, with Breuer as her student" (475). Mitchell (1992) provides us with an alternate reading of the Breuer/Pappenheim encounter: "The madness that came via her father's death . . . enabled Anna O. and Breuer to descend together to the 'Mothers'" (103). Mitchell argues that hysteria is the result of a crisis at the loss of the maternal (hence, the disturbance of language) and that Breuer saw in Bertha his own lost mother.

her life to saving young girls from prostitution, crusading against the
trafficking of women. She worked tirelessly to save them from ex-
ploitation and abuse, whether sexual or psychological, perhaps motivated by her own experiences of violation. Pappenheim played an important role in bringing about social reforms for women and was
especially active in Jewish women's organizations.[58] Regardless of the
fuel behind her efforts, the fact remains that the once helpless psychoanalytic patient emerges as a powerful figure of female liberation. Pappenheim transformed her hysteria into feminist activism; hers was a
performance of sexual politics. The case study of Anna O. demonstrates the two-way flow of power, which allows both analyst and
analysand to employ strategies of manipulation, negotiate new identi-
ties, and imagine alternative social realities. Neither Anna O. nor Elektra ends up the victim of an imposed pathology. Each transforms her
hysterical diagnosis into a powerful healing performance. Anna stumps
Breuer through her carefully staged "private theater" and goes on to
treat the social ills that threaten the lives of young girls. Elektra choreographs a "dancing cure" in her fiery revenge speech, which promises
her father a victory *Reigen*. Throughout the drama, she performs this
literal and symbolic dance. Elektra thus usurps rhetorical power from
her mother, restores her father's lost honor, heals her author's lost faith
in language, and even triumphs over death itself.

58. Pappenheim translated Mary Wollstonecraft's *A Vindication of the Rights of Woman*
and wrote a play entitled *Women's Rights* (Hunter 1983, 478). For more detailed discussions
of Bertha Pappenheim's life and work, see Fritz Schweighofer's *Das Privattheater der Anna
O.* (1987), Helga Heubach's edition of Bertha Pappenheim's *Die Anna O.: Sisyphus: Gegen
den Mädchenhandel* (1992), and Melinda Guttmann's *The Enigma of Anna O.* (2001).

Choreographing a Cure

RICHARD STRAUSS'S *ELEKTRA* AND
THE IRONIC WALTZ

The story of the Viennese Elektra and her troubles with Freudian hysteria does not end with Hofmannsthal's drama. The operatic adaptation by Richard Strauss (1864–1949) premiered on January 25, 1909, six years after Reinhardt's first production of *Elektra*, breathing new life into the character and opening up new controversies. While Hofmannsthal's drama was a great local success, it was the international nature of opera and the genre's ability to transcend linguistic and cultural boundaries that brought fame to the name Elektra and arguably cemented her status as an archetype of twentieth-century hysterics.

In his most avant-garde opera, Strauss adds an ironic twist to the heroine's hysterical diagnosis through the musical psychology of dance motifs. Elektra undermines her diagnosis of hysteria in a dialogue with Hofmannsthal's libretto and with Strauss's clever manipulation of the Viennese waltz. The familiar dance motif functions as a remedy for Elektra's neurosis and the larger cultural pathology of the period but also parodies the naïve frivolity and decadence of the waning Habsburg Empire. Elektra's *Totentanz* extinguishes the ironies of the waltz and, in contrast to Anna O.'s talking cure, performs a dancing cure, healing the wounds of the Atrean court. Strauss in turn puts on a medical hat and manipulates the pathology of the dance further yet to perform a "musical cure."

In 1900, three years prior to writing *Elektra*, Hofmannsthal approached the successful composer Richard Strauss with a proposal for a ballet libretto called *Der Triumph der Zeit*. While Strauss responded positively toward the draft the young poet sent, calling it a work of "great poetic beauty," he declined the offer, saying he had plans for his own ballet (Strauss and Hofmannsthal 1952, 16).[1] The two men would not collaborate on a joint project until five years later. This time it was the composer who contacted Hofmannsthal, inspired by a performance of *Elektra* at the *Kleines Theater*.[2]

Though the libretto showed immediate promise, considerable changes were needed before it would suit Strauss's requirements.[3] The most significant alteration is the drastic reduction in text, most notably in the speeches between Elektra and her mother, but also in the recognition scene, which shrank from eighty-six to twenty-three lines.[4] While this scene was severely cut, it is one of the only places where Strauss actually requested more lines, apparently to extend Elektra's ecstasy. Joanna Bottenberg (1996, 109) interprets this as the suspension of the drama to allow a lyrical outpouring of emotion in musical time. But it was the dance in Hofmannsthal's *Elektra* that most inspired Strauss. Perhaps the composer recognized its potential to unite words and music in an opera that would speak to the cultural aesthetic of the times. His earlier opera *Salome* provided a model for such an endeavor.

The protagonists of both *Elektra* and *Salome* are defiant young women, both suffer under oppressive circumstances, and of course both are dancers, some would say possessed dancers. Both operas are also set in ancient times and contain popular motifs of orientalism, exoticism, and of course a seductive and sexually deviant femme fatale. *Salome* had just debuted when the composer first saw Hofmannsthal's *Elektra* in 1905. If *Salome* had shocked audiences with its daring avant-garde harmonies and startling brutality, Strauss had even greater plans for his new mythical material. However, there were mixed reactions to *Elektra* when it premiered in Dresden as part of the Richard Strauss *Festwoche*. With the standing ovation it received and the great jubila-

1. "von großer poetischer Schönheit"
2. The relationship between the cultured, dandyish Hofmannsthal and the beer-drinking Bavarian Strauss has been likened to that of a flute and a bassoon (Simon 1992, 16). Hofmannsthal once remarked on the composer's "neglect of the higher standards of intellectual existence," but was much more flattering toward the end of his life (quoted in Kennedy 1995, 67). For a discussion of the working relationship between composer and librettist see Indorf (2002, 231–232).
3. Most of the early criticism focuses on how unfaithful Hofmannsthal and Strauss were to Sophocles' Attic tragedy, but Malcolm Davies (1999, 49–53) demonstrates that the opera is actually quite faithful to Sophocles' tone and theme, pointing in particular to the composer's and dramatist's talents at exploiting Sophoclean irony.
4. For a detailed commentary on the Strauss-Hofmannsthal opera, see Gilliam (1991).

tion accorded the spectacular performance under the direction of Willi Schuh, *Elektra* appeared to be a huge success. And yet following the premiere in Prague, a one-word telegram was wired to Strauss: "Failure" (Strauss 1953, 156). The composer had created what some would deem a cacophony of chromatic dissonance, and the critics were duly harsh. The opera's music has been compared to "a witches' cauldron, from which rise the most pungent and acrid fumes" (Carner 1971, 26). It was not long before spiteful cartoons appeared in the press showing patrons clutching their ears in agony at the screeching emanating from the stage and especially from the orchestra pit, where an unprecedented one hundred and thirteen instruments blared intolerably (Indorf 2002, 229).[5] Strauss wrote in his memoirs that it had been his aim to challenge the listening habits of his audience: "I penetrated to the uttermost limits of harmony, psychological polyphony and the receptivity of modern ears" (Strauss 1953, 155).[6] This statement indeed aptly sums up the effect of *Elektra* on many who heard it. Strauss not only ignored the conventions of opera but also tested the limits of the genre.

Waltzing Ironies

Imbedded among the avant-garde harmonies is a familiar dance form of the waltz, the musical signature of Vienna's decadent ballrooms.[7] At first glance, the lighthearted motif introduced by Strauss presents a sharp contrast to the Dionysian *danse macabre* that serves as a catalyst for Elektra's triumphant exit. Upon closer examination, however, we see that the waltz undergoes a metamorphosis and eventually acts as a figurative springboard for the dance that will serve as the opera's finale. The dance form appears numerous times in various contexts and is clearly at odds with the subject matter. The *Reigen* could be interpreted as just another sign of Elektra's apparent hysteria, but it turns into a tri-

5. Strauss included such rarities as the recently invented Heckelphone, the potent bass oboe. The composer was at the time by his own admission enamored with the dynamic setting of *fortissimo* (Strauss 1953, 156).

6. The alternation of harmonic tonality and atonality in *Elektra* has been widely debated. The opera is by some standards Strauss's most daring foray into modern sounds and was a decisive influence for Alban Berg's *Wozzek* (Gmeiner 1999, 80). But Stefan Kunze (1998, 505–506) argues that the presence or absence of atonality is not enough cause to say that *Elektra* constitutes musical "progress." He notes instead that the subject matter demands a different treatment than his later opera *Rosenkavalier*, which is much more harmonically balanced.

7. Strauss took great interest in dance and even claimed that he wanted to "modernize dance" ("den Tanz erneuern") in his ballet *Josephs Legende* (1914) (Woitas 2001, 411), but Monika Woitas demonstrates that Strauss's most lasting mark on dance was actually with *Elektra* and not in his compositions intended specifically for dance (421).

umphant victory dance and indeed dispels rumors of the Atrean princess's madness.[8]

The waltz first appears during Elektra's opening monologue as she outlines her plans for revenge. Her words tell one story, the music another. She sings of the slaughter and bloodshed of matricide, a speech filled with sorrow, vengeful rage, but also triumphant jubilation:

> When all this has been achieved and purple pavilions have been erected from the fumes of blood drawn up by the sun, then we shall dance, your blood, all around your grave: and over the bodies I will fling my knees up high, step by step, and they who will see me dancing like that, even if they see only my shadow dancing from a distance, they will say: a magnificent feast is being prepared here for a great king by his flesh and blood, and happy is the man who has children who dance around his mighty grave such royal victory dances! (Hofmannsthal 1994, 16–17)[9]

This revenge song is accompanied by a rhythmic reminder of the waltz, an aural allusion to diametrically opposing images of flowing gowns and happy couples twirling around an elegant ballroom to the brisk and regular tempo of the dance. But this is not quite an ordinary waltz; Elektra's own description of her stomping victory dance, kicking her knees up high in bacchic celebration, radically contradicts such images of splendor and grace. This chasm between subject matter and music foreshadows the ecstatic joy of Elektra's death dance in the opera's finale. What Strauss offers here is not the music of frivolous entertainment but instead a contorted, even deviant, version of the familiar dance form. The ambiguity presented by this disfigured terpsichorean theme plants in the ears and minds of the audience a seed that will grow into the *Reigen* that ends Elektra's life, a dance that, like this initial waltz, is both ecstatic and morose.

---

8. Bryan Gilliam (1999, 251) argues that *Elektra* is one of the first operas to take gestural, theatrical elements as a primary source of inspiration. Similarly, London Green (1999, 402) posits that Rose Pauly shaped the character of Elektra through her compelling performance and had a lasting influence on the reception of the opera. My own reading shows how the composer blends dramatic performance and music to put a new twist on Hofmannsthal's drama.

9. "Wenn alles dies vollbracht und Purpurgezelte aufgerichtet sind, vom Dunst des Blutes, den die Sonne nach sich zieht, dann tanzen wir, dein Blut, rings um dein Grab: und über Leichen hin werd' ich das Knie hochheben Schritt für Schritt, und die mich werden so tanzen sehn, ja, die meinen Schatten von weitem nur so werden tanzen sehn, die werden sagen: einem großen König wird hier ein großes Prunkfest angestellt von seinem Fleisch und Blut, und glücklich ist, wer Kinder hat, die um sein hohes Grab so königliche Siegestänze tanzen!"

Hofmannsthal's decision to end the play with the dramatic *Totentanz* can hardly have been a mere whim, since Elektra's death dance presents a stark contrast to Sophocles' bleak and enigmatic final scene. The poet had more than a passing interest in ballet and mime. He had written ballet libretti and numerous dance reviews and was intensely interested in the new dance forms. Isadora Duncan, who mimed the free-spirited maenad in her ecstatic interpretations of the dances of ancient Greece, made her Viennese debut in 1903, the same year that Hofmannsthal wrote his *Elektra*. It is likely that Hofmannsthal witnessed one of her spectacular performances, which were the talk of the coffeehouses and literary salons.

Hofmannsthal had other, more personal reasons for turning to dance. He held the nonverbal arts of music and dance in high esteem, praising them for their ability to transcend the expressive inadequacies of language. A little over a year before beginning work on *Elektra*, the poet had confessed in his famous "Chandos-Brief" his utter frustration with words, which were for him no more than empty shells and "moldy mushrooms" (Hofmannsthal 1951a, 13).[10] The collaboration with Strauss on an opera was a perfect means for him to overcome his linguistic uncertainties, made plain by the heroine's final words in the play: "Be silent and dance" (Hofmannsthal 1954, 75).[11] In an overwrought and manipulative dialogue with the waltz, Elektra performs a dancing cure and thus heals her author's linguistic anxieties, but she also speaks to the general cult of nervous hysteria at the close of the fin-de-siècle period. In chapter 3, I discuss the significance of the dramatic action in *Elektra* as a response to Hofmannsthal's language crisis, but here I will focus on dance and musical dance forms and the unique capacity of these media to express in kinetic and sonic terms.

Strauss's incorporation of the waltz motif is much subtler than Elektra's ecstatic *Totentanz*, so subtle in fact that it has been granted little scholarly attention. It has often been assumed that the music of this opera reflects the tormented unconscious of the hysterical mourning daughter (Jäger 1991, 145). Lawrence Kramer (1993) not only labels Elektra a hysteric but compares Strauss's treatment of her with Otto Weininger's misogynist portrayal of women and suggests that the "vocal shrillness and orchestral mayhem" mirror Elektra's "abnormality" (142). While Kramer is right that *Elektra* was written on the heels of Weininger's blatant attacks on all things feminine, indeed in the

10. "modrige Pilse"
11. "Schweig und tanze"

same year as his 1903 *Sex and Character,* it is also true that through
Strauss's use of the waltz motif, the Atrean princess successfully manipulates the misogynist message to her benefit. A careful analysis of leitmotivs in *Elektra* refutes the notion that the music reflects the psychological unconscious of the text. On the contrary, as Sonja Bayerlein
(1996) demonstrates, Strauss adapts the Wagnerian leitmotiv into a
more fluid system, which interacts directly with the libretto to create
an integrated psychological portrait of each character. Moreover, Bayerlein concentrates not on the heroine's symptoms of hysteria but
rather on her "repressed femininity" as the chief source of her unrest
(68–71).[12]

Unlike the Sophocles tragedy, which climaxes with the recognition
scene between Electra and Orestes, Hofmannsthal's drama centers on
the psychological battle between Elektra and her mother and reaches a
pinnacle of intensity with the heroine's collapse. The music does appear to echo this dramatic structure, representing the madness of Elektra and her world. And yet the waltz and the multiple messages it delivers seriously question this hypothesis.

Music and Words: A Polyphony of Voices

The relationship of words to music has always been a subject of much
controversy. One critic praises Strauss for translating Hofmannsthal's
psychologically complex narrative into simple musical symbols and suggests that music is a form of shorthand code for language (Jäger 1991,
145). On the other hand, Theodor Adorno (1978) argued concerning the
relation between music and language: "Music is an intentionless language" (2:252).[13] This implies that unlike language music cannot be interpreted because it carries no specific meaning, and thus mood and
emotion in music are connotative rather than denotative. Plato, too, declared rhythm and melody subordinate to words because language has a
superior representational capacity. Schopenhauer agreed with Plato
that music is absolute and unmediated, which makes it the vehicle for
the expression of true will but denies its capacity to convey pleasure,
pain, sorrow, or horror:[14] "Music acts directly upon the will, *i.e.,* the
feelings, passions and emotions of the hearer . . . unlike all the other
arts, it does not express the *Ideas,* or grades of the objectification of the

12. "verdrängte Weiblichkeit"
13. "Musik ist eine intentionslose Sprache."
14. Similarly, Edward Hanslick (1986) declares that music cannot signify emotion or
ideas per se, declaring that "love and anger occur only within our hearts" (9).

will, but directly the *will itself*" (1964, 3:232). While Schopenhauer elevated music above all other art forms, he nonetheless questioned its communicative potential.[15]

By the end of the romantic era, the concept of music as an absolute, nonsignifying totality was being challenged. Program music began to test the narrational and mimetic limits of musical forms, and Strauss was among the many prominent composers to cultivate this genre. Freud's psychoanalytic theories of the unconscious were also an important influence on the changing perception of music and cast doubt on the notion of music as an unmediated art form. If consciousness itself is divided and mediated, then music, too, must be allowed to function as both message and medium.

Carolyn Abbate (1991) calls this capacity of music to express on multiple levels a "polyphony of voices." Here, voice is "not literally performance, but rather a sense of certain isolated and rare gestures in music, whether vocal or nonvocal, that may be perceived as modes of subjects' enunciations" (ix). Abbate distances herself from Edward Cone's notion of the "composer's voice" as the sole narrator of the musical piece and proposes that there may be a plurality of voices, each with its own intentional autonomy. Such voices do not constitute a linear narrative driving the plot forward but interact separately and even express contradictory messages. The resulting incongruence is a source of pleasure, says Abbate, because of the tension that builds among the voices. If we consider Strauss's *Elektra* in terms of Abbate's "polyphony of voices," we must rule out the possibility that the music functions as an unconscious of the text, revealing the hidden psychological processes at work in Elektra's mind. The multiple voices created by Strauss's clever use of the Viennese waltz challenge the heroine's hysterical diagnosis.[16]

---

15. In *The Emancipation of Music from Language*, John Neubauer proposes that social circumstances paved the way for Schopenhauer's theory of music as a means of achieving divine transcendence. With the waning of absolute church authority and religious beliefs, instrumental music expanded its role from frivolous entertainment to a serious medium capable of filling the spiritual vacuum. Schopenhauer's thought allowed secular music to attain an almost sacred status as a vehicle for transcendence.

16. Susan McClary (1991, 80–82) investigates the musical representation of madwomen from a feminist perspective, arguing that composers have been attracted to narratives involving female hysteria because the subject matter offers tremendous opportunity to show off their compositional skills by ensuring there will be moments of wild dramatic energy. She goes on to say that the musical representation of hysteria is the result of a conflict between rigid musical structures and the desire to violate these disciplinary models. This very scenario may be said to be at work in Strauss's *Elektra*, with the heroine caught in the middle of the struggle.

As we have already seen, the presence of the waltz in Elektra's opening monologue creates an overload of conflicting images, both textual
and aural. Elektra's monologue begins not with the imposing Agamemnon motif but with a plaintive lament. Elektra does not sing the leitmotiv that has been associated with her character. Instead the English horn
and Heckelphone together insert the plaintive triad trailing off in as-
cending semitones. The fact that Elektra's musical signifier appears in
the orchestration and not in her own voice is just one indication that
there is more going on in the subtext than first meets the eye or ear. In
this first segment, Elektra can hardly be seen as a hysterical maenad. Instead, we encounter a dignified princess, who narrates the events that
have led to her present situation and outlines a rational plan for revenge.

The frenzied, rhythmic reference to the waltz at the end of Elektra's
monologue is fleeting and barely fulfills the musical requirements of
this form. It is in 6/4 time, and although we hear a dotted rhythm, it is
pounding rather than lilting. It begins just after §56 at the moment
when Elektra sings the last word promising her victory dance, "Then
we shall dance, your blood, all around your grave,"[17] and lasts for only
eight fleeting bars.

Paradoxically, the bacchanalian dance motif is juxtaposed with a
soaring, tuneful melody, which is more reminiscent of the ballroom
than is the waltz itself. This sentimental motif appears just before §46
and at §62 in its complete form, and as a fragment at §59, moving up
through the registers in different instrumental groups. The motif en-
circles Elektra's maniacal victory dance like elegant bookends. Strauss
plays with time signatures, oscillating between 2/2 and 6/4, a sign of
schizophrenia or an inside joke—either way his musical genius shines
through. Günter von Nau (1971) labels this welcome relief from the
chromatic tensions of Elektra's waltz the "ecstasy-motif" (422),[18] while
Christopher Wintle (1988) calls this same motif "Good Family" (81; see
fig. 1). This melody will here be renamed "nostalgia" for a number of
reasons. The whole orchestra pulls back, softens, and slows for this
moment of sanity with its regular four-measure phrases. The nostalgic
motif finally allows the orchestra and audience to catch their collective
breath. At §46, the strings are doubled by the first horn to conjure up
patriarchal institutions like the hunt and the battle—this motif has elements of both *eros* and testosterone.

---

17. "Dann tanzen wir, dein Blut, rings um dein *Grab.*"
18. "Seligkeits-Motif"

"Nostalgia Motif" (Wintle 1988, 81).

The nostalgia melody takes off with great promise but leads nowhere in a halting repetition and hesitation, leaving the audience full of suspense and anticipation. The motif brings with it a welcoming tonicizing effect to lessen the strain of the brutal waltz with its driving rhythm (it shifts from the C-minor Agamemnon motif into A-flat major without changing key signature), but there is no cadence and it is left unresolved. While this rich and sonorous motif evokes wistful memories of times long gone and the Habsburg Empire itself, the frenzied rhythm of Elektra's waltz affirms the new century, the age when technology and industry take precedence over high art and culture. One could even equate Elektra's chaotic waltz with the awkward newness of Berlin and the nostalgia motif with Vienna's Old World refinement and high culture. Strauss's major musical influences were German, and though he himself was a Bavarian, he is allied in *Elektra* with the future-oriented German capital, whereas Hofmannsthal is firmly situated in the cultural and literary milieu of Vienna, a city preoccupied by a certain wistful sentimentality or even nostalgia for its imperial past.

Vienna: A Parody of Nerves

Richard Strauss was acutely aware of his cultural milieu and would have been conscious of the powerful aural reference of the waltz to the father of the quintessential Viennese dance, Johann Strauss. Richard, who was at pains to distance himself from with whom he only coincidentally shared a name, exploited Vienna's most potent musical convention for its evocations of innocence and nostalgia. In *Fin-de-siecle Vienna*, Carl Schorske writes of Arthur Schnitzler's far-reaching interpretation of the waltz in ways that are also suggestive for Richard Strauss: "[Schnitzler] understood not merely the traditions of the world of the waltz but also the psychology of its individuals in their increasingly eccentric relation to the dissolving whole." The waltz stood for "the disintegrating moral-aesthetic culture of *fin-de-siecle* Vienna," claims Schorske (1980, 15). Strauss remained at a comfortable distance from the decaying metropolis, both temporally and geographically. Once the turn of the century was well behind him, Strauss, with the wisdom of hindsight, could comment musically on the social upheaval of those times. He notes in his memoirs, for example, Johann Strauss's remarkable ability to capture a historical moment: "At a time when the whole world around him was tending towards increased complexity, increased reflectiveness, his natural genius enabled him to create from the *whole*" (Strauss 1953, 77). This last statement applies equally to Richard Strauss, who possessed a gift for ordering complexity—while the waltz metaphor's multiple voices deliver conflicting messages, the composer keeps a tight control over the whole of his composition. Strauss is calculating in his use of the waltz to parody Vienna's reputation as a neurotic city.

Throughout his life, the composer had a somewhat tormented relationship to the Austrian cultural capital. Strauss was appointed artistic director of the Vienna Opera in 1919, but a dispute with Franz Schalk led to his resignation in 1924. Prior to Strauss's appointment, Hofmannsthal had voiced his reservations, knowing that his colleague, an entrepreneur and an advocate of the nouveau riche, would shake up the Old World conservatism of Viennese opera patrons (Kennedy 1995, 67). But Strauss never missed an opportunity to make a joke, and it is possible that he saw even Vienna's sacred institutions as fair game. He once described this aspect of his character: "I am the only composer nowadays with some real humor, a sense of fun and a marked gift for parody" (quoted in Kennedy 1995, 1), a talent he was already beginning to hone when he wrote his *Elektra*. It is possible that despite the opera's serious subject matter, Strauss could not resist testing Vienna's pressure points. If this is the case, then the insertion of the waltz in the orchestration surrounding Elektra's monologue may also parody the epidemic of Freudian hysteria into which Hofmannsthal's heroine was born in the early years of the twentieth century. In contrast to this collective *crise de nerfs*, the operatic Elektra comes across as relatively sane.

Strauss brings back the oral and aural irony for an encore during Elektra's confrontation with Klytämnestra by sprinkling the dialogue with the motif von Nau (1971, 422) calls "Joy."[19] Wintle (1988, 68) calls

19. "Freude"

it "rocking," conjuring up notions of nurturing, maternal qualities (see fig. 2). This melody is reminiscent of the nostalgia motif because of its lyrical consolation. Strangely, and not coincidentally, the nostalgia and joy motifs are more waltzlike than Elektra's victory dance. With their soaring, tuneful quality and lilting beat, they perform an aural reference to the Viennese waltz with all its associations of a splendid, if now almost forgotten, era. They are a welcome relief in an orchestral landscape dominated by clashing dissonance and harmonic tensions.

"Joy Motif" (Wintle 1988, 84).

But coupled with Elektra's quick wit and biting verbal irony, the joy motif becomes a weapon and turns Klytämnestra into a helpless victim. Elektra's joy is her mother's tortured anguish. Ironically, the motif first appears in Klytämnestra's vocal line at §148 and §165 when she attempts to persuade her daughter to give her a remedy for her terrifying nightmares. It crops up again in the orchestration accompanying her description of her affliction. Once her mother has fallen into the trap set for her, Elektra torments her with a deadly riddle, the clever wordplay designed further to confuse Klytämnestra. Elektra takes great pleasure in her diagnosis that when the right blood flows, her mother will be free from the tormenting dreams that haunt her, and she leaves her to guess who will be the victim of the sacrificial ax.

> Klytämnestra: Speak then!
> Elektra: Can't you guess?
> K.: No, that's why I ask.
> Say the name of the sacrifice!
> E: A woman.
> K: One of my servant women, tell me!
> a child, a virgin? A woman
> who is known by man?

E.: Yes, one who is known, that's it.
K.: And sacrificed how? At what hour? And where?
E.: At every place at every time of the day or night . . .
(STRAUSS 1990, §§207–211)[20]

Klytämnestra sings faster and faster until she reaches a staccato frenzy, so great is her need for the knowledge her daughter withholds, and she begs Elektra not to play games. "Don't talk in riddles" (§215),[21] she says. This is hardly the graceful pace of Viennese *Gemütlichkeit*, yet the melodic and harmonic peace of Elektra's joy motif that dominates the orchestration is sickly sweet as Klytämnestra sings: "I'm glad that for once I don't find you obstinate" (§216).[22] The nonchalance of the lilting beat parodies Klytämnestra's naiveté by drawing aural attention to the saccharine-laced irony of Elektra's tongue as she reveals that it is her mother who must die. The teasing becomes increasingly absurd as Klytämnestra digs herself even deeper into the grave Elektra has prepared for her. The irony here effectively invites the audience to take Elektra's side, bidding them to join in the shameless taunting and ridiculing of her mother. The juxtaposition of the lyrical comforting melody and Elektra's devilish words allows the daughter to usurp rhetorical power from her mother and the oppressive situation of the Atrean court. She turns the tables, such that Klytämnestra now takes on the role of the patient and Elektra that of the doctor.

These waltzlike motifs appear in encrypted forms numerous times, but the last and most magnificent example is after the final note of Elektra's duet with Chrysothemis in the closing scene. Immediately thereafter, we hear the most extensively developed example of Elektra's ecstasy motif (von Nau 1971, 421; Strauss 1990, §§247–250; see fig. 3), another lyrical waltzlike melody normally associated with the recognition scene between Elektra and Orestes. This is followed by the dotted

20. "Klytämnestra: Rede doch!
Elektra: Kannst du mich nicht erraten?
K.: Nein, darum frag' ich.
Den Namen sag des Opfertiers!
E: Ein Weib.
K: Von meinen Dienerinnen eine, sag!
ein Kind, ein jungfräuliches Weib? Ein Weib,
das schon erkannt von Manne?
E.: Ja erkannt! das ist's.
K.: Und wie das Opfer? Und welche Stunde? Und wo?
E.: An jedem Ort zu jeder Stunde des Tags und der Nacht."
21. "Gib mir nicht Rätsel auf."
22. "Ich freue mich, dass ich dich heut' einmal nicht störrisch finde."

rhythm and pungent chromaticism of what is being called here Elektra's dance of revenge (at §250a). This symphonic interlude maps Elektra's psychological state. Both of these motifs are references to dance forms, foreshadowing her final maenadic performance, but with diametrically opposing messages. The first, waltzlike melody speaks to the blissful rapture Elektra experiences at restoring the honor of her father's name, but also nostalgically reminds of the waltz's heyday in 1870s Vienna when the ballrooms were in full swing. The revenge dance is a demonic death dance, in which Elektra celebrates the thrill of Klytämnestra's bloody murder.

"Ecstasy Motif" (Wintle 1988, 86).

The nostalgia motif dominates Elektra's last words, in which she pledges to carry the weight of all human happiness and concludes with a message of optimism and hope: "For whoever is happy like us only one thing is fitting: to be silent and dance" (§§256a–259a).[23] It is telling that all references to the waltz come to an abrupt end when Elektra takes the first steps of what will turn out to be her death dance. At the exact moment when it would finally be appropriate to insert a dance motif, Strauss pulls back on the heavy orchestration. Most of the instrumental lines have fixed chords while the strings play the lonely triadic Elektra motif. Strauss dispenses with frivolities and drops the ironic veneer in this most serious of moments. The composer's acute sense of dramatic energy is one of his most valuable gifts. The two events in the opera that might be considered what Cone (1989, 132) calls "occasions for song" are Elektra's opening lament for her dead father and her final dance.[24] And yet in the latter case, the performer re-

23. "Wer glücklich ist wie wir, dem ziemt nur eins: schweigen und tanzen!"
24. Edward Cone (1989, 132) defines occasions for song as brief "phenomenal" or self-reflexive moments in an opera when a character suddenly becomes conscious of his or her singing. Often they arise when there is a reason to sing aside from the conventions of the

mains mute, and Strauss figuratively echoes this silence by extinguishing the waltz motifs just before the dancer's own demise. In this last rendition of the distorted waltz and the metaphoric silence that follows it, there is no irony. Elektra's death is a serious matter. This exit performance suggests a parallel with the abrupt end of the age of imperial splendor that haunted Europe just as Agamemnon haunted Argos. The delicate and breezy waltz dies along with Elektra. The dance conjures up paternal images of the waning Habsburg Empire but also aurally recalls the composer's musical forebears, such as Johann Strauss and Richard Wagner, as well as his own father's considerable influence. In the end, this opera is at least as nostalgic as it is avant-garde.

It should not go unnoticed that the waltz is a purely instrumental form and not the accompaniment for text, demonstrating the autonomy of music as its own expressive medium, but also emphasizing the silence of the voice. If Strauss had known his Freud as Hofmannsthal did, he would have realized that silence is one of the symptoms of hysteria. Perhaps he had heard of "Fräulein Anna O." and knew of her apparent aphasia and of the subsequent analysis she would later call her "talking cure."[25] Strauss knew relatively little about psychoanalysis and was not likely aware of Freud's theory of dreams and the unconscious (Bayerlein 1996, 14). Still, the instrumental quality of the dance melody demonstrates the expressive capacities of nonverbal art forms, a device he used to great effect in his earlier opera *Salome*. Strauss no doubt takes his lead from Hofmannsthal, who makes abundantly clear in his stage directions that this dance is not subject to the limits of language and calls it a "nameless dance" (Strauss 1954, 55).[26]

If Hofmannsthal takes Anna O.'s talking cure and turns it into a dancing cure, Strauss takes the metaphor one step further and performs a "musical cure." The composer's clever and subtle use of the waltz motif speaks to the climate of decay, nostalgia, and grief in fin-de-siècle Vienna. Moreover, if Elektra's stomping victory *Reigen* is seen as an orgiastic frenzy, the waltz allows her to demonstrate her sound mind and her talents as a cunning manipulator within the Atrean court. Ultimately, Strauss's opera helps Elektra throw off the yoke of her hysterical diagnosis for good.

---

genre. Common examples are love serenades or tavern songs, but they can also be instrumental, such as the famous horn solo at the beginning of act 3 of Wagner's *Tristan und Isolde*. While Elektra's dance is not an "occasion for song" per se, it is a self-conscious performance within the opera.

25. For a full discussion of the case study of Anna O., see chapter 3.

26. "namenlosen Tanz."

5

Oedipus Endangered

ROBERT MUSIL'S *THE MAN WITHOUT QUALITIES*

Robert Musil's portrayal of the Electra myth in *The Man without Qualities* forms a bridge between Hofmannsthal's fin-de-siècle adaptation and the later images of American poets H.D. and Sylvia Plath. Musil's narrative masterpiece of Viennese modernism is situated precariously on the cusp between the old world and the new. The action takes place in the ominous prewar year of 1913, but the orientation of the novel is forward-looking and innovative, challenging old stereotypes and outdated institutions of power, prestige, and privilege.[1]

Where Hofmannsthal's *Elektra* hints at the threat to Oedipus by upstaging the masculine neurotic with the female hysteric, Musil anticipates Heiner Müller's approach in waging open war on Freud's psychological everyman. He figuratively castrates his leading male and replaces him with an androgynous Electra and a hermaphroditic utopian union of the sexes. Musil enters the debate on the role of woman in modernity and anticipates future theories of gender, sexuality, and subjectivity in ways that scholarship is only just beginning to consider.[2] He thus paves the way for H.D.'s and Plath's more con-

---

1. Musil documented his concern to confront the future, writing in his diary: "The facts of contemporary life have outgrown the concepts of old" (quoted in Bernstein 2000, 36).
2. Early critics saw *The Man without Qualities* as a book about men and the world. One critic wrote: "Musil's book is one of the most masculine . . . that has ever been written" ("Musils Buch ist eins der männlichsten . . . , die je geschrieben worden sind") (quoted in

sciously feminist readings of Electra. H.D. has her Electra negotiate
sibling relations with Orestes, who is then relegated to the sidelines,
but in Plath's poetic reconstruction of the myth, the brother is altogether excised from the cast.

Musil spends little time on the problem of Oedipus, instead compos-
ing a neat dismissal: "I am afraid that after another generation or two
there will no longer be an Oedipus!" (Musil 1998, 325).[3] There are those
who would argue that Musil's prediction has not come to fruition—
after all, there are plenty of new discussions of Freud's Oedipus complex.[4] Oedipus would appear to permeate every fiber of our modern
cultural consciousness. But taken on a metaphorical level—Oedipus as
the psychological everyman with a single, unified, and undeniably masculine subjectivity—the question is open to debate. If Musil had in
mind the complexity and ambiguity present in the discourses of gender,
sexuality, and subjectivity, then he was definitely right—Freud's oedipal
model is no longer relevant. Either way, Musil's decision to devote several decades, mountains of paper, and the monumental effort of com-
posing a work such as *The Man without Qualities* not to Oedipus but to
the myth of Electra speaks volumes. He wrote a scant three-page essay
on Oedipus and some two thousand pages as a thinly veiled allegory of
Electra. With the sheer quantity of his work, Musil makes a clear argument for the dominance of Electra over Oedipus.[5]

The myth of Electra permeates the novel like a musical leitmotiv,
but there is more at work here than a mere retelling of the Greek myth
transposed into modern times. The sibling incest mimed by Ulrich and
Agathe provides the framework for the first threads of a new relational
ethics as a space of intersubjectivity.[6] Musil invokes Ernst Mach's theo-

---

Kraft 2000, 108). A number of studies have now begun to tackle the long-neglected question of gender in Musil's writing, including Luft (2003), Jonsson (2000), Seidel (2001),
Kingerlee (2001), and Kümmel (2001). Musil was a writer ahead of his time, looking
modernity and modern subjectivity squarely in the face as only a handful of other writers
were doing, among them Joyce, Proust, Kafka, and Mann. Critics have been slow to engage with Musil partly because he did not fit the mold of Austrian letters and partly because of the complicated publication history of *The Man without Qualities* (see note 8).

3. "Ich befürchte, daß es nach ein bis zwei Menschenfolgen keinen Oedipus mehr
geben wird!" (Musil 1955c, 502).

4. See for example Julia Kristeva's *The Sense and Non-Sense of Revolt: The Powers and
Limits of Psychoanalysis* (2000), Henk de Berg's *Freud's Theory and Its Use in Literary and
Cultural Studies* (2003) and Diane Jonte-Pace's *Teaching Freud* (2003).

5. Musil's comments on Freudian psychoanalysis are by and large negative, but he did
make favorable comments on the theory of narcissism in 1932 (Kingerlee 2001, 150).

6. My argument about Musil's linking of sexuality and subjectivity with ethics parallels
that of David S. Luft (2003), who writes: "Musil believed that the task of his generation
was to rethink gender identity and conventions, that the move beyond bourgeois conventions about sexuality and gender was linked to the move beyond the bourgeois ego and to
the exploration of the genuine sources of ethical motivation" (x). Luft goes on to say that

ries of the provisional ego and sensation body in his interpretation of
the Atrean myth to challenge the subject position of the oedipal model.
The novel's narrative trajectory eventually transcends Mach's "unsalvageable self" and moves beyond the cliché of a Viennese crisis of
identity. Through an investigation of the semiotics of the body and experimentation with gender in the form of androgyny, hermaphroditism, and the "new woman," Musil engages in a larger argument with
modernity and the culture of militarism and morality. At the end of his
Oedipus essay, the author ventures the question: "Will we get an
Orestes instead of an Oedipus?" (Musil 1998, 325).[7] With *The Man
without Qualities* Musil answers his own question—neither Oedipus nor
Orestes will dominate the action. Electra will play the lead.

   An icon of Austrian literary modernism, Musil (1880–1942) was
born in Klagenfurt and lived through one of the most tumultuous periods in Austrian history. He studied engineering and philosophy, earn-
ing a doctorate in 1908, and even attempted a military career before
devoting himself to a life of letters. Although he belonged to the Austrian upper bourgeoisie, Musil was educated not at a classical Gymnasium but at military boarding schools, which had the lasting effect of
making him scrupulous about personal hygiene and orderliness.

   Musil's life and work from about 1924 until his death while exiled in
Switzerland were solely dedicated to the production of one mammoth
masterpiece of literary modernism, which, by the author's own admission, had become a historical novel in the process of its creation (Musil
1995, 1767).[8] Often compared to Joyce's *Ulysses* and Proust's *A la
recherche du temps perdu*, Musil's novel, though of epic proportions, is
compact in its chronology. *The Man without Qualities* presents a precise
silhouette of the waning Habsburg Empire, suffused at first with biting
irony, which is then suddenly replaced by a poignant, almost sentimen-

---

"gender appears in *The Man without Qualities* as a metaphor both for reconciling thinking
and feeling and for the duality of force and love in human affairs" (127). In his insightful
and convincing reading, Luft emphasizes Musil's exploration of the "role of love in human
knowledge," and it is my own opinion that *The Man without Qualities* might even anticipate
Emmanuel Lévinas's philosophy of ethics and alterity, for example in *Totality and Infinity*
(1969).
   7. "Werden wir statt des Oedipus einen Orestes bekommen?" (Musil 1955c, 504).
   8. The first volume of *The Man without Qualities*, published in 1930, received such praise
that Musil began to dream of a Nobel Prize. Under pressure from his publisher and his
readers, he released the second volume in 1933. It was not as successful, owing in part to
the political climate but also to its less than polished state, as Musil himself thought. *The
Man without Qualities* was banned in Germany and Austria in 1938, and the censorship
would eventually extend to all his works, which made conditions worse. In dire financial
straits throughout the remaining years of his life, Musil labored increasingly over the
manuscript, though with little progress.

tal lyricism that risks descending into the worst kind of kitsch. The seemingly endless dialogue and diatribe on such lofty subjects as love, morality, freedom, mysticism, and social deviance, contrasted with scheming political intrigue aimed at the general glorification of a pathetically outdated empire, is strategically crammed into one anticipatory prewar year.[9]

The mounting tension also revolves around Musil's protagonist, Ulrich, whose main claim to fame is his *Eigenschaftslosigkeit*, the total absence of any defining characteristics or traits. At the ripe age of thirty-two and entirely lacking in professional ambition, this son of a prominent Austrian aristocrat decides all at once to take a year off from life, during which he hopes to make some meaningful discovery about the nature of humanity and the world. As time slows down and the plot all but grinds to a halt, mired in pages and pages of idle contemplation, the reader's patience and the writer's capacity are stretched to the limit.[10] The novel is infuriatingly masterful in taking on subjects of grand scale that hold great promise and result in ever larger circles that lead to an inevitable vortex. *The Man without Qualities* is about something and nothing at the same time. And yet the resulting creative intensity is never resolved, for the work remains a novel fragment.[11] It is

9. After meditating and hypothesizing upon the nature of love in conversations mostly with Agathe, but also with anyone who will listen (Clarisse, Bonadea, Diotima), Ulrich boils the problem down to its essential questions: "how to love your neighbor, whom you don't know, and how to love yourself, whom you know even less . . . and how to love at all" ("wie man seinen Nächsten liebe, den man nicht kenne, und wie sich selbst, den man noch weniger kennt, . . . wie man überhaupt liebe") and "what love 'actually' is" ("was Liebe 'eigentlich' ist") (Musil 1978, 4:1223–1224). Not only are these burning questions with regard to his relationship with Agathe, but Ulrich feels compelled to include "millions of loving couples" in his equation. This is just one example of how our protagonist ensures his own failure by setting himself impossible tasks. His musings on other subjects are of equally preposterous proportions.

10. Indeed, the praise for *The Man without Qualities* has not been unanimous. Peter Handke called the work "a megalomaniacal and unbearably opinionated work right down to the individual sentences" ("ein bis in die einzelnen Sätze größenwahnsinniges und unerträglich meinungsverliebtes Werk") (in Luserke 1995, 96), and another critic claimed: "The pillars of narrative construction gradually sink into the quicksand of the essay" ("Die Pfeiler der narrativen Konstruktion versinken allmählich im Treibsand des Essays") (Moser 1980, 176).

11. *The Man without Qualities* is a fragment in the sense that it is an unfinished manuscript, but also in the sense that it is confused and inconclusive, especially toward the end. It is debatable whether this is a result of the unfinished nature of the project or rather of an intentional aesthetic transformation within the text. My reading supports the latter interpretation: Musil struggles to provide narrative closure, in part owing to the lack of plot toward the end. His characters have abandoned their social roles, but they have not replaced their former lives with any clear plan of action. Loredana Marini (2001, 137) argues convincingly that Musil is a "fragmentist" in all his writing and that the unfinished nature of his works reflects the problem of the modern hero who, being a man without qualities, cannot have a story either. Though many critics and scholars insist on a clear distinction between the published segments of *The Man without Qualities* and the posthumous papers,

as if the characters have been cut off in midsentence as the anxiety of pending war is frozen in the air. The author never has to orchestrate the suicide, murder, or *Liebestod* of the protagonist and his sister, for they are figuratively terminated in the dangling threads of the novel's refused conclusion.

The Man without Qualities presents its anti-oedipal polemic in the subtlest of ways. The pervasive paradigm of Oedipus and his complex are present at the outset, with Ulrich as sole protagonist in an apparently oedipal struggle with power and tradition. But just as the climax is beginning to unfold and Musil's oedipal hero is faced with his first real challenge, his role is usurped by his other: Electra. At the halfway point in the novel, when Ulrich's plan to transform himself and the world has proven entirely futile, the narrative is abruptly shaken by the death of Ulrich's father. This precipitates an upheaval of dramatic proportions in the protagonist's life and initiates a significant shift in tone. The narrator dispenses with the clever, ironic ploys that poke fun at everything from the self-satisfied society dames with their lavish wardrobes and secret affairs to the petty and obsequious ways of the Austrian civil service with its ludicrous and antiquated bureaucracies. A new narrative voice emerges as the Atrean myth of Electra seeps through the pages of the third book and stains the characters with the painful legacy of patricide and sibling incest.

The patriarch's sudden death, precipitating haunting reverberations of Agamemnon's ghost, coupled with the much-anticipated reunion between Ulrich and his long-absent sister, Agathe, constitutes the peripeteia in the novel. Electra's story is unearthed in this poignant recognition scene. Never mentioned by name, the myth has been scraped to its bare bones, reduced to a few crucial clues. The first of these is the death of the father.[12] The children seem almost pleased at

---

I treat Musil's latter drafts and notes as part of the whole. These chapters may be rough and unpolished, but they nevertheless provide important clues to the author's intentions on a number of key points.

12. The death of the father refers equally to Ulrich and Agathe's biological father, the patriarchal figure of the aged emperor Franz Joseph, as well as the terminally ill Habsburg Empire itself. Franz Joseph's seventieth jubilee, to be celebrated on December 2, 1918, is the subject of the great "Parallel Campaign," an elaborate planning committee with which Ulrich becomes involved. The whole scheme revolves around the attempt to overshadow the German celebration of Wilhelm II's jubilee in June of that year. Ulrich's father explains: "Since December 2 could not of course by any means be moved back before June 15, we came up with the brilliant idea of declaring the whole year of 1918 a Jubilee year" ("Da der 2. XII. natürlich durch nichts vor den 15. VI. gerückt werden konnte, ist man auf den glücklichen Gedanken verfallen, das ganze Jahr 1918 zu einem Jubiläumsjahr unseres Friedenkaisers auszugestalten") (Musil 1978, 1:79). This scheme reveals the full extent of the ludicrous activities within the government (especially since "Parallel Campaign" dissolves into a social club) and the lengths to which the Austrians will go to uphold their his-

the passing of their overbearing father. However, the recurring sense of loss and confusion in the second half of the novel is akin to that felt by the Atrean children at the brutal murder of Agamemnon.

The other major element of the myth's structure is precisely the anagnorisis of Electra and Orestes. During the much-anticipated recognition scene, the earth ought to cease rotating on its axis for one long moment of gaping silence. Musil heightens the suspense of this encounter by maneuvering his subjects into place and then delaying their meeting in much the same way as does Sophocles in his Attic version. And yet there is something artificial and contrived about this first meeting. This is merely a trial run for the real recognition scene, which transpires much later in the novel.

Ulrich arrives at the family home following the father's death, exhausted and disheveled after his trying train journey, only to learn that Agathe, whom he labels his "unknown sister" (Musil 1978, 3:674),[13] is indisposed and cannot possibly see him right away. He is confused by this inhospitable welcome and is unsure what to make of it since he barely knows this mysterious sister of his (they have seen each other on very few occasions since their early childhood). Conscious of the power dynamic at play, Ulrich surmises that her reluctance to rush to greet him gives Agathe the upper hand in the situation. Finally, after an agonizing hiatus, the siblings are poised to enter the scene. In contrast to the Electra myth of antiquity, in which Orestes disguises himself as the messenger of his own death, here brother and sister both know what is at stake in this reunion. Or at least they think they do.

In subtle rebellion at having been abandoned upon his arrival—"She should at least have come to greet me right away"[14]—Ulrich decides to wear "a baggy woolen pajama . . . with black and gray checks, almost a Pierrot outfit" (Musil 1978, 3:675).[15] Little does he know that his sister has taken the same exaggeratedly casual attitude toward her dress, and has donned an almost identical lounging suit. When Ulrich enters the room, he is confronted with a Pierrot "who, at first glance, looked peculiarly like himself."[16] Equally flabbergasted, Agathe exclaims: "I

---

torical supremacy over the Germans. The campaign is a ridiculous and desperate attempt to resuscitate a dying tradition and the prestige it once evoked, and a symptom of a larger philosophical problem of the "nonempty gap" (Ryan 1991, 216) that invades much of the rest of the novel in different forms.

13. "unbekannte Schwester"

14. "Sie hätte mich doch wenigstens in der Wohnung gleich begrüßen sollen."

15. "einen großen, weichwolligen Pyjama . . . beinahe eine Art Pierrotkleid, schwarzgrau gewürfelt"

16. "der auf der ersten Blick ganz ähnlich aussah wie er selbst"

didn't know we were twins" (3:676).[17] Though suspenseful and anxious, this recognition scene differs fundamentally from the Greek myth. Where the emotions of the Hellenic versions range from shock and dismay to disbelief and bittersweet tears, Ulrich and Agathe seem more awkwardly surprised and somewhat clumsy in their first interaction. They must wait patiently for the second anagnorisis to recognize each other truly. Once they get over the incredible coincidence of their matching outfits and the uncanniness of the doppelgänger experience, the siblings revert almost immediately, as if out of adolescent shyness, to conversational banalities such as the sports they prefer.[18] Still, the meeting is not without lasting consequences. Even if they are as yet blind to the true nature of their bond, Ulrich and Agathe begin to function as one indivisible unit. From this point forward, they progressively refer to their status as hermaphrodites, as Siamese twins, and consider that they are inextricably linked in a platonic, perhaps even mythical, union.[19]

Ulrich and Agathe in turn mime this artful meeting of Pierrot with him/herself.[20] Their extraordinary encounter constitutes an identity crisis for Musil's protagonist with lasting repercussions. The mere pos-

17. "Ich habe nicht gewußt, daß wir Zwillinge sind."

18. Surely it is no coincidence that the identical disguise is that of Pierrot, the notoriously ambiguous circus figure, descended from early European *commedia dell'arte*. He has been known as Pucinella, Punch, Pedrolino, or Petrushka, the simpleton and fool who exposes and ridicules his masters. This melancholy clown suffers slightly from schizophrenia, appearing at once mischievous and playful, then macabre like the jealous and cynical operatic figures of Rigoletto and Pagliaccio. But the aspect of Pierrot's personality of most interest here is the ambiguity surrounding his gender identification. Traditionally gendered male, in the late nineteenth and early twentieth centuries Pierrot was increasingly played by women, for example Frank Wedekind's Lulu character. This double articulation of Pierrot as feminine man and masculine woman irreparably alters the nature of the siblings' reunion. They no longer identify as man and woman, with all the erotic overtones implicit in the Attic recognition scenes. Instead, they meet as brother and sister, as twins, perhaps even as each other's other. On the history of Pierrot, see Thomas Kellein's *Pierrot: Melancholie und Maske* (1995) and Martin Green and John Swan's *The Triumph of Pierrot: The Commedia dell'Arte and the Modern Imagination* (1986).

19. The twin metaphor was so significant in Musil's understanding of the novel that he first intended to title it "The Twin Sister" ("Die Zwillingsschwester") (Kingerlee 2001, 139).

20. Perhaps Musil knew of Mallarmé's fascination with the self-identical play of murder, incest, and suicide orchestrated by Pierrot, the mime. In a brutal and bizarre drama, Pierrot illustrates his murder of the unfaithful Colombine. He ties her to the bed while she is sleeping and begins to tickle her feet, such that her "ghastly death bursts upon her among those atrocious bursts of laughter" (quoted in Derrida 1981, 199). Pierrot simultaneously plays the murderer and his female victim, thus initiating the collapse of both gender and subject/object boundaries. A single character takes on a form of oscillating androgyny, in his illustration of what Derrida calls a "masturbatory suicide." While Musil's invocation of Pierrot likely has a different aim, the analogy is a useful one.

sibility of an oedipal scenario is forever banished from the novel, since Ulrich's consciousness is now unmistakably and irreversibly split, as if severed at the root into two distinct, platonic halves. Freud's Oedipus has as his sole purpose the pursuit of a unified and developmentally complete consciousness. Oedipus may, in his emergent state, waffle somewhat in his object choice, but this ambiguity gives way in the end to a secure and singularly masculine subjectivity. Freud (1905) is adamant on this point: "Anyone failing to [master the Oedipus complex] falls victim to neurosis" (226). According to this view, Ulrich and Agathe's relationship is a sign of neurosis, for it is the successful mastery of the oedipal stage that awakens and instates the incest taboo.[21] Contrarily, I would argue that the siblings are able to negotiate an ethical pact precisely because they do not fall victim to the restrictive social initiation of the Oedipus complex.

Musil, who himself underwent psychoanalysis following a nervous breakdown in 1928, initially follows Freud in setting up sexual relations as a crucial cultural model.[22] However, Musil's system veers significantly from accepted theories in his insistence upon the coexistence of *eros* and intellect in a move toward a revolutionary, sexual ethics.[23] Moreover, he repudiates the cultlike status and seemingly unscientific approach of the psychoanalytic establishment. While Musil seems to have set out, in part, to refute the primacy of Freud's principal paradigm, Freud's theories are by no means his sole reference point. He wrote his doctoral dissertation, "Beitrag zur Beurteilung der Lehren Machs," on the pre-Freudian psychology of Ernst Mach (1838–1916), a physicist who gave the Austrian public a new formulation of the monist doctrine of positivism.[24] Mach's famous dictum proclaiming the unsal-

21. The sibling incest between Agathe and Ulrich is metaphorical in nature—their bond is not really sexual. Rather, they use the fuel of *eros* to orchestrate a quasi-transcendent union, which I will address later in this chapter.

22. Musil was treated by a student of Victor Adler's, a member of Freud's inner circle who had left owing to differences of opinion. During and after his analysis, Musil absorbed a great deal of Adler's thought, but he had also studied the Gestalt theories of Max Wertheimer, Wolfgang Köhler, and Kurt Koffka while in Berlin (Timms and Robertson 1992, xi). Perhaps Musil's ambivalent stance toward psychoanalysis had to do with his own struggles with depression, but it may also be that he abhorred Freudian psychoanalysis in particular because of the conflict between Adler (whom he greatly respected) and Freud. He had three serious bouts of depression during his lifetime (1913, 1916, 1928), possibly because of the enormous pressures he placed on himself (Kingerlee 2001, 136–137).

23. Musil parts company with Freud upon the fundamental issue of biology. Freud insists upon the "biological foundation of the Oedipus complex," thereby rendering it an essential part of human sexual development. For Musil, this is a simplistic view, which fails to take into account the significance of social, psychological, and indeed ethical factors.

24. A genius of many talents, Mach was, among other things, a physicist, an engineer, a psychologist, and a philosopher. He is known for his theories of epistemology and positivism and for his experiments in optics, acoustics, electronic induction, physiology, and

vageable self, "*das unrettbare Ich,*" became a powerful catchphrase and dominated the psychological landscape of Viennese modernism. Adopted by the influential cultural critic Hermann Bahr, it became a ubiquitous axiom of the crisis in language and the crisis of identity itself. In Mach's own words: "The 'I' is not a monad isolated from the world, but rather a part of the world" (quoted in Frank 1983b, 32).[25] As such, and this is Mach's central argument, subjectivity can exist only as a bundle of sensations and as a fiction of its own perceptions of the world. Or as Musil interprets: As soon as one attempts to analyze the self, "it dissolves into relations and functions" (Musil 1978, 8:1403).[26] This is demonstrated in *The Man without Qualities* when all that appears tangible and malleable in its characters slips through one's fingers like the finest silt.

The Man without Qualities simultaneously engages with and critically evaluates Mach's theories, and the Electra myth serves as a platform for this dynamic dialogue. The novel denies Freud's exclusive oedipal narrative, all the while leapfrogging Mach's deconstructive metaphysics and opening up a space for an alternative ethical relations. It is the encounter of the mythological siblings in the guise of Ulrich and Agathe together with Musil's experimentation surrounding their negotiations of subjectivity and positionality that provides the basis for a new ethics to emerge.

The author makes no attempt to outline a systematic theory of ethics. In fact, an ethical *system* is an oxymoron: "Where there are regulations," laments Musil, "morality is established" (Musil 1978, 8:1305).[27] In *The Man without Qualities*, morality is shown to be static and artificial, while ethics functions as an ongoing fluid and relational project: "Morality is in its essence . . . bound to repeatable experiences" (8:1093),[28] whereas "Immorality achieves its heavenly right as a drastic critique of morality" (3:959).[29] Later in the novel, such statements become bolder and more anarchic in tone: "Nothing is solid. Every ordering leads to absurdity" (5:1834).[30] In much of this enigmatic

---

photography. He held posts alternately as professor of mathematics, physics, and philosophy and has been inducted into the Fluid Mechanics Hall of Fame as one of the leading pioneers of supersonic aerodynamics. He is perhaps most famous for his discovery of the unit of the speed of sound, appropriately labeled the "Mach."

25. "Das Ich ist keine von der Welt isolierte Monade, sondern ein Teil der Welt."
26. "löst es sich in Relationen und Funktionen auf"
27. "Wo eine Regelmäßigkeit sich einstellt, dort hat sich eine Moral gebildet."
28. "Moral ist in ihrem Wesen . . . an wiederholbare Erlebnisse gebunden."
29. "Das Unmoralische gewinnt sein himmlisches Recht als eine drastische Kritik des Moralischen!"
30. "Nichts ist fest. Jede Ordnung führt ins Absurde."

section, the narrator speaks in axiomatic phrases, spitting out philosophical epithets and leaving the reader to decipher his code. Unwit-
tingly, we become schooled in the doctrines of Mach, which will then
be mutated through Musil's clever manipulation of character and narrative development.

Recognition Scene

Musil once vowed never to analyze a character, and apart from a few
lapses he allows his protagonists the freedom to experience their own
fluid shifts. One scene in particular aptly demonstrates Musil's narrative technique and relational theory. In a chapter entitled "Beginning
of a series of wonderful experiences," found near the beginning of the
posthumous papers, Ulrich and Agathe are engaged in preparing for
yet another evening out with friends.[31] Already running late, the two
are dressing hastily, Ulrich acting as ladies' maid to his sister in the absence of qualified maidservants. The narrator outlines in the minutest
detail this scene, in which Agathe dons a silk stocking—her body becomes the object of an artist's gaze. Ulrich loses his cool distance, helpless in the face of the powerful kinetic force connecting him and his sister; the painting "seemed to have lost its frame and passed so
unmediated into Ulrich's body" (Musil 1978, 4:1082).[32] Without warning, Ulrich leans over his sister from behind and bites into one of the
folds on her tenderly exposed neck.

   This moment marks a crucial turning point in the sibling relationship and warrants being labeled a *second recognition scene*. In antiquity's
myth of Atreus, anagnorisis is a one-time-only event, as there is no

---

31. The posthumous papers are divided into two sections: the first is a group of twenty
chapters which appear relatively intact and have undergone the first stages of the intense
polishing to which Musil subjected all his work. The second section consists of notes,
sketches, and drafts for future chapters or versions of other chapters. There is much repetition, and the writing is disjointed and almost fantastic in nature. We witness an unraveling of character and plot such that the whole first three books of Musil's masterpiece almost appear to come apart at the seams before our very eyes. When we read this section,
everything that has come before seems like a fiction, and these dreamlike, visionary final
musings become the real novel. Here Musil experiments with various alternative scenar-
ios, including the possibility of Ulrich's having sexual relations with a number of the
women in the text: Agathe, Diotima, Clarisse. This testifies to Musil's own complaints that
publishing the work piecemeal limited him severely; he considered the novel a continual
work in progress, experimental in nature, and felt that the release of early chapters distorted the entire shape of the work (Pike 1996, xii). Perhaps one of the most important
contributions of the posthumous papers is the light they shed on Musil's concept of mysticism and what he called the "other condition" ("anderer Zustand").
   32. "schien ihren Rahmen verloren zu haben und ging so unvermittelt in den Körper
Ulrichs über"

need for Orestes and Electra to repeat the act of seeing each other for the first time.[33] However, Musil's rendition suggests that Ulrich and Agathe never really *saw* each other during the Pierrot scene. They were too absorbed in establishing the pecking order of sibling hierarchy. Ulrich was still acting his spoiled playboy routine, and Agathe was preoccupied with plotting the end of her marriage. Only now does the narrative's ironic veneer finally slip away altogether to reveal the quasi-mystical union of two souls.

And at frequent intervals following the first recognition scene, Ulrich and Agathe critically evaluate their status alternately as the two halves of Plato's original human (3:903), as Pygmalion, as the Hermaphrodite (1978, 3:905), and as the Siamese twins (3:908; 3:936; 3:945). They even describe themselves as hermits (3:801). In fact, very early on, Ulrich shows incredible insight into his dependent relationship to Agathe, the sister who will allow him to love himself. His self-analysis reveals his lack of this ability, to which she is the apparent remedy: "I now know what you are: you are my self-love! . . . I've always been missing the proper love for myself . . . in a certain sense . . . and now, by some fluke or by fate, it has been embodied in you instead of myself!" (3:899).[34] After lengthy debate and consideration, Ulrich solidifies and confirms this hypothesis:

> Even I have to be able to love something, and since she is a Siamese sister who's neither me nor herself, but just as much me as herself, she is obviously the only intersection of everything! (3:945)[35]

This kind of analysis abounds in the chapters leading up to the second recognition scene, but the tone is cerebral and sterile in nature. Ulrich

33. Classical and neoclassical drama often includes a recognition scene as a means of driving the plot forward. Aristotle accorded it great importance and developed criteria for anagnorisis, which included some kind of false inference. Whether deliberately contrived or not, there is necessarily a misunderstanding concerning the true identity of a character (Dupriez 1991, 433–434). While Ulrich and Agathe do not appear to fall prey to such Aristotelian false inference, there is arguably a misunderstanding. For they never get beyond the Pierrot costume to see the true nature of their relationship. Thus, this chapter constitutes a second recognition, one that seems to run almost the entire course of the novel without full resolution. Ulrich and Agathe are in a constant state of *seeing* each other for the first time.

34. "Ich weiß jetzt, was du bist: Du bist meine Eigenliebe! . . . Mir hat eine richtige Eigenliebe . . . im gewissen Sinne immer gefehlt . . . und nun ist sie offenbar, durch Irrtum oder Schicksal, in dir verkörpert gewesen, statt in mir selbst!"

35. "Auch ich muß doch etwas lieben können, und da es eine Siamesische Schwester, die nicht ich noch sie ist, und geradesogut ich wie sie ist, offenbar der einzige Schnittpunkt von allem!"

may have softened around the edges somewhat since the arrival of his sister, but his thinking is still mired in an intellectual, even clinical, quagmire. What transpires with this second anagnorisis is clearly on a different plane.

Following the initial description of Ulrich lunging in a vampiric maneuver toward Agathe, the whole scene is repeated in extreme slow motion, this time emphasizing the somatic distortions of this single gesture. In a cinematic frame-by-frame analysis, we learn that Agathe has been liberated into weightlessness and has lost her balance. The event has called all muscles into play but simultaneously paralyzes their limbs (4:1082). The siblings abandon ordinary language for a kind of corporeal code, such that "the sibling nature of their bodies transmuted itself as if they grew out of a single root" (4:1083).[36] Indeed, they suddenly recognize their collective blindness as if a cloudy film has been peeled back from their eyes:

> They looked into each other's eyes with such curiosity *as if they were seeing each other for the first time.* And although they would not have been able to explain what had happened, since their participation in it had been too fleeting, they still thought they knew that they had just chanced to find themselves for a moment in the midst of that shared condition on the border of which they had been hesitating for such a long time. (4:1083, my emphasis)[37]

Ulrich and Agathe are granted the gift of a special vision, which affords them insight into the nature of their relationship as they stand on the crest between their past and their future. They see that they have been hovering at this precipice since the night of their first meeting. They have been trying all along to articulate in ordinary language what they have now experienced physically as an "other condition."[38] What was an accident of bodily gesture—Ulrich leaning over Agathe—becomes a

---

36. "Der geschwisterliche Wuchs der Körper teilte sich ihnen mit, als stiegen sie aus einer Wurzel auf."

37. "Sie sahen einander so neugierig in den Augen, *als sähen Sie dergleichen zum erstenmal.* Und obwohl sie das, was eigentlich vorgegangen sei, nicht hätten erzählen können, weil ihre Beteiligung daran zu inständig war, glaubten sie doch zu wissen, daß sie sich soeben unversehens einen Augenblick inmitten dieses gemeinsamen Zustands befunden hätten, an dessen Grenze sie schon so lange gezögert . . . hatten."

38. "anderer Zustand." Musil introduces the term "other condition" in the third book to refer to Ulrich and Agathe's experiment in creating an alternative, imaginary social reality. The author never clarifies this ambiguous epithet, perhaps because defining it might ruin the magic of the quasi-utopian twosome the siblings attempt to nurture and sustain.

catalyst for something more. Even picking up the phone and canceling their engagements for the evening has no effect in sobering Ulrich. The phone calls act as a caesura and set the scene for the next phase of Ulrich and Agathe's collective being.

For what seems like an eternity after Ulrich's daring overture, the siblings remain silent. Only their glances meet as they navigate through unknown territory using a new somatic language. They sense that their movements are censored by some warning, a higher force that has nothing to do with moral codes. When they finally regain the use of their voices, the two delve into a forgotten tongue, borrowing vocabulary and imagery from romantic poets such as Tieck, Schlegel, and Novalis. As if from nowhere, Ulrich blurts out to Agathe: "You are the moon. . . . You have flown to the moon and he has given you back to me again as a gift" (1978, 4:1084).[39] With these prophetic words, he places his sister in the role of female redeemer in the romantic tradition.[40] She embodies his reflection as a mirror image, thus also strengthening their hermaphroditic bond. Not only has Agathe been returned to him, but also implicit here is that Ulrich has been given back to himself, that he has found love for himself through his love for his other half.

Breaking the spell in the most annoying manner, the narrator interrupts our romantic scene to inform us that we are in the midst of an artificially altered reality and must not fully integrate into this magical world. Soon, however, the narrator forgets his task of waking the reader and carries on with such cliché romantic epithets as the all-encompassing corporeality of the night far from the harsh light of day, which facilitates a state of "limitless selflessness" (4:1085).[41] If this scene were extracted from its context, one might think it part of Novalis's *Hymns to the Night*, with its lovers "shrouded in the dark night"

39. "Du bist der Mond. . . . Du bist zum Mond geflogen und mir von ihm wiedergeschenkt worden."

40. We need only think of examples such as the "beloved" in Novalis's *Hymns to the Night*, Lucinde in Schlegel's novel of the same name, or the many Wagnerian redeemers: Senta, Elisabeth, Brünnhilde, and Isolde. These women all sacrifice themselves to facilitate the transcendence of the male hero, often an artist struggling to realize his creative potential. While Agathe's role in *The Man without Qualities* does not fit easily into this paradigm, there are elements of this tradition at play in the novel, especially in this critical chapter. Ulrich does most of the talking, and his sister acts more as facilitator to his experience of discovering self and subjectivity. As we shall see, this model breaks down when it becomes clear that Ulrich cannot simply overcome his existential angst even once he has found his Platonic mate. From Ulrich's mature perspective, Wagner's predictable plots will seem foolishly simple. In the final sections of the narrative, Agathe emerges as the dominant force in the guise of the new woman.

41. "grenzenlose Selbstlosigkeit"

108

CHAPTER 5

(1978, 177)[42] or from Wagner's *Tristan und Isolde*,[43] where the magical couple feels their love threatened by the jealous and deceitful day.[44]

Musil's sexual imagery, borrowed from his romantic predecessors, could not be more blatant. The sensual moon, icon of intoxicating desire, beckons irresistibly and invites the siblings into a magical union of the flesh. And yet, like magnets that attract and repel with equal intensity, the moon seems to pull them toward each other and keep them apart. Still, they are aware of love's fever in their bodies and gaze longingly toward the celestial sphere, as if transplanted from Caspar David Friedrich's iconographic painting of lovers mesmerized in lunar observation. Just when their metaphysical union threatens to dissolve into a sexual consummation, Ulrich adds a puzzling corollary by comparing Agathe to "Pierrot Lunaire." The narrator again severs the bond with any romantic paradigm with this clinical analysis of the archetype: "The pale mask of the lonely lunar Pierrot . . . expressed his love of moonlit nights such that it became a joke" (4:1086).[45] For a number of reasons, the siblings are kept from confirming their love in a sexual union of the flesh: the first is Ulrich's admission that their scene has slipped into a sentimental debauch, trivialized to the point of kitsch (4:1086). Then the Pierrot allegory returns from the first recognition scene, bringing with it the overtones of androgyny, hermaphroditism, and general confusion over sexual identification. Historically, the figure of Pierrot represents ambivalence and mystery, but here it can be seen as the symbol of Ulrich and Agathe's strange metamorphosis into

42. "in dunkle Nacht gehüllet." There are numerous references to Novalis in *The Man without Qualities*. Agathe is in the habit of quoting Novalis—"Whatever can I do for my soul, which inhabits me like an unsolvable riddle?" ("Was kann ich also für meine Seele tun, die wie ein aufgelöstes Rätsel in mir wohnt?") (3: 857)—even though she confesses that she believes in no soul. She leaves the answering of such questions to her brother.
43. Wagner, too, figures prominently in the novel; his music is the source of tension between Clarisse and Walter, Ulrich's childhood friends. They play duets of his music on the piano and become entranced by its romantic fervor; Walter even compares their suffering to that of Tristan and Isolde. Wagner functions as a backdrop in the novel (Clarisse's brother is conspicuously named Siegfried), representing a now defunct world where authenticity was still a goal and sentimentality did not have to become kitsch.
44. Along with the ubiquitous romantic characterization of night as a refuge from the harsh realities of the light, both Novalis and Wagner speak of a new kind of sight: for Tristan and Isolde, to be "night-sighted" ("nachtsichtig") (Wagner 1968, 80) means being able to see the false lies of the strict moral and social codes imposed by day. And Novalis's lovers have access to the night's loving sun, "beloved sun of the night" ("liebliche Sonne der Nacht") (Novalis 1978, 151), a secret inner piercing light fueled by passion. Ulrich and Agathe's new extended vision features some of these same characteristics, allowing them access to a higher plane, but also freeing them from a static and repressive moral system.
45. "[Die] bleiche Maske des mondlich-einsamen Pierrots . . . drückte also die Vorliebe für Mondnächte beträchtlich ins Lächerliche hinab."

one character. Like Heiner Müller's Hamlet, who is subsumed under the rubric of Elektra, Ulrich too is feminized and eclipsed by Agathe's electric presence.

Pierrot symbolizes the unknown force that has marked the siblings for some "higher purpose" (4:1083).[46] With the return of a rather pathetic Pierrot, the siblings realize they are nothing but characters in their own plot. Nevertheless, brother and sister both understand that they have experienced, if only for a fleeting moment, a hint of what the narrator names "feelings of ecstasy" (4:1086).[47] Indeed, elsewhere the narrator calls Ulrich the last romantic (5:1844).[48] In many ways, the siblings' journey to another reality comes across as clichéd and sentimental, rescued from the vices of kitsch at the last minute by common sense that breaks through the false veneer. Having recognized that they are characters in their own play or figures in a painting, they take the necessary steps to close the scene. Agathe unexpectedly chirps, "Gute Nacht!" to her brother, and then, as though waking suddenly from a dense slumber, she closes the curtains with such haste that the tableau of the two of them standing in the moonlight vanishes suddenly and without trace (4:1087). The romantic dream is eclipsed as quickly as it emerged.

In a larger sense, Ulrich and Agathe's romantic encounter illustrates Musil's attempt to compensate for a loss of authenticity in the world around them, but the scene also mimes the loss of oedipal subjectivity as their primary self-conscious identification. Their collective mourning for what was and their yearning for what might be color the narrative as they linger on the cusp between meaning and irony, between

---

46. "höhere Ahnung." That Ulrich and Agathe do not consummate their love is in some ways a strange reversal of Wagner's erotic philosophy in *Tristan und Isolde*. While Wagner was an unabashed fan of Arthur Schopenhauer and his philosophy of will-negation, he allowed himself certain liberties in its application. The *Liebestod* makes for a perfect Schopenhauerian climax, with Isolde as otherworldly redemptress, and yet their physical union of the flesh contradicts the philosopher's doctrine of asceticism. While Musil's motives are clearly not the same as Wagner's, his decision to deny Ulrich and Agathe's sexual desires contradicts the romantic imperative of erotic love and paves the way for them to transcend their earthly existence (and here this might be translated as the fixed moral codes of Viennese society) toward the construction of a relational ethics, with Schopenhauer's will-negation acting as the driving force.

47. "Seligkeit des Gefühls"

48. Manfred Frank (1983a) interprets *The Man without Qualities* as part romantic allegory and part romantic critique. He points to the appropriation of key concepts regarding the construction of the self and argues that Musil adopts Novalis's critique of Fichte's self-determining self in favor of a self determined by a nonself. He demonstrates that Ulrich and Agathe's foray into romanticism represents a quasi-religious aspiration, which abolishes totalizing systems and unfolds as an anarchic project.

sincere love and debauched vulgarism. But like the mythological characters whose roles they mime, they too must make a decision and move
forward. Typically, a recognition scene is followed by the stunned silence at having *seen* for the first time, and yet Electra and Orestes both
know they cannot gaze forever into each other's eyes. They have a task
before them. Their love alone will not redeem the kingdom of Argos,
and they take up their swords and head off to battle. So, too, must Ulrich and Agathe confront their future together.

Ernst Mach's Sensation Body

In the middle of the prolonged romantic scene, Ulrich feels the need to
theorize their relations and explains: "We exchanged bodies without
touching each other" (4:1084).[49] The body emerges as a central metaphor for their relationship, be it a physical body or rather a "sensation
body," as postulated by Mach. It is no mere coincidence that the catalyst that finally allows Ulrich and Agathe to understand the depth of
their connection is a single physical gesture. What cannot be understood on a cognitive level must be approached on the corporeal level.

In a very early paper, *The Analysis of Sensations*, Mach relates an anecdote from his youth of coming across Kant's *Prolegomena to All Future
Metaphysics* in his father's library, which precipitates his later inquiry
regarding the "superfluity of things in themselves." He explains that
one day "the world, including my own selfhood, suddenly appeared to
me as a coherent mass of sensations, in which my sense of self was only
and simply a stronger cohesion" (Mach 1911, 24). In his later work,
Knowledge and Error, Mach further outlines his theory of the ego's construction through its fundamental interdependence with the body's
spatial surroundings and with the body's experience of sensations:
"There is something all but unexplored standing behind the ego,
namely our body" (1976, 8). Inasmuch as the body is the only vehicle
for knowledge of the self, the ego is equally vulnerable to errors of perception: "The imagination rounds off incomplete findings . . . thus oc-
casionally falsifying them" (7). In other words, the dependence upon
outside forces and the processing of them as internal circumstances of
sensation can lead to delusion. This propensity to confuse knowledge
and error based upon a misunderstanding in the interpretation of in-
coming data renders the self a fundamentally unknowable entity, such
that "an isolated ego exists no more than an isolated object: both are

---

49. "Wir hatten unsere Körper vertauscht, ohne uns zu berühren."

provisional fictions of the same kind" (9). As a "provisional fiction," the self is nothing more than a sensation cluster, connected to plants, animals, and objects via its sensory perceptions. Essentially, humans are not much different from machines, argues Mach: "some kind of weird and wonderful automata" (18). Far from despairing at this fatalistic view of the ego, the psychologist insists that this model of human development is actually liberating because it frees us first of all from the mind/body dichotomy and then from a static, fossilized notion of self.

Mach's phenomenological and pragmatic approach to the perception of the self is important for Musil's project in a number of ways. First, as we have observed, the characters in *The Man without Qualities* are shown to be fluid entities, without ground. Initially, it seems like a reasonable task to remedy this, and Ulrich tells his sister optimistically: "We are going to try to ground you" (1978, 3:959).[50] Eventually, the narrator recognizes the impossibility of such a project and describes another version of being: "one that in principle cannot be justified" (5:1752).[51]

Another important factor for Musil's characters is Mach's theory of emotions as part of the overall experiential phenomena of the body: "At first glance, feelings, affects and moods of love, hate, anger, fear, depression, sadness, mirth and so on, seem to be new elements. On closer scrutiny, however . . . they mark certain directed modes of bodily reactions known from experience" (Mach 1976, 17). Ulrich echoes Mach's theory when he elaborates his own thoughts on love to Agathe: "There is first of all a physical experience, which falls in the category of skin irritations" (Musil 1978, 3:941).[52] Love is, for Ulrich, first and foremost a physical-mechanical experience rather than one of the soul.

This assertion is illustrated by the fact that their mutual experience of love is that of sharing and even exchanging bodies. Ulrich describes a sensation that affects his body when he is close to a woman, "as though he had himself been given a second, much more beautiful, body of his own" (3:898).[53] Being twins is not enough; they must be Siamese twins, physically connected such that all physical sensations are shared. The narrator begins to spout Mach-like phrases on the coexistence of emotion and physical sensation, such as Ulrich's dream "of being two bodies in one" (4:1060).[54]

50. "Wir suchen einen Grund für Dich."
51. "welches wir im Grunde nicht begründen können"
52. "Das ist erstens ein körperliches Erlebnis, das zur Klasse der Hautreize gehört."
53. "als sei ihm da selbst ein zweiter, weit schönerer Körper zu eigen gegeben worden"
54. "zwei Menschen zu sein und einer"

Clearly, Musil engages with Mach's theories in order to understand
the nature of his characters' subjectivity. But he eventually goes beyond
Mach's corporeal aesthetics and challenges his mentor. Musil supports
the notion of the ego as an unstable cluster of physical sensations, essentially a nothingness, which is at every moment being redefined according to new spatial and sensational circumstances. The author parts
company from Mach when he develops this model into a complex set of
social relations. Not only is the ego a fluid entity, but for Musil it inter-
mingles and interferes with other sensation beings. Ulrich and Agathe
are determined by their respective somatic perceptions; however, they
also codetermine each other's beings through their interactions.

Further exceeding the limits of Mach's theories, Musil seems dissat-
isfied with the notion of the unsalvageable self and the pessimistic view
that the ego is really nothing but an accident of error and false perception. Instead, he proposes and demonstrates an alternate, some would
say utopian, perspective. Recognizing the inherently unsettled nature
of their collective being as sensation clusters, Ulrich and Agathe embark upon a path of discovery through the catalyst of love. Without
love, their status as Siamese twins or shared hermaphrodite would be at
best ridiculous and at worst pathetic. It is love that compels them to
seek some better alternative to the status quo. "Love," affirms the narrator, "is the great anti-reality" (4:1319),[55] and this is the inspiration for
the siblings' quest to imagine a reality beyond the limits of morality.
Indeed they risk everything to enter into their ethical pact, an experiment of gargantuan proportions.

Ulrich is the more articulate of the two about his desire for the siblings to meld fully with each other. Throughout the novel, he repeatedly voices the wish to abandon his masculine identity and become his
female other. At the outset of the novel, we see Ulrich as Oedipus, but
it becomes clear that his goal is to undergo a Kafkaesque metamorphosis and to become Electra in body and spirit. He recalls as a child seeing his sister all dressed up for a birthday party and longing desperately
to be a girl. But later in the novel, it is his love for Agathe that awakens
in him a deep yearning to be a sister at any cost (4:1311).

But to be a sister is far more than simply to unite fully as sibling
Siamese twins. It becomes a code word for a particular way of being
that Ulrich and Agathe begin to cultivate consciously after their mystical recognition; they step deliberately beyond the confines of moral
codes and strict social structures and withdraw into their imaginary

55. "Liebe ist die große Anti-realität."

hermaphroditic state. Ulrich affirms this alternative definition of soror-
ity: "The 'sister' is a manifestation of the 'other' part of emotion that
comes from the turmoil of this emotion and the desire to live differently" (4:314).[56] Together, Ulrich and Agathe acknowledge their existence as that of the "third sister," the intermingling of "I" and "you."[57]

The New Woman

Ulrich's desire to embody Electra and womanhood itself in the form of
his/a sister is foregrounded by the rise of a new ideal of femininity in
the novel. Very early on, we find evidence of a dichotomy between two
categories of women, characterized by body type: the round, soft, maternal woman and the hard, tight, boyish girl. The female characters in
the novel are equally divided among these two categories: Diotima,
Bonadea, and Leona all fall into the maternal group, while Clarisse,
Gertha, and Agathe are more androgynous and boyish. Diotima, Ulrich's confidante and cohort in the "Parallel Campaign," is described as
embodying "an ideal of beauty . . . that was Hellenic . . . with a bit
more flesh" (1:109).[58] She has a large, warm body with feminine curves
and several rolls of voluptuous fat on her neck. On the other hand,
Clarisse's small, nervous body is hardly maternal but rather "hard and
boyish" (1:354).[59] Over time, this tendency accelerates until she becomes an emaciated rack of bones, devoid of feminine flesh.

   In his slow eradication of the maternally connoted female body from
the novel, Musil refers tacitly to the legacy of J. J. Bachofen or even
Otto Weininger. As discussed in chapter 1, in Bachofen's anthropological study of mythology, *Mother Right,* the primitive, maternal principle,
finally gives way to the laws of paternity precisely when Electra decides
to avenge Agamemnon's death.[60] The legendary misogynist Weininger,
who abhorred all things maternal, saw in women the roots of social disease. He was disgusted by the so-called bisexuality of culture and the

   56. "Die 'Schwester' ist ein Gebilde, das aus dem 'anderen' Teil des Gefühls ersteht, der
Aufruhr dieses Gefühls und das Verlangen, anders zu leben."
   57. Near the end of the posthumous papers, the three sisters are mentioned, referring
to the trio of Ulrich, Agathe, and the fictional world they have created, which itself is
granted object status. Musil's notes are by this point chaotic and convoluted. The author
contemplates Ulrich's and Agathe's respective thoughts of suicide, albeit not without a
glimmer of hope. Ulrich vows that they will not kill themselves until all other avenues have
been exhausted.
   58. "ein Schönheitsideal . . . , das hellenisch war . . . mit ein bißchen mehr Fleisch"
   59. "hart und knabenhaft"
   60. See chapter 1 for a discussion of Bachofen's *Mother Right* and its relevance for the
Electra myth.

feminization of the ego and considered this phenomenon a symptom of
decadence and social decay. Musil can hardly be said to uphold either of
these theories. He observes and comments upon the same phenomenon
of gender ambiguity and experimentation; however, he introduces this
new construction of femininity in order to celebrate women's liberation
from their maternal responsibilities and their newfound ability to interact with a free-floating set of gender signifiers.

Musil theorizes this concept in an essay entitled "Woman Yesterday
and Tomorrow" (1929),[61] where he begins by describing an outdated
version of femininity. Nineteenth-century women's bodies are depicted as caricatures with tiny waists, hands, and feet, a rosebud mouth,
and great cushions of fat (Musil 1955a, 642). Female bodies were prud-
ishly buried beneath wads of fabric, which had the opposite of the desired effect, creating "an incredibly artificial enlargement of the erotic
surface" (641).[62] In an early chapter of *The Man without Qualities*, the
narrator expounds upon these same points almost word for word, pos-
tulating that the extensive clothing of the traditional woman was something of a civilized aphrodisiac. Maternal and corpulent, these women
were sexual beings.

The ideal of woman changed, proposes Musil, with the Great War.
The new woman sheds her camouflaging layers and her maternal role
all at the same time: "She is boyishly thin, sociable, athletically tough,
and childish" (Musil 1955a, 645).[63] She remains physically immature
and is principally concerned with matters of how to prevent reproduc-
tion. This fact is made evident in *The Man without Qualities* when Ulrich's friend and confidante, Clarisse, maintains a self-imposed chastity
in spite of her husband's tireless pleading for conjugal relations. Another of the protagonist's female companions, Gertha, also denies herself and Ulrich the pleasures of the flesh when, at the height of passion,
a twisted scream hurtles from her body in a violent purging of all sexual impulse.

Called "a woman with qualities" by one critic, Agathe too falls
squarely within the bounds of the new woman (Jonsson 2000, 197).[64]
When Ulrich sees her for the first time in feminine attire, he mistakes
this costume for a disguise. Women's clothing is a foil more jarring

61. "Die Frau gestern und morgen."
62. "eine ungeheuer künstliche Vergrößerung der erotischen Oberfläche"
63. "Sie ist knabenhaft mager, kameradschaftlich, sportlich spröd und kindisch."
64. Albert Kümmel (2001, 431) concurs that lacking qualities is a problem unique to
men in Musil's world.

than the Pierrot pajamas of their first meeting.[65] Her body is tall and thin with broad shoulders, all of which contributes to Ulrich's confusion surrounding her gender status. In fact, his very first remark about her appearance notes the sexually ambivalent and immature nature of her body. He is so shocked that he is incapable of determining whether his initial fascination with her arises out of curiosity or sexual desire.

This prepubescent, androgynous, and even asexual image of Agathe acts as a mirror for Ulrich's construction of his own masculinity. Musil never writes an essay on "Man Yesterday and Tomorrow" or the nature of the new man. But Ulrich's own self-conscious analysis of his character and his relationship to Agathe speak to a larger shift in the development and manifestation of masculinity, a shift that threatens the oedipal scenario. This is not a man whose sexual development is either predictable or complete. He refuses to identify with or emulate the kind of man his father was and purposefully casts off the shadow of the domineering man. The absence of his biological mother precludes any oedipal mother-son conflict. And, while he appears to go through a period of infatuation with maternally connoted women, Ulrich, unlike Oedipus, does not take part in the ritual of usurping the power of the maternal in order to assert his masculine, sexual supremacy. Mother figures simply fade away when the new woman takes center stage as the dominant cultural and corporeal aesthetic.

The demise of the oedipal scenario is inversely proportionate to the rise of the Electra myth. When Ulrich is finally ready to turn his back upon his father's world for good, the myth of Atreus is introduced. The son leaves behind the security of paternal inheritance and the solid oedipal subjectivity it connotes. Following the father's death and the recognition scene, Agathe and Ulrich slowly begin their retreat from the world; they abandon the life of Viennese high society and begin their self-imposed exile as recluses. The two of them lose any clear sense of identity they might have had and enter a zone of liminal, postoedipal subjectivity. By the end of the posthumous papers, the two have practically fused into one being, so complete is their union. Agathe describes a dream she has had, in which she entered her body lying on the

65. Ulrich is annoyed that Agathe is not more assertive in her role as a new woman and suggests that her inability to stand up to her husband is detrimental to both of them (3:684). As the novel progresses, Agathe becomes increasingly independent, even straying from Ulrich's jurisdiction. One day, Ulrich cannot find Agathe anywhere, but when he realizes he is unneeded, he is no longer concerned that she should embody the new woman. Instead, he behaves like a selfish and jealous husband.

bed, only to discover that it was her brother's body. She is startled by this uncanny sensation, which takes the doppelgänger motif of Siamese twins one step further. The dream continues with her taking her brother's body into her arms, lifting it up high in exaltation. Their bodies melt into each other and become indistinguishable. The dream represents a state of utopian bliss, a simultaneous stasis and complete fusion of subjectivities that Ulrich first mentioned in the moonlit scene. There is a religious sense of awe to this scene, as though Agathe were Mary Magdalene lifting Christ's dead body to become one with it.

Agathe's dream also signals a shift in her overall role in the novel. She becomes the driving force behind their collective actions, exemplified by Ulrich's repeated desire to become her, to meld with her. As Ulrich casts off his allegiance to Oedipus, Agathe accepts the role of Electra, courageous and defiant. She asserts her independence and sets her own agenda, and Ulrich, like Orestes, seems happy to follow. Though her task is not that of orchestrating a literal matricide, her characterization as the new woman acts as a figurative matricide. She extinguishes the maternal element in herself, just as Musil postulates its erasure from the cultural imagination.[66]

Agathe's new role is foreshadowed by Ulrich's own suggestion, shortly after their first meeting, that the siblings might also take on the roles of Isis and Osiris as they perform the alchemy of becoming symbolically one. Musil explores this theme elsewhere in poetic form: "Isis und Osiris" (1923) reveals the grizzly story of Isis stealing her husband's male member: "And the sister separated the sleeper from his sex and ate it" (Musil 1955b, 597).[67] In exchange, she gives him her heart, which he consumes. The poem parallels the siblings' quasi-incestuous relations in *The Man without Qualities* in that Osiris, like Ulrich, is figuratively emasculated, though Ulrich like Oedipus is a willing victim. In both the poem and the novel, however, the brother/lover's sacrifice is rewarded when he gains access to the coveted trophy: his sister's heart. Such a metaphor of cannibalistic ritual is perhaps a more profound symbol of the depth of their union than sexual consummation itself.[68]

---

66. Such a figurative matricide need not be seen in a negative light. Musil uses Agathe to question and redefine the nature and role of femininity. But ultimately, he sees her emergence as the "new woman" positively, gaining strength and rejuvenation. In building a bridge of regendered ethical relations, Musil allows Agathe's expression to extend beyond the confining limits of maternity.

67. "Und die Schwester löste von dem Schläfer / Leise das Geschlecht und aß es auf."

68. For a discussion of the Isis-Osiris myth in *The Man without Qualities*, see Sebastien Seidel's *Dichtung gibt Sinnbilder: Die Sehnsucht nach Einheit. Das Lebensbaum-Mythologem und das Isis-Osiris-Mythologem in Robert Musils Roman "Der Mann ohne Eigenschaften"* (2001)

The novel starts off with Ulrich as a solitary oedipal protagonist in a quasi-bildungsroman quest for a purpose and meaning in life. By the end of the unfinished work, we are on much less solid ground. Agathe and Ulrich have melted into each other to the extent that they function as one character, with Agathe or the androgynous new woman as the dominant force. In a parallel to Müller's *Hamletmaschine*, Oedipus has been abandoned and Electra and Orestes have become one.

Unlike Müller's Electra, whose anarchic view privileges destruction as the only ethical stance, Musil's characters embrace the possibility of creating and nurturing an alternative reality through their own ethical relations. Musil refutes Freud's oedipal subject in part by looking to Mach, whose metaphysical skepticism constructs the subject as a provisional fiction of physical sensations. Mach's pessimistic pragmatism, however useful as a provisionary model, does not provide all the building blocks for Musil's project. He does not want his version of Electra and Orestes to end up in a void or in a relational cul-de-sac.

Nietzsche and the Abyss

Musil looks to Nietzsche to complete his vision of an alternative relational ethics. Present as a backdrop throughout *The Man without Qualities*, Nietzsche first surfaces through Ulrich's close friend Clarisse.[69] Ulrich gives her the complete works of Nietzsche as a wedding present, and indeed the unspoken force of Dionysus appears to threaten her stability: "Something indeterminate tore itself loose inside her and threatened to fly away with her spirit" (1:62).[70] Clarisse even proposes a "Nietzsche Year" as a parallel to the ridiculous jubilee year planned for Emperor Franz Joseph. Her obsession reflects the extent to which this philosophy dominated the cultural landscape in Musil's Vienna. Clarisse's rather shallow reception of Nietzsche—she cherishes the weighty tomes but seems not to have read them—and her worship of him as a statuesque icon act as a counterpoint to Musil's larger conversation with the philosopher toward the end of the novel. The author's

---

and Roger Kingerlee's *Psychological Models of Masculinity in Döblin, Musil, and Jahnn: Männliches, Allzumännliches* (2001, 165–174).

69. Musil makes frequent reference to Nietzsche throughout his diaries, remarking later in life that he understood little of the philosopher in his youth and yet considers him a "decisive influence" ("entscheidender Einfluß") (quoted in Mehigan 2001, 87). For a detailed discussion of Musil and Nietzsche, see Wolfgang Rzehak's *Musil und Nietzsche: Beziehungen der Erkenntnisperspektiven* (1993).

70. "Etwas Unbestimmbares riß sich dann los in ihr und drohte mit ihrem Geist davonzufliegen."

allegiance to Nietzsche permeates his prose, especially in the third
book and posthumous papers.

"All ordered society puts the passions to sleep," asserts Nietzsche in
The Gay Science, a message paralleled by Musil's conviction that morality is a narcotic that lulls even sharp minds into a dull, sleepy trance.
The author sees in Nietzsche the potential for a different kind of drug,
perhaps one that stimulates productive insomnia to "reawaken the
sense of comparison, of contradiction, of joy in the new, the daring, the
untried" (Nietzsche 1976, 93). The characters in *The Man without Qualities* are engaged in a Nietzschean experiment of audacious joy, through
which they escape ordered society to imagine something new. Agathe
and Ulrich risk everything to break free from social mores, and their
actions echo the narrator's aphoristic bluntness: "Everything is moral
except morality" (3:1024; 5:1853).[71]

The creative tension of the characters' unfinished and permeable
subjectivities recalls Nietzsche's invitation to move beyond one's own
self in an explosion of Dionysian excess. Musil demonstrates his theory
of ethical relations through the perpetual metamorphosis of his characters and their courageous endeavors to harness their love and sketch a
new vision of intersubjective being. In so doing, he shows modern individuals how to recreate themselves constantly and to embrace the
chaos of the changing world around them.[72]

Agathe and Ulrich may engage in a Nietzschean experiment of joy,
which leads to their hermaphroditic fusion into a plural Electra character and an unspoken denigration of a singular oedipal subject. However, their coexistence does not culminate in the kind of Dionysian
frenzy performed by Hofmannsthal's Elektra in her *Totentanz*. Instead,
their challenge is to walk an ever-narrowing precipice between two extremes: utopia and anarchy.[73] Like Nietzsche's tightrope dancer, who

71. "Alles ist moralisch, nur die Moral nicht."
72. Though Nietzsche's thought offers utopian possibilities for Musil's characters, if left
on this course the siblings risk falling victim to a vacuous and apolitical sentimentality.
Mach's theories constitute the pragmatic anchor for this ideal couple on the margins of society and lend much-needed leverage to the symbolic silence of their self-imposed exile.
73. Critics (Schärer 1990, Luserke 1995) have accused Musil of indulging in utopian
fantasies, which provide no real political alternative for the corrupt and decrepit society he
seeks to undo. Musil counters this criticism with this diary entry: "The contemplation of
the 'other condition' is something other than a trance" ("Das Kontemplative des A.Z. [an-
deren Zustands] ist aber etwas anderes als der Trance") (quoted in Kochs 1996, 786). The
author keeps his characters from succumbing to the utopian trance by having them tread a
thin line between their ideal vision in a self-exiled alternative reality and the threat that
their dream will implode into a destructive anarchy. In the end, it is the continual encounter with the other that keeps Ulrich and Agathe alive to the challenge of resisting the
status quo and attempting to embrace a different version of reality.

symbolizes the courage necessary to transcend the limits of the subject, they are confronted on either side by a cliff and a bottomless abyss. Perhaps the impossibility of succeeding at such a feat is what prohibits Musil from completing his masterpiece. The novel refuses to end with Electra and Orestes walking hand in hand into the sunset. On the contrary, it simply peters out as Ulrich and Agathe teeter ever closer to the edge of the abyss. In order to stay alive, they must reject the slumber of moral stagnation and stay awake to imagine new ways of being in the world.

6

Resurrecting Electra's Voice

H.D.'S *A DEAD PRIESTESS SPEAKS*

Where Musil and Müller challenge Oedipus directly, Freud's masculine archetype is conspicuously absent in the work of H.D. (1886–1961).
Instead, the modernist poet places Electra in a triadic relationship with
mother and brother. In the subtle poetic images of *A Dead Priestess
Speaks*, the Atrean princess learns new respect for the villainized
Clytemnestra, transforming this powerful maternal force into her own
mature femininity. Following Musil's model of hermaphroditic sexuality, H.D. makes the sibling relationship between brother and sister
central to the development of Electra's subjectivity. Like Musil's Isis
and Osiris metaphor, the duality of masculine and feminine becomes
almost indistinguishable, with Electra and Orestes mimicking Siamese
twins. We come to know H.D.'s Electra through her connection to but
subtle erasure of her brother. In the end, masculinity is subsumed
under a new creative and maternally connoted femininity, a covert criticism of Oedipus's singular subjectivity.

The American poet H.D., born as Hilda Doolittle in the Moravian
community of Bethlehem, Pennsylvania, is best known for her early
imagist phase prior to World War I. At this time, she was heavily influenced by Ezra Pound's methodically sparse verse, which advocated
the "direct treatment of the thing." H.D.'s poetic resurrection of
Electra represents a radical departure from the tight, crystalline per-

fection sought by the imagists; Electra is the muse behind the development of a new, mature poetic voice. The Electra poetry is
H.D.'s response to war and loss. She lost her brother to the war, and
her father died soon after; as if that was not enough, the poet and her
unborn child almost succumbed to Spanish influenza. But the poetry
is also a response to the suffering of women in a male-dominated
world. Virginia Woolf invokes Electra's story to parallel women's and
girls' limited access to the power of myth on account of their lack of
a classical education: "[Sophocles'] Electra stands before us like a
figure so tightly bound that she can only move an inch this way, an
inch that. . . . She will be nothing but a dummy, tightly bound"
(1992, 95).[1] Electra's silence is akin to women's ignorance, and Woolf
urges them to follow the example of the defiant and even violent
mythological heroine: "Electra bids him utterly destroy—'Strike
again'" (96). She counsels her readers to turn to the Greeks to make
sense of the "vast catastrophe of European war," a subject that otherwise risks falling into sentimental poetry. Woolf concludes that "it is
to the Greeks that we turn when we are sick of the vagueness, of the
confusion, of the Christianity and its consolations, of our own age"
(106).[2]

Heeding Woolf's words, H.D. takes the tightly bound dummy and
unravels her binding clothing in an attempt to overcome the shattering
experiences of the Great War and regain her voice. Like others of her
generation, H.D. felt silenced by the breakdown of personal and public
values in the wake of World War I and responded to these traumatic
events with a quest for a new aestheticism based on the intoxicating
beauty of a Greek statue. The words the poet chose for her gravestone
epitomize her reading of antiquity, "Greek flower, Greek ecstasy," a vision that she explains in "I Said" (1919):

1. While Alicia Ostriker (1985, 317) advocates a feminist revisionist mythmaking, she
cautions that it is important to keep in mind that myth belongs to "high culture" and that
it has been filtered by religious, educational, and literary authority. Rachel Blau Duplessis
(1986, 15) and Susan Stanford Friedman (1981, 234) both point out that one of H.D.'s primary motives is to confront the process of masculine mythmaking and find a new place for
women in a male-dominated tradition.

2. Woolf's argument is somewhat complicated by the fact that she is against translation
as a means of making the classics available to a wider audience, although her opinion might
have been different if there had been any reader-friendly translations in her time. While
she encourages the teaching of classics to girls and women, inevitably access to such training is restricted to the educated elite, regardless of their sex. Woolf reveals her own complicity with the regime of secrecy in that she provides no English translation of her own
Greek citations.

you may not seem a Greek to yourself,
you may not seem a Greek to another,
but anyone who stands alone,

. . . .

anyone to-day who can die for beauty,
(even though it be mere romance
or a youthful geste)
is and must be my brother.

(H.D. 1983, 323)

Loss was all around H.D. In addition to losing her cherished
brother and her father, the poet also lost her literary mentor. Once
heralded by Pound as the perfect emblem of his times and christened
"H.D. Imagiste," she was then abandoned (Korg 2003, 27). The paternal modernist rejected what he perceived as the emptiness of formalism
and along with it H.D., the voice that had best epitomized such purity.
There is bitterness in H.D.'s manifesto-like declaration of the need for
a new Hellenism:

> The mind, in its effort to disregard the truth, has built up through the
> centuries, a mass of polyglot literature explanatory of Grecian myth and
> culture.
>
> But the time has come for men and women of intelligence to build up a
> new standard, a new approach to Hellenic literature and art. (H.D. 1983, 328)

When H.D. appropriates mythological figures in her attempt to witness the atrocities of war and the horrors of manmade modernity, she
provides us not only with a revision of her characters' stories but with a
revision of mythopoesis itself. In her autobiographical novel,
HERmione, H.D. writes: "Mythopoetic mind (mine) will disprove science and biological-mathematical definition" (quoted in Morris 2003,
153). Mythopoetics rejects all that is associated with the modern world
of men. The logic of science is replaced with the art and beauty of science. Accordingly, H.D.'s poetic style shifts away from the scientific
model proposed by Pound. Gone are the crisp edges of imagism—
H.D. learns to sand down the hard surfaces of her poetry with the tools
of semantic overdetermination, lexical slippages, allusion, and ellipsis.
In short, her postwar poetry creates a new kind of hermeticism. As discussed by Rachel Blau Duplessis, Susan Stanford Friedman, and Cassandra Laity, among others, H.D.'s new Hellenism is a direct attack on
the male-dominated modernist mythopoetics of Pound, Eliot, and

Yeats.[3] She challenges the vision of Greek heroics that makes a cult of war and adventure. In its place, she fosters a hermetic world with a code language of flowers, stone-cold hands, and sleek statues symbolic of sensuous beauty, sexual liberation, and illicit love. In *Paint It Today*, the protagonist exemplifies H.D.'s abhorrence of the typical quest structures of male mythmaking: "Large epic pictures bored her, though she struggled through them" (quoted in Duplessis 1986, 20). Here, epic might be equated with the genre of Pound's *Cantos* or Eliot's *Wasteland*.[4] H.D. did exploit the epic genre in *Trilogy*, and yet she did so as a deliberate departure from the grandiose works created by her male counterparts (Friedman 1990, 352).

While Friedman (1981, 209) places H.D. "squarely in the center of this modernist mythmaking tradition," even if her poetics emphasize a more religious, esoteric, syncretist, and personal reading, Cassandra Laity and Norman Kelvin offer a perspective more in line with my own reading. They contend that H.D.'s mythopoetics are not so much a rebellion against the male modernists as a backward gaze and willful appropriation of a decadent-symbolist Hellenist aesthetics practiced by fin-de-siècle writers (Kelvin 2000, 170). Oscar Wilde, Walter Pater, and Algernon Charles Swinburne, with his morbid scenes of statuesque, corpselike figures and cold, deep graves, glorified a version of spiritual and rejuvenating friendship as well as same-sex love (Laity 1996, 48).[5] These same images fascinated H.D. and acted as her early muse. While the male modernists strove to eradicate the connection between antiquity and the effeminate and fragile aesthete so prevalent in symbolist poetics, for H.D. the Platonic doctrine of these late-ro-

3. Pound, whose early influences included Swinburne, Rossetti, and Morris, vehemently rejected aestheticism, calling it "a masturbatory phantasmagoria" (quoted in Laity 1996, 48). Ironically, H.D., who began as an imagist and followed Pound's doctrine of the "direct treatment of the thing," turned to the very writers her mentor had rejected as part of his youthful infatuation. Pound felt that he had matured beyond his romantic-influenced early work, and it could be that he was threatened by H.D.'s recuperation of the very poets he rejected.
4. Eliot (1975) prescribes a new "mythical method," praising Joyce's "parallel to the *Odyssey*, and the use of appropriate styles and symbols" (175) as a prototype for a modern recuperation of mythological forms: "In using the myth, in manipulating a continuous parallel between contemporaneity and antiquity, Mr. Joyce is pursuing a method which others must pursue after him" (177–178). H.D.'s endeavors diverge from Eliot's suggestion precisely in her reception of the classics, which does not involve the imposition of method, a "controlling" or "ordering," but rather entails a widening of the lens angle to include alternative versions of reality, blurring rather than focusing mythmaking in a narrative poetics.
5. Here, we might even think of Mallarmé's portrait of antiquity in "Hérodiade" or Baudelaire's *Les Fleurs du mal* and the general influence of symbolist aesthetics on this decadent fin-de-siècle aesthetic.

mantic and Pre-Raphaelite images provided a defense against the terror of war she associated with the heroic legends of violence and conquest. Wilde's encoded homoerotics can be read as misogynist or at least unsympathetic to a version of femininity that focuses on fertility and creativity, and yet H.D. had a different reception. She embraced the icon of the nude male body of Greek statuary, often summoned as a Victorian Hellenist object of the male gaze. Whereas Musil questioned sexual identity and militarist masculinity in particular through the image of hermaphroditism, H.D. appropriated this homoerotic image toward a vision of the androgynous youthful body, which signifies transgressive female desire and lesbian erotics in the writing of Virginia Woolf, Radclyffe Hall, and Colette.[6] H.D.'s romantic-Victorian model of antiquity is centered on an ideal of morbid beauty as a symbol of gender ambivalence. It serves as a frame for her poetic politics, rejecting the violence of war and the unnecessary suffering it imposes on those who are left behind.

Poet-Prophet-Priestess: Resurrecting a Voice

H.D.'s work is explicitly concerned with the recuperation of the classics and the role of "Greekness" in defining a modern sensibility. There is a significant shift in her approach to mythmaking, issuing from the trauma of the war and its aftermath, though more specifically attributable to the therapy the poet sought out to remedy her lost voice.[7] H.D. underwent an initial analysis with Freud in the spring of 1933, an experience that would have a profound effect on the ongoing dialogue with myth as intertext. As Friedman (1981) puts it: "Freud's equation of cultural myths with personal dream involved her in a self-conscious attempt to define the links between tradition and individual vision" (212). Her encounter with psychoanalysis led H.D. to modify her incorporation of the classics as an intricate web of hermetic allusions: the poet began actively creating new myths, paralleling the resurrection of her

6. Lisa Rado suggests that H.D. was influenced by Otto Weininger's groundbreaking (if misogynist) theories of a permanent bisexual condition in *Sex and Character* (1903): "A common denominator among these new theories of gender differentiation was the hypothesis that sexuality had a function beyond the reproductive . . . the artistic" (Rado 2000, 63). Deirdre Pettipiece (2002, 9), on the other hand, argues that H.D.'s understanding of sexuality came from a unique blend of her Moravian cultural roots and Darwin—a strange mixture of spirituality and evolutionary science. The spiritual equality of the sexes was the resulting philosophy, embodied in the notion of the hermaphrodite or androgyne.

7. In her letters to her lifelong lesbian companion Bryher, H.D. openly discusses her writer's block in 1933 and 1934 (Friedman 1981, 30), although she later characterizes this silence as an "incubation period" for the emergence of a new H.D. (9).

own poetic voice.[8] This rebirth is most apparent in her poem cycle *A Dead Priestess Speaks*, where H.D. turns to the Electra myth among other motifs to demonstrate her new models of femininity.[9]

But it was the "professor," as the poet refers to her mentor in *Tribute to Freud*, who urged her to use her writing to discover and develop this new voice. It was in response to haunting visions such as the one she labeled her "jelly-fish experience of double ego" (H.D. 1974,116) that H.D. sought out Freud's treatment.[10] She felt stifled and desperately "wanted to be let out":

> I wanted to free myself of repetitive thoughts and experiences—my own and those of many of my contemporaries. I did not specifically realize just what it was I wanted, but I knew that I, like most of the people I knew, in England, America, and on the Continent of Europe, were drifting. We were drifting. (13)

Freud considered the poet more of a student than an analysand, and indeed the sessions can be seen as a catalyst for the ensuing dialogue with and translation of psychoanalysis as an intertextual project. While she was very enthusiastic about this new world of dreams and symbols, H.D. was far from an uncritical consumer of psychoanalysis. She took

---

8. A good example of this practice of altering myths to form new models of female empowerment is H.D.'s poem "Eurydice." Here, the speaking "I" takes the subject position of the wife who remains so silent in the classical versions of the myth. Eurydice blames Orpheus (whose name goes tellingly unmentioned) for his "arrogance" and berates him for forcing her back to life: "if you had let me rest with the dead, / I had forgot you / and the past" (H.D. 1983, 51). She blames him for summoning her out of her peaceful death only to be forced once again to face the black depths of "this colourless light." Eurydice berates her "ruthless" husband for intruding on the solitude of the dead that she had come to cherish, a little place for her spirit to grow, finally glorifying her newfound comfort: "before I am lost, / hell must open like a red rose / for the dead to pass" (55).

This poem enacts the very opposite scenario from that expressed in *A Dead Priestess Speaks*. While Eurydice found solace in the silence of Hades and admonished Orpheus for imposing his will, the speaking subject in *Priestess* expresses pleasure at being freed from the enclosure of the underworld and rejoices like Persephone in her newfound voice. In the poem "The Master," the old man to whom the speaker refers is Freud, a welcome Orpheus figure envisioned here as bestowing "wisdom" and "measureless truth," thus aiding her in the process of resurrection (451ff.).

9. H.D. later writes that these "nine poem-sequences or choruses belong in technique and emotional content, exactly to this transitional period. . . . They are hardly a bridge, they are threads in a tapestry" (quoted in Burnett 1990, 156).

10. H.D. (1974) describes the experience: "bell-jar or half-globe as of transparent glass spread over my head like a diving-bell and another manifested from my feet, so enclosed I was for a short space in St. Mary's, Scilly Isles, July 1918, immunized or insulated from the war disaster" (116). This effect of a doubled vision distorting the world around her recurs as an image throughout the poet's writing and can be viewed as one metaphor for the way in which mythology is woven through her poetry, as a lens through which to see the world.

on the role of critic and interpreter, documenting her treatment in
Tribute to Freud as a case study, a hieroglyphic testimony riddled with
allusions to myth.[11] Indeed, H.D. was not content to be either
analysand or student, and definitely not a case study in female hysteria
such as Anna O. Instead she figuratively dons the robes of prophetess,
priestess, or even goddess.[12] The poet describes the professor sitting in
his office, "a curator in a museum, surrounded by his priceless collection of Greek, Egyptian, and Chinese treasures" (116). He is also an
archeologist, digging up, collecting, and preserving the past in an attempt to make sense of the human psyche through the timelessness of
myth. While H.D. took from psychoanalysis the relationship of dreams
to the world of myth and what she called the "associative method,"
working with the semantic slippages of language, her use of myth differs from Freud's.[13] The poet recalls in *Tribute to Freud* that "the Professor said that we two met in our love of antiquity. He said his little
statues and images helped stabilize the evanescent idea" (175). And yet
Freud and H.D. diverged in their reception of this antiquity. Whereas
for Freud the myths of Oedipus and Electra are paradigms developed
into a model for human psychosexual development, for H.D. myth or
mythological characters are not absolute archetypes. Rather, each leg-

---

11. Examples of mythological characters who figure in *Tribute* are Hermes, "the Messenger of the Gods and the Leader of the Dead" (H.D. 1974, 8), or Janus, "the roman
guardian of gates and doors," the god of beginnings and ending, symbolizing H.D.'s quest
for a new voice. Both of these gods, who in some sense mediate the threshold between life
and death, signify the role the poet designates for Freud as "midwife to the soul" (116),
master of H.D.'s resurrection.

12. H.D. has been criticized for her Freud-friendly reading of psychoanalysis, ignoring
his problematic view of female sexuality (Fields 1974, xxxviii). It is true that she dedicated
her memoir to Freud, whom she called the "blameless physician," and yet the poet's reception of his work must be viewed in the context of her own experience of analysis. It is also
important to keep in mind that if H.D. felt that Freud helped her regain her voice and
overcome her personal crisis, her gratitude should not be understood as a blanket acceptance of his theories. She does relate incidents of disagreement between herself and Freud:
"I was rather annoyed with the Professor in one of his volumes. He said (as I remember)
that women did not creatively amount to anything or amount to much, unless they had a
male counterpart or a male companion from whom they drew their inspiration" (H.D.
1974, 149). And yet the overriding message that Freud seems to have conveyed is that H.D.
needed to work through her war trauma in her writing. Ironically, it is through writing
that the poet unravels the trauma of this male-gendered muse. She casts Freud at first as
Apollo to her Pythia, then castrates the sun god through the image of "blindness."

13. H.D.'s style has been criticized for being excessively associative, often using lexical
similarities to link ideas and images (Fields 1974, xxxix), and yet this is clearly an intentional tactic. She emphasizes the importance of cryptic hieroglyphics: "SIGNET—as from
sign, a mark, token, proof; signet—the privy seal, a seal; signet-ring—a ring with a signet
or private seal; sign-manual—the royal signature, usually only the initials of the sovereign"
(H.D. 1974, 66). H.D. uses her encoded initials to mold her identity. In many ways, the author constructs her own subjectivity as a myth.

end is made up of fragmented images and allusions, which she employs to construct a plurality of subject positions. No one myth dominates her writing, which freely evokes myths in quick succession, combining Greek, Roman, and Egyptian traditions, maintaining a fidelity to age-old legends while constructing new stories.

In *Tribute to Freud*, H.D. writes, "I let death in at the window" (117), referring to her attempt at "unravelling the tangled skeins of the unconscious mind and the healing implicit in that process" (16). The otherness of the unconscious is revealed through the poet's analysis with Freud, which she characterizes as a liminal or threshold experience, illustrated by her observation of the picture entitled *Buried Alive* in Freud's waiting room at Berggasse 19 in Vienna (131). H.D. actively seeks out the surprise of her own writing as a near-death experience, prophesying: "Perhaps I will learn the secret, be priestess with power over life and death" (117).

The poet realizes this power to mediate between life and death, literally to negotiate her own symbolic resurrection, through her poetic voice, spoken through the dead priestess-cum-Electra. H.D. transforms her underworldly priestess figure into a new vision of Electra in the course of her poem cycle *A Dead Priestess Speaks*. This complex intermingling of mythological characters and images acts as a mediating journey for Electra, one punctuated by an important encounter with Clytemnestra. Electra comes to understand her mother in a dialogue of love and respect that has been denied both women throughout antiquity. Moreover, it is through this renewed maternal bond explored in Electra that H.D. realizes her true poetic potential and emerges into the celestial light of day as a confident and mature voice.

The secret of writing functions like a dreamworld to cloak the "I," as evidenced by the speaker in the title poem of this collection: "They may read / the pattern / though you may not, / I, being dead" (H.D. 1983, 371). This statement plays in complicated ways with the subject perspective: the "you" refers to both reader and speaker, neither of whom has access to the secret code. The speaker must be the author of this unreadable "pattern" but is denied the right to decipher it because, as she has told us, she is dead. The "you," designating the reader, is also denied the special knowledge of her words. Only the furthest removed "they" are privileged to encode the wondrous pattern. And yet, by announcing that she is dead, the "I" constructs her own identity as "other" to herself. This conundrum is typical of H.D.'s poetry in this cycle and indeed in much of her later work. Hermeticism functions as a rhetorical trope, expressing the sensation of being "buried alive," hesitating between this world and the next. In her discussion of melancholia, Julia Kristeva (1989) observes that people experience trauma as a falsity of language, which attempts to compensate for the lost object "buried alive": "The dead language they speak . . . conceals a Thing buried alive. . . . It shall remain walled up within the *crypt* of the inexpressible affect" (53). This claustrophobic image recurs in H.D.'s *Dead Priestess*, and yet it is precisely through a renewed language, replacing the dead one, that the poetic voice manages to exit from the enclosure of the metaphoric underworld.

H.D.'s dense semiotic clusters contain the power of the priestess's oracles, and the speaker in this poem claims to possess such a mighty force:

> I wore white,
> as fitting the high-priestess;
> ah, at night—
> I had my secret thought, my secret way,
> I had my secret song
>
> (1983, 372–373)

She tells us of the surprise that only the priestess (as the dead other) can write, and yet this does not mean that she is immune to suffering. Finally she tells the story of the pain and anguish caused by war, be it the Trojan War or the Great War. We learn that this travesty was the cause of her own death, that help came "too late":

> how my heart cried,
> O, I was never pure nor wise nor good,
> I never made a song that told of war
>
> (1983, 376)[14]

Part of the secret of this poem is the identity of the speaker behind the mask of "Delia," a Roman version of Artemis. The choice of this

14. War is not the only cause of her suffering—she laments that she is caught in the arms of an "angry lover" (H.D. 1983, 376), perhaps a reference to the poet's failed marriage to Richard Aldington, or her earlier engagement to Pound, but more likely to her painful liaison with D. H. Lawrence. While these biographical details are not central to the interpretation of the poem cycle, the poet does mention all of these men in her discussion of her analysis. It is all the more relevant to consider possible allusions to her biography since H.D. constantly plays with her own life, in the roman à clef *Paint It Today*, in her memoirs, *Notes on Thoughts and Vision*, in the obvious punning on her initials in *HermeticDefinition*, and in the autobiographical metaphor in *Helen in Egypt*.

name also solidifies a connection to the writer's own life, since this is the pseudonym used for her autobiographical text: "H.D. by Delia Alton." Part of the fascination with H.D.'s clever self-referentiality is that she is consistently both subject and object of her own discourse. The addition of various mythological characters into this equation makes for an entangled and perpetually shifting subject position.[15] H.D.'s story shows up as a palimpsest beneath the tale of Artemis, goddess of the hunt, protector of wild creatures and defender of virginity. Here, the speaker-writer laments that she was "too late" to end the war and prevent needless suffering. We must recall that Artemis enters the Atrean myth when she stops the fleet headed for Troy, refusing to grant the necessary winds until Agamemnon sacrifices his daughter, Iphigenia. Artemis feels wronged by Agamemnon because he slew her most beloved stag when hunting, and so she decides to avenge herself by taking from Agamemnon something that is equally precious to him: Iphegenia. The goddess is doubly rewarded when Agamemnon dies because he sacrificed his daughter. The water that brings him home turns from the wondrous symbol of glory, "dark and purple," to "his *wine-dark sea*" (1983, 372).

Though Electra's sister Iphigenia is a virgin, deserving for her burial a "simple white / pure slab of untouched marble" (1983, 376), the goddess feels tainted because she failed to put an end to war and imagines being taunted for her sins: "Delia of Miletus is a whore" (374).[16] Delia is modeled on the women who were helpless to prevent their sons, brothers, and lovers from leaving for battle following promises of "the glory of the war" (372). For those left behind and numbed by the horror of mass death, the only remaining task was to write "an epitaph / to a dead soldier" (371).

However, the speaker plays more than one role, for she is also the "high-priestess," invoking the Pythia at the shrine of Delphi.[17] While

15. Friedman (1990, 75) observes that just as *Roland Barthes by Roland Barthes* taught us the linguistic construction of identity, the self as a product of naming, so too H.D.'s "Delia" confirms that the Other is always writing the self.

16. It is also significant that in some versions of the myth Artemis is said to be the twin sister of Apollo. Her bid to stop the Trojan War by arresting Agamemnon's fleet creates a clear opposition to Apollo's oracle urging Orestes to commit matricide. The contrast between Artemis's pacifism and Apollo's brutal decree is intensified in light of their filial relations.

17. Apollo's priestess, Pythia, was named after Python, a huge female serpent said to have protected the original oracle, which was in the hands of Gaia. Apollo killed the serpent and took over the shrine but retained Pythia as his priestess. The power of his oracles is forever indebted to the earth goddess Gaia (Grant and Hazel 1993, 290; Walker 1988, 832). It is unlikely that H.D. was oblivious to this aspect of the legend, since her treatment

this female speaker has knowledge of the most powerful words, she is
nevertheless responsible for delivering Apollo's oracle demanding that
Orestes commit matricide. The speaker implies that the priestess is innocent, and yet she is blamed for the perpetuation of the cycle of violence and cruelty that incites Clytemnestra's murder. The allusion to
Artemis and Pythia constructs the female voice as victim, forced to
carry out the male-dominated strategies of destruction, as suggested by
the priestess's lines:

> I was not pure,
> nor brought
> purity to cope
> with the world's lost hope
> (1983, 369)

The speaker, as mediator and messenger of death, also bears resem-
blances to Persephone, the archetypal figure of death and resurrection.
If the speaker as Artemis/Pythia is destined only to suffer for what she
could not prevent, the triumph of Persephone and Demeter over
Zeus's omnipotence offers hope for a future of liberation and rejoicing.
The goddess of the underworld overcomes her fear of Hades, of being
"buried alive," instead promising great fertility and creative spirit.
Through Persephone, the cycle of war and hatred is replaced with one
of resurrection and renewal. There is nothing arbitrary in H.D.'s careful shaping of the speaker's voice, "the line I drew with weaving, the
fine thread" (377), a secret pattern to be read only by a select few. In this
respect, the narrative subjectivity is both mythical and mythological,
consenting to none other than a "hermetic definition."[18] H.D.'s hermeticism is as frustrating as it is provocative. There are times when it
seems unnecessarily elliptical, as if the poet sends her reader on a treasure hunt with only the faintest of clues. It may appear arrogant, and yet

---

of myth thrives on such connections to female power. Through Pythia, Python, and Gaia,
H.D. is able to connect the roles of priestess, prophetess, and goddess within the speaker
of the poem, creating a forceful and persuasive female figure. We might also consider the
link between the Pythia's delivery of oracles and the writer's creative genius, and yet, as the
poet makes clear in her discussion of dream with Freud, an oracle is always plurivocal:
"The Priestess or Pythoness of Delphi sat on the tripod while she pronounced her verse
couplets, the famous Delphic utterances which it was said could be read two ways" (H.D.
1974, 51).
   18. By "mythical" I mean what the OED calls "a widely held but false notion," and
"mythology" refers more generally to the study of myths. I make this distinction to incorporate into H.D.'d hermetic poetic landscape both fictions of the self (created by herself or
projected from others) and narratives of antiquity.

we can also see the poet's obscurity as an invitation to imagine new myths and stories. Because we are provided with incomplete versions, the reader must finish the telling and invent the treasure herself.

Electra and Orestes: Twin Statues and the S/word

Electra emerges among a series of mythological figures, all symbolizing resurrection: Psyche, Persephone, Eurydice, Osiris, and even Lazarus. While Electra's story is not about reincarnation per se, the myth is inserted into the poem cycle in such a way as to imply her ascension from the underworld parallel to the liberation of the poet's voice. Inspired by Euripides' *Electra*, H.D. constructs the myth anew through a dramatic dialogue between Electra and Orestes, in which the siblings negotiate the aftermath of violence. It is "too late"—the murders have been committed and the two are left to wrestle with their guilt, as expressed by the wholly un-Sophoclean chorus: *"woe for the children's fate"* (1983, 388). Where Sophocles praises the children's actions and casts them in a rosy hue, Euripides projects a gloomy future. Their world has been transformed into purgatory in the wake of the cruel massacre manifested by the curse of Atreus, and, like the dead priestess, Electra and Orestes find themselves condemned to the land of the living dead.

Quite unlike many of the Electras so far examined, H.D.'s heroine begins with a lament for Clytemnestra that reads more like a love song. She likens her mother's story to an undiscovered flower, camouflaged by the ashes of war:[19]

> and I thought of rhododendron
> fold upon fold,
> the rose and purple and dark-rose
> of her garments.
>
> (1983, 378)

In the eyes of Electra, the murderous queen is the victim of her own violence. Strangely, however, when H.D. sets up a reflexive relationship between subject and object—"To love, one must slay / . . . / to love, one must be slain"—the perspectives of mother and daughter meld

---

19. H.D. continues her attempt to redeem Clytemnestra's name in *Helen in Egypt*, where Helen rewrites her twin sister's story: *"By identifying Clytemnestra with Iphigeneia, 'as one before the altar,' it seems as if Helen were trying to re-instate her"* (1961, 77).

into one lump of pain. In fact, there is no explicit mention of the mother, and the indeterminate "she" remains nameless for the first few pages of the poem, like the secret of the unopened flower: "no one knows / what I myself did not, / how the soul grows" (378). This same epithet is repeated with the variant "that the soul grows in the dark," referring again to the dark of the tight rosebud or to the obscurity experienced by the dead priestess.

H.D. appropriates the floral vocabulary from her decadent-symbolist influences such as Mallarmé and Wilde, and yet she rewrites the semantic horizon of flowers such as the rhododendron or the rose. For Wilde and Pater, certain flowers were highly encoded with images of homoerotic love and sexual liberation, but for H.D. this opening flower stands for the figure of the mature woman who emerges out of the tight rosebud of prepubescent youth or androgynous sexuality. The rhododendron is a recurring image throughout this poem cycle, and each time it is evoked, it strengthens the metaphor of mature female sexuality and the self-assured creative fertility of the poetic voice.

The enigma of the mother is not revealed until Electra's second speech, when "the whole earth in flame" announces "rose / rose / rose, / O rhododendron-name, mother." Here, her daughter sees clearly for the very first time. Electra mourns the fact that Clytemnestra had to die for the world to see her true colors:

no one knows the color of a flower
till it is broken,
no one knows the inner-petal of a rose
till the purple
is torn open;
no one knew
Clytemnestra

(1983, 381)

The poem is constructed through a series of couplings, allowing H.D. to play with the ambiguities of subject position. The dialogue oscillates between Electra and the Choros, Electra and Orestes, Electra and Clytemnestra, Electra and Pythia. These exchanges are carried on simultaneously, enriching the positionality of the Atrean princess. Electra's first two speeches are interspersed with statements from the Choros, which relates the story of Apollo's oracle and Agamemnon's death. They warn of the dangers of the curse—*"tread not here / where wine is spilled, / red, / red / on marble*" (380)—in contrast with the "white / pure slab of untouched marble" (376) meant for the dead priestess's grave in the previous poem. And yet the Choros confirms the afterlife of the murdered: "Never let it be said, / they are dead." They prophesy that "Clytemnestra, Electra and Death / are burnt like star-names in the sky" (383). H.D. seems also to be invoking here the first Electra, one of the seven Pleiades, daughters of the Titan Atlas. They are said to have been so distressed at the death of their sister, Hyades, that they all killed themselves and were subsequently placed in the sky as a cluster of stars used as tools of navigation (Grant and Hazel 1993, 275). Hence H.D.'s association of Electra with her mother and death.

Electra's Persephone-like journey to the underworld and back as an affirmation of Clytemnestra (Demeter) is implied through H.D.'s allusion to the earlier Electra, but it is also present through the unity of the poem cycle, that is to say, through the affinity between the speaker of the previous poem and the "dead priestess." This connection not only is apparent in the speakers of these two first poems but functions as a "subject rhyme" that continues throughout the collection, where the theme of death and resurrection (signaling a new feminine creativity) recurs in many guises, including that of a female Christ figure, Calypso, Dodona, Hyades, and Aphrodite. And yet H.D. is doing more than resurrecting her own creative voice through the figure of the dead priestess. Indeed, she is altering the iconography of her poetic muse. Her early poetry is defined partly in terms of the symbolist movement, which made an aesthetic out of morbidity and constructed a decadent worldview from images of faded beauty. While H.D. embraced these symbols and incorporated the neoromantic fin-de-siècle poetics into her version of Hellenism as a contrast to the sterile vision put forward by her male modernist counterparts, in *Dead Priestess* H.D. seems to be recoding her symbolic vocabulary surrounding death. In this poem cycle, the death is encoded no longer as decadent morbidity but rather as "productive decay," in Benjamin's sense of allegory (see chapter 2); death is symbolic of female fertility and creativity in the image of Persephone.

From Androgynous Greek Youth to Maternal Sexuality

An alternate reading of the daughter's figurative death is H.D.'s quest for a mature voice. Electra and Orestes are figured as "statues / by a temple-gate," encoded as the decadent and neoromantic image of the androgynous or hermaphroditic Greek youth, making up the two halves of the Platonic third sex, as witnessed by the Choros's lines: "*They are fair, / they are tall, / they stand twin-statues/ by a city-wall*" (385). In H.D.'s early work, twins seem to symbolize a prelapsarian androgyny, whereby brother and sister form a complete sex. Twins of the same sex also hold up same-sex love as an exalted form of friendship.

H.D. is fascinated by doubles of all kinds, such as the coupling of the sisters Helen and Clytemnestra in *Helen in Egypt*, "twin-sisters of twin-brothers" (H.D. 1961, 74) or that of Osiris and Isis, Demeter and Persephone, or Orpheus and Eurydice. In *Tribute to Freud* the poet writes of the doubles in her family history: "There were two's and two's and two's in my life. There were the two actual brothers (the three of us were born within four years). There were the two half-brothers; there were the two tiny graves of the two sisters" (H.D. 1974, 31). H.D.'s initials are twinned with and inverted in D. H. Lawrence's name, alluded to in *Tribute* (141) and echoed in the opposition of *A Dead Priestess Speaks* to Lawrence's *The Man Who Died*.[20]

In her later work, the twinning of Helen and Clytemnestra no longer seems to be inspired by the ideals of androgyny, hermaphroditism, or homosexuality but rather represents the perfection of gynocentric love, a sisterly kindness and mutual understanding, a secret shared only by women. This imagery is introduced in the long-overdue reconciliation of Electra and Clytemnestra, where the daughter first recognizes her mother's beauty as an opening rhododendron rose.

Following the traumatic experiences of the war, H.D.'s ensuing analysis with Freud, and the painfully mute "incubation period," the new voice emerges as that of a mature, self-assured, and maternally identified woman, most evident in *Helen in Egypt*. Laity (1996) points out that twins are still an important image, though now transformed into the "abject body associated with the cult of the femme fatale" (64). "Femme fatale" is perhaps too strong a term for Clytemnestra here, but Electra's compassion for her mother can be read as a transition of subject perspective to a femininity allied with fertility and creativity. What we witness in the intersection of "Electra, Clytemnestra and Death" (1983, 383) is part of this transition period that leads to the acceptance of a powerful and passionate female sexuality, which H.D.

---

20. Gary Burnett (1990) argues that this work deals with "Christ's late attempt to come into 'touch with the flesh' and sexuality with the priestess of Isis" (159), whereas H.D.'s priestess rejects the "angry lover," declaring that it is "too late" (see Burnett 1990, 155–173).

previously rejected in favor of a male-gendered androgyny. We might also interpret this as a metaphorical incorporation of the lost mother on the part of her daughter:[21] it is as if the newfound wisdom of maturity enables Electra to understand, indeed to embody her mother's version of the story. It is through the mutual experience of death uniting mother and daughter, in which Electra is cast in the role of her suicidal Pleiadic predecessors, that the Atrean princess emerges like Persephone resurrected in the form of the maternal Demeter. Just as Electra and Orestes are constructed as "twin-statues," symbolizing the perfect pairing of gender in a utopian hermaphroditism, Electra and Clytemnestra also embody an ideal image of femininity as a coupling of prepubescent girl and mature womanhood. But this partnership is about more than myths of mothers and daughters. It is about H.D.'s coming to terms with her literary fathers, be they Pound and Lawrence or Wilde, Pater, and Swinburne, allegorized in Electra's rejection of the selfish and arrogant Apollo. Electra's incorporation of and resurrection as Clytemnestra symbolize H.D.'s realization that she does not need the Victorian symbolist figure of the Greek statue in order to make a powerful poetic statement, but that she can rely on the formidable strength of the priestess/prophetess/goddess model of femininity.

Orestes crumbles in the wake of the murder, blaming his actions on Apollo's words: "He said 'strike' and he struck me; when I struck Clytemnestra, I struck myself. I cut right through myself, and I am nothing but the cold metal, I am cold, the sword, I don't feel anything at all" (1983, 384). Orestes' admission that he is "nothing but the cold metal" is surely a reference on H.D.'s part to her earlier decadent-influenced poetic voice. At one time she viewed the metaphor of cold immortality as one of purity and classical beauty. But used in this context, it has clearly lost its appeal, now signaling nothing but the dispassionate numbness of murder.

Orestes now looks to Electra to be his Pythia, "a sort of sister," and begs her to hold him up: "Stand up, stand up, O Electra, don't fall." However, she makes clear where her loyalties lie: "Why should I stand while Clytemnestra lies?" (385). Orestes feels abandoned by his sister, calling her "—you devil," but she returns his words, calmly and courageously accepting herself for what she is: "Only Electra" (386).

21. Incorporation is a term used by Freud but also by Klein and Kristeva to discuss the mourning subject's desire to absorb the lost object into the ego. In psychoanalytic terms, this is the subject's attempt to heal the gaping wound left by the irrecoverable loss of the mother. Of course, language is another vehicle for suturing over that loss.

She repeats her argument that "no one knew / Clytemnestra" (387), reiterating the image of the flower bud that opens to reveal "the inner petal of a rose," and yet her efforts fall on deaf ears. The siblings argue issues of justice and action, but it all comes down to a problem of semantics:

> Orestes: It was you who said, slay.
> Electra: Long ago—yesterday.
> O.: But now—the shadows have not moved.
> E.: There are no shadows when the whole is black.
> O.: Would you take back the deed, take back the *sword?*
> E.: Only the—*word.*
> O.: The *word* was God.
> E.: Who is to say whether the *word* was daemon, God or devil?
>
> (1983, 387, MY EMPHASIS)

H.D.'s subtle use of language plays cleverly with the complexity of justice. Electra juggles images and words, first establishing that there is no distinction between right and wrong, light and dark, when "the whole is black," then signaling the vanity of Apollo, whose "word" so easily becomes a "sword." Electra's self-designation as Pythia—"I was the sister, I was the priestess, I was alone" (1983, 385)—makes her not a neutral messenger or mask for the sun god's words, but her own woman. She is aware that the power of the word cannot be left to a god or to her literary fathers, nor, for that matter, to the Apollo-like establishment that spoke the word that started the war. Indeed, the last lines of the poem stage a formal rejection of the once-prized Greek statue of the androgynous youth: "Un-sexed, / inhuman, / doomed" (388). H.D.'s now-mature Electra equates Apollo, the voice of a male god masquerading as a female priestess, with the unspeakable horrors of violence, be it matricide or war. Apollo does not even have the courage to deliver his oracles himself, instead setting up Pythia to take all the blame. Electra realizes that justice is never a black and white issue but is clouded by the ambiguity of language, the word made sword. While she accepts her complicity in the matricide, this new Electra recognizes the need for an independent, sexualized, and assured voice to speak against cruelty and destruction of any kind. The Choros, as in Sophocles, mirrors Electra's sentiments, and yet, like the Euripidean chorus, it does not condone the actions of the children. Instead it affirms the triumph of the mother's authority, also symbolizing H.D.'s sexually mature and maternal poetic voice:

> *Out on the sea*
> *the ships toil grievously,*
> *soon they will come,*
> *finding that they have lost*
> *Clytemnestra*
> *and home.*
>
>   (1983, 388)

Hope in the Song: Coda

After a hiatus of nearly a hundred pages, Electra and Orestes return to recapitulate their theme song. Wedged between the Atrean dialogues are several poems, all of which in some way enact the theme of resurrection.[22] The poet-speaker is created and recreated in the vision of a post-Apollonian priestess, the Pythia *sans* sun god. When brother and sister return, Orestes has changed his tune, decrying Apollo's intervention and even denying him the status of deity:

> not God,
> not God
> to betray with a nod
> youth into battle . . .
> why did I follow
> a song?
>   (1983, 466–467)

At first Electra expresses nothing but anger and hatred at the destruction caused by "not God," saying: "men, men, my brother, / will slay us, / men will lift stones / obeying the writ of their altar" (467). Then she suddenly bursts forth in praise of the powers of her own creative voice:

---

22. Among these poems is "The Master," where H.D. most explicitly treats her analysis with Freud. The aging father of psychoanalysis is cast partly in the role of an obstinate Apollo ("I was angry at the old man, / I wanted an answer"), and yet it is precisely the frustration that leads the speaker to let go of her need for this "very beautiful" old man and follow his advice to find her own voice: " 'you are a poet' " (H.D. 1983, 454–455). If at the outset H.D.'s speaker sees herself as Freud's Pythia, her perspective has changed by the end of the poem: "men will see how long they have been blind, / . . . shall see woman, / perfect" (460). This meditation on her analysis seems a deliberate attempt on the part of the poet to make sense of her contradictory relationship to Freud. She genuinely liked the man she had come to know and felt indebted to him for the success of her therapy, but she could not reconcile this view of Freud with the man capable of writing such misogynistic theories of female sexual and psychological development.

Orestes, fly first,
there is shelter
there is hope
in the song.
(467)

Even so, Orestes is beside himself, made distraught by his guilt, claiming responsibility not only for the matricide but also for sister-murder:
"How can I go, / O my sister, / and leave you to death? / mine was the
sword" (467). In quiet dignity, as the "priestess with the power over life
and death" (1974, 117), Electra responds: "I am older, / a woman / . . . /
God, God, / he is gone" (1983, 468). In one easy sentence, the confident sister shows herself worthy of the title of Atrean princess, carried
by the strength of her mother and her own figurative death experience.
The "song" no longer belongs to any "God" but has been transposed
into her own language, the word of the priestess, not the Apollonian
sword. These lines offer conviction and faith, the promise of a renewed, independent, and powerful female voice. While the Choros in
the first Electra-Orestes poem predicted doom and scorned the children's actions—"*woe, woe for those who spent/ life-blood / in hate*" (1983,
388)—this brief dialogue confirms the resurrection and rejoices that
"the dead priestess speaks."

The Death of Hysteria

H.D.'s poetic enactment of Electra initiates a radical departure from
the myth as told in the Attic tragedies, as she has the heroine renegoti-
ate her familial relationships in tandem with the poet's own quest for a
new voice. Still, there are elements that betray the influence of previous Electras.[23] Specifically, the presentation of the heroine's implied
death experience as a descent into the underworld and her subsequent
resurrection bear the mark of Hofmannsthal's innovation with the
"dance of death." Although his fin-de-siècle heroine does not have a
chance to rise from the dead, her triumphant end is configured as a

---

23. Other feminists have attempted to vindicate Clytemnestra from the accusation of
ruthless murderess bestowed upon her from Homer onward (Irigaray, Hirsch, Cixous,
Kristeva). Few, however, have managed to include Electra as part of this story. Many feminist writers concentrate on reinterpreting Clytemnestra's story but do not deal with the
problematic element of Electra's involvement in matricide. H.D. handles this difficulty by
telling a new version altogether whereby Electra begs forgiveness for her part and finally
assumes her mother's role. But in her later work, *Helen in Egypt*, in which H.D. revisits
Clytemnestra's story from Helen's perspective, Electra is conspicuously absent.

pseudo-redemptive performance in the same kind of transfiguration as H.D.'s Electra experiences through her "song." Here female creativity serves the same function as the ecstatic dance.

Hysteria, however, is conspicuously absent from H.D.'s characterization of the Atrean princess. There is no hint of insanity on Electra's part—only Orestes is haunted by a guilt bordering on madness, as in Euripides' *Orestes*, in which Electra is charged with the task of rescuing her brother from the ravages of lunacy. In this loosely biographical reading of H.D.'s Electra poems in the context of the *Dead Priestess* collection, the poet writes her testimony of trauma through the enactment of a mythological figure as other. This Electra is not a hysteric like Anna O. but a powerful priestess and master of her own oracle precisely because this trauma is displaced in language, in the repetition of words and fragmented images. And while H.D.'s fascination with twinning, hermaphroditism, and androgyny can be compared to Musil's equally fascinating experiments with his Electra and Orestes characters in *The Man without Qualities*, H.D. comes to a very different conclusion, partly in that she comes to any conclusion. Musil leaves his Agathe and Ulrich in limbo, stuck somewhere between their Siamese status and a new life as individuals. Where Musil foregrounds new models of sexuality based on the erasure of militaristic masculinity and the triumph of boyish femininity, H.D. deliberately moves away from the ideal of Greek androgyny. Both authors create strong models of female sexuality for their Electra characters, albeit on different terms.

H.D. rescues her mythological heroine from a disastrous situation, resurrecting her from the silence of the underworld and deploying her as the muse of a newfound creativity. This Electra not only speaks in the powerful voice of the priestess/prophetess but also initiates a reconciliation with Clytemnestra, reinstalling and reincorporating the mother as part of her healing process. H.D.'s version of the legend banishes the hatred and violence synonymous with what she views as a male-dominated war machine in favor of a feminine politics of renewal, where beauty, *eros*, and fertility triumph and culminate in an aesthetics of hope and peace. H.D. has this Electra refuse the psychoanalytic couch. The poet chooses to transform her pain into pen marks on a page, focusing on female empowerment and creativity as home remedy.

While H.D.'s engagement with Electra is on the surface an intensely private exercise in reclaiming and appropriating voice, confronting her own sexual identity, and coming to terms with maturity, this poetry coincides with an increased interest on her part in the public sphere and

140   CHAPTER 6

politics.[24] H.D. was deeply affected by the visible rise of fascism and the blatant anti-Semitism she witnessed in Vienna in 1933 and 1934 during her analysis with Freud. From this point forward, she began making more direct political statements on subjects ranging from the Spanish Civil War to the necessity for American participation in World War II. Much later, she writes of her alter ego, the priestess from *A Dead Priestess Speaks:* "We are through with experimenting. We are in the mid-thirties, not the mid-twenties. But there must be a new means of expression, of self-expression, of world-expression. . . . The storm is coming" (quoted in Taylor 2001, 144). Like Electra, who would not be cloistered inside the intimate world of the family, H.D. uses myth as a platform to launch a more publicly minded spirit of engagement with the world.

24. Georgina Taylor (2001, 137ff.) argues that H.D. has been wrongly criticized for being intensely private, unconcerned with audience, and largely apolitical. She cites numerous examples of the ways in which the poet engaged actively in the public sphere with contemporaries and through publications in widely read magazines. Perhaps her public persona has been ignored because her audience was largely made up of women contemporaries such as Marianne Moore, Violet Hunt, Ethel Colburn Mayne, and Alice Toklas, and of women readers.

A Poetics of Survival

SYLVIA PLATH'S ELECTRA ENACTMENT

The Electra poems of Sylvia Plath (1932–1963) teeter daringly on the edge between myth and mythology, between intense animation and immobile perfection. Early critics accurately assessed the importance of myth for Plath's work, in particular Judith Kroll in *Chapters in a Mythology* (1976), which traces moon imagery and other motifs back to Robert Graves's *The White Goddess*. Myth is clearly a cornerstone of Plath's poetic oeuvre. But mythology has clouded much of our efforts to understand the genius of her craft, mythology surrounding the cultural icon of poet suicide, forever fossilized as a youthful émigré in postwar Britain and an up-and-coming poet married to a successful writer.[1]

The readings of Plath's Electra poetry offered here will attempt to uncouple the writing from the writer, to see the poetry through the lens of a mythological character, moving away from biography toward the concerns that fuel Plath's poetry: negotiating human relationships, family dynamics, women's changing roles in society, and survival under difficult circumstances. As Tracy Brain (2001) puts it, quoting Plath's own words, her "writing is very much about the things of this world" (6).

---

1. Tim Kendall (2001, xi) notes that a recent study devoted more time to "The Plath Myth" than to the poetry and that this constitutes a worrying trend in Plath studies. The publication of a half dozen new biographies since 2002 plus a Hollywood film indicates the urgency for critics to counter this interest in biography with serious analysis of her work.

More recent scholarship has shed light on the political Plath, on her engagement with the Cold War (Peel 2002), the Holocaust (Hungerford
2003), the environment, and national identity (Brain 2001). The focus of
my argument, however, will be on the vibrant life force evident in her
poetry, indeed the nascent energy that Taïna Tuhkunen-Couzic (2002)
calls "embryonic writing" (46). Of particular interest to me are the mechanics of Plath's writing, the pounding rhythms and the sonic harmonies she achieves, all as part of a successful mourning process, what
Julia Kristeva (1989) has called a "poetics of survival" (73).

   In "Electra on Azalea Path," the poetic persona announces: "I borrow the stilts of an old tragedy" (Plath 1981, 117), revealing Plath's use
of the Electra myth as a balancing act and an attempt to achieve equi-
librium in an unstable intertextual matrix. Plath turns to myth in her
efforts to make sense of experiences of loss that resist articulation in
ordinary language. The stilts symbolize the difficulty of witnessing
such pain, the business of walking in shaky shoes, but they also attest to
the incredible resourcefulness of someone who invents prostheses to
replace missing limbs. We might read it too as a clever inversion of real
world events, since Plath's father died after his leg was amputated because of diabetic gangrene. In the microcosm of the poem disability is
transformed into the stuff of circus magic. The poet's "borrowing" suggests an imperfect palimpsest, something that does not quite fit. There
is also a measure of impermanence in this image, like little girls swap-
ping clothes for an afternoon. The term "tragedy" refers equally to the
classical genre of antiquity and Plath's own aesthetic reworking of loss.
Helen Vendler (2003) surmises that once Plath has translated Greek
tragedy into the architecture of a poem, "the task of [Electra] is relieved by a new perception of the ruin, an aesthetic one" (131). Following the logic of Walter Benjamin, Plath works with the tangible remains of loss as the raw material of aesthetics, producing mourning in
and through the beauty of decay. But lest we think this too serious an
endeavor, Vendler reminds us that Plath's genius is her ability to con-
cretize human emotion, to "mingle wit and tragedy" (133). In *Loss: The
Politics of Mourning*, David Eng and David Kazanjian (2003) argue that
this focus on materiality "generates a politics of mourning that might
be active rather than reactive, prescient rather than nostalgic, abundant
rather than lacking, social rather than solipsistic, militant rather than
reactionary" (2). It is these active, prescient, and militant aspects that I
want to allow to surface in Plath's engagement with Electra.
   I want to begin by discussing Plath's poetics of incorporation in the

context of theories of mourning by Freud, Melanie Klein, and Julia Kristeva. I will examine in some detail the poems where Plath most explicitly adopts the persona of Electra—"Electra on Azalea Path," "Colossus," and "Daddy"—and will show how metaphors of orality are transformed into what I call "reverse incorporation." Freud distinguishes between normal and pathological responses to loss, between mourning and melancholia, the latter of which is characterized by a narcissistic regression to the cannibalistic phase of infantile development. I hope to demonstrate that although Plath's early poetry is dominated by metaphors of consumption, there is a gradual shift away from the incorporation of the lost object and a move toward renewed object relations, where the speaker is cared for and protected through the experience of mothering. As with H.D., the mature Plath moves beyond her identification with Agamemnon's daughter and comes into her own when she begins to engage with the maternal, to confront her worst fears about Clytemnestra, and to make the link between creativity and the nurturing role of motherhood. The poet's conversation with mythology does not end when she discards Electra's voice; rather, Plath refers in her elegy "Edge" to "the illusion of Greek necessity" (1981, 272).[2] In this last invocation, things Greek become both impossible and indispensable, aptly summing up the poet's ambivalence toward the power of myth to signify omnipotent truth and to be nothing but hoax, a trompe l'oeil. Ultimately Plath leaves it up to the reader to decide which version to accept.

An Aesthetics of Mourning

It was Plath and not her critics who first revealed her poetic persona as that of Electra, explaining her poem "Daddy" in a BBC radio interview: "Here is a poem spoken by a girl with an Electra complex. Her father died while she thought he was God" (Plath 1981, 293). She does not say that she enacts the mythological figure as the poem's speaker, instead invoking the Freudian term "Electra complex" to refer to a psychological model that functions as a rhetorical trope. Electra is not so

2. Jahan Ramazani (1993, 1143) considers Plath's contribution to the genre of the elegy and traces her influence on American poets like Sexton, Rich, Wakoski, Kumin, Kizer, and Olds. Ironically, it is Plath herself who becomes the object of painfully romantic and nostalgic elegies, mythologizing her life as a tragedy with Oresteian proportions. Even though Plath's writing is contemporaneous with H.D.'s later work, and the poets' birth dates are separated only by a few decades, Plath remains frozen at the age of thirty in the collective cultural psyche. It is as if the poet had been cryonized at the time of her death, despite the fact that if she were alive today she would be in her seventies.

much the subject as subjective positionality, a mediator or a platform for the construction and destruction of paternity in the image of Agamemnon. Radically opposing images of the father dominate Plath's poetry from beginning to end: rage, revenge, hatred, and humiliation are countered by love, admiration, and inspiration. The heroine of the Oresteian legend provides a means of establishing this relationship as obsession, fascination, even fetish. As Jahan Ramazani (1993) puts it: "The Electra-myth may be a smokescreen" (1147); Agamemnon is invoked, made larger than life, then reduced to a mere ghost.

Except for the daughter and her constant apostrophic invocation of the father, all elements of the Electra myth have been stripped away. Unlike H.D., Plath does not engage with Orestes but rather excises him from her poetic landscape. Indeed, even Oedipus is dismissed with one terse line in "Ravage": "O Oedipus. O Christ. You use me ill" (1981, 116). Plath does not take the time to tell Electra's story as it happened but picks up where the action left off. The bodies are strewn across the stage, but the spotlight is on Agamemnon's corpse, and his death exists as a distant, elliptical memory, shrunk into three scant lines in "Electra on Azalea Path":

> *The day your slack sail drank my sister's breath*
> *The flat sea purpled like that evil cloth*
> *My mother unrolled at your last homecoming.*
> (1981, 117)

Frederike Haberkamp (1997) calls Plath's insertion of the myth "clumsy," suggesting that it appears only to "lend the proper symbolic dimension and resonance" (29). J. M. Bremer (1991b, 312) views the Aeschylean intrusion differently, suggesting that the three lines in italics, while they are not a direct quotation from the *Oresteia*, are spoken by an Electra character embedded within the poem. Vendler (2003, 119) points out that Electra's viewpoint is made all the more intimate through the omission of proper names. Plath thus allows Electra to voice her own interpretation of the events, and the mythological heroine is introduced as a double for Plath's primary poetic persona. The following lines admit this willful appropriation:

> I borrow the stilts of an old tragedy.
> The truth is, one late October, at my birth-cry
> A scorpion stung its head, an ill-starred thing;
> My mother dreamed you face down in the sea.
> (PLATH 1981, 117)

The first voice returns to set the record straight—"The truth is . . ."—
dismissing the neat Aeschylean rendering of the myth, which explains
the father's death from everyone's perspective save that of Electra. It is
indeed telling that Plath chooses the *Oresteia* as her intertext and not
either of the later *Electra* tragedies of antiquity. This Attic trilogy gives
Electra the fewest lines. She is sidelined for most of the action, echoing
Plath's own sentiments that she "felt cheated" when she visited her father's grave, the incident that inspired this poem (Plath 1982, 298). Not
only does the poet at last allow the Atrean princess a say in the matter,
but because this Electra is the most elusive of the three versions in antiquity, Plath has a clean slate upon which to draw her vision of Aeschylus's heroine.

However sketchy Plath's reference to the Electra myth may appear,
the poet's consistent use of metaphors of incorporation nevertheless
forges a link to the history of the house of Atreus and its cannibalistic curse. Throughout the *Collected Poems*, we find repeated and intense images of orality (eating and being eaten, devouring, chewing,
mouthing), corresponding to Freud's theory in "Mourning and Melancholia" that incorporation is an important part of the process of griev-
ing: "The ego wants to incorporate this object into itself, and, in accor-
dance with the oral or cannibalistic phase of libidinal development in
which it is, it wants to do so by devouring it" (Freud 1917, 249–250).
This desire to bring the lost love object into the self is in fact a regression from a more developed object-choice to an expression of primary
narcissism. Melanie Klein (1975b, 345) elaborates on Freud's thesis in
"Mourning and Its Relation to Manic-Depressive States," suggesting
that oral fixation or a consumption compulsion as a response to trauma
marks a return to the very early stages of infancy when the child incor-
porates "good" and "bad" objects as partial representations of the
mother's body. The child's initial desire to destroy the "bad" objects
leads to sadistic and masochistic behavior, which, when recuperated in
later periods of mourning, results in guilt and self-destructive tendencies. For Klein, the metaphoric incorporation mediates the experience
of loss: "The individual is reinstating his actually lost loved object; but
he is also at the same time re-establishing inside himself his first loved
objects" (369).

Kristeva (1989) agrees with Klein that incorporation is closely linked
to the mourning of a lost loved one. However, she maintains that this
act conceals an aggressiveness toward the dead person, illustrating with
a first-person narrative account: "I love that object, but even more so I
hate it; because I love it, and in order not to lose it, I imbed it in myself;
but because I hate it, that other within myself is a bad self, I am bad, I

am non-existent, I shall kill myself" (11). Plath's poetic personas mirror
this love-hate obsession with the father as a lost object that needs con-
tinually to be ingested or introjected, as if she is trying to create a new
image of paternity as a part of the mourning self.

Esther Greenwood, the young intern at *Ladies' Day* magazine in
Plath's novel *The Bell Jar*, confesses her fascination with consumption:
"I'm not sure why it is, but I love food more than just about anything
else. No matter how much I eat, I never put on weight" (Plath 1963,
25). This passage does not reveal the extent of Esther's anxiety, but we
are left wondering if she could have avoided the breakdown and subsequent suicide attempt depicted in the novel if only she had been able to
realize her dream of being fully identified with her father, the lost love
object represented by her love of food. And yet, as Kristeva (1989)
points out, incorporation, if taken to its full extreme, leads to a total
narcissistic identification, "a *loss* of the essential other" necessary for
the existence of the subject: "Depression is the hidden face of Narcis-
sus, the face that is to bear him away into death, but of which he is un-
aware while he admires himself in a mirage" (5). Thus, if it is to be an
effective tool of mourning, incorporation must remain at the liminal
stage, a consumption of the parts but not the whole.[3]

The connection of Plath's lyric speaker's situation to the *Oresteia* is
indeed partial, a case of covert intertextuality, invoking the terrible
scourge that infected the Atrean house, plagued by the curse of the
family romance: a dead father and a hateful mother. Toward the end of
Aeschylus's *Agamemnon* we learn more of the history behind the cycle
of revenge and hatred. Aegisthus recounts the terrible crime against his
father, Thyestes, who was fed his own children by Agamemnon's father, Atreus:

> Thyestes was the guest,
> and this man's godless father—
> the zeal of the host outstripping a brother's love,
> made my father a feast that seemed a feast for gods,
> a love feast of his children's flesh.
> He [Atreus] cuts the extremities, feet and delicate hands
> into small pieces, scatters them over the dish

3. Ewa Ziarek (1993) cautions against an overzealous acceptance of Kristeva's theory of
melancholic depression and suggests that there is always a "violence in the symbolization
of the other" (70). Incorporation itself is an act of brutality—it may obliterate the boundaries between inside and out, self and other, but it also negates the other in an effort to suture over the "open wound within the ego" (71).

and serves it to Thyestes throned on high.
He picks at the flesh he cannot recognize,
the soul of innocence eating the food of ruin—
look, (*pointing to the bodies at his feet*)
that feeds upon the house!

(AESCHYLUS 1966, 1620–1631)

This scene is in fact a repetition of an earlier calamity: it was Tantalus of Lydia who offended the gods by feasting them on his son's flesh, for which he was condemned to starve in Hades, "tantalized" by food and drink just beyond his reach. Thus, it is plain to see that the atrocities committed in this myth are the result of the crimes of the father brought to bear on the children. And it is this legacy that Plath paints in her poetic invocation of the Atrean legend through a subject rhyme with her own accursed family romance.

According to Klein (1988a, 30), the infant's fear of being devoured by the parent is a reaction to its own desire to assimilate and possess what is external to the self. Essentially, the desire to consume and the fear of being consumed amount to the same thing. Plath's imagery of incorporation is the reverse of the scenario related by Aegisthus in the *Agamemnon*—instead of the father eating his children, the speaker devours the father, miming a graphic feast perhaps as homage to this history, a performance of cultural memory, but also to save herself, to put an end to the curse. What the two scenes of conspicuous consumption have in common, however, is a destabilizing of the boundaries between inside and outside. In *From Communion to Cannibalism*, Maggie Kilgour (1990) questions the absoluteness of this opposition: "The idea of incorporation . . . depends upon and enforces an absolute division between inside and outside; but it is in the act itself that opposition disappears, dissolving the structure it appears to produce" (4). She goes on to say that the interior always takes precedence, attempting to control the threatening outside, precisely in the act of bringing it inside.[4]

This desire to control the lost object through incorporation is demonstrated in one of Plath's earlier poems, "The Thin People," where the speaker expresses the same perpetual state of hunger Esther Greenwood experiences in *The Bell Jar*:

---

4. One of the most obvious representations of incorporation is eating, a necessary function of the body, but this may also account for the strict social and religious practices around food. It would seem that the taboo against cannibalism that Freud postulates in *Totem and Taboo* (1913) is tied to the fundamental cultural need to regulate the relations of inside and out.

They are always with us, the thin people
Meager of dimension as the gray people

. . . .

It was during the long hunger-battle
They found their talent to persevere
In thinness, to come, later

(1981, 64)

Similarly, the poetic persona in "On the Plethora of Dryads" learns to squelch her insatiable desire: "Without meat or drink I sat / Starving my fantasy down" (1981, 67). And in "I want, I want," we encounter an equally grievous image of a forlorn creature: "Open-mouthed, the baby god" who "cried out for the mother's dug," but for whom only "sand abraded the milkless lip" (106). There are numerous examples where the speaker expresses a desire for oral satisfaction, or rather shows pity for the helpless and weak who must go hungry and neglected. Both Klein and Kristeva confirm that the drive to incorporate the dead other in the process of mourning recalls the originary loss of the mother, a repetition of what Freud calls the *"impossible mourning for the maternal object"* (quoted in Kristeva 1989, 9). As such, the object of mourning—in Plath's and Electra's case, the father—becomes confused with the primary grief over the lost mother. The speaker in "Poem for a Birthday" reflects this ambivalent relationship to the mother, beginning with the image of bounty, which soon gives way to the natural wilting that accompanies such a cornucopia:

The month of flowering's finished. The fruit's in,
Eaten or rotten. I am all mouth.
October's the month for storage

. . . .

Mother, you are the one mouth
I would be tongue to. Mother of otherness
Eat me. Wastebasket gaper, shadow of doorways.

(1981, 131–132)

The boundaries between inside and out, subject and object are utterly destroyed in this poem, which functions as an elegy to maternal fertility, as portrayed by the flowers and fruit of late summer. The speaker does not wish to incorporate the mother per se but offers her own body as surrogate or prosthesis, to be spoken by the mother's tongue. The words "Wastebasket gaper" perform this ritual rhetorically by inverting "wastepaper basket" to create a distorted image of the mouth as a crude, gaping hole, a receptacle for garbage symbolic of the otherness of the mother.

And yet the desire to invade and be inhabited by the mother's body is simultaneously a drive to negate and thereby usurp her power, since, as Kristeva (1989) puts it, "Matricide is our vital necessity, the sine-qua-non condition of our individuation" (27–28).[5] But for the depressive or melancholic, this process is interrupted, instead leading in two directions: either the self is obliterated to save the mother from fatal negation—"In order to protect mother I kill myself while knowing . . . that it comes from her"—or the mother is transformed into the "death-bearing she-Gehenna," so that "I do not kill myself in order to kill her but I attack her, harass her, represent her" (Kristeva 1989, 28). Plath's speaker in the poem "Maenad" concludes: "The mother of mouths didn't love me" (1981, 133). And finally in "Stones," the last poem of the sequence, the "I" recognizes that the web of self-hatred and rage against the father and by proxy the mother is the result of unrequited love for the lost object:

> Love is the uniform of my bald nurse.
> Love is the bone and sinew of my curse.
> (137)

The speaker comes to the same conclusion in "Electra on Azalea Path": "It was love that did us both to death" (1981, 117). Inevitably death only interrupts the love between father and daughter. Such a curse is indeed no different from the one that mires Electra and her family. The Atrean princess has inherited the cannibalistic crimes of her forefathers in the same way that Plath's speaker is haunted by paternal loss and the desire for introjection, what Kristeva (1989) calls "melancholy cannibalism . . . this passion for holding within the mouth . . . [that] manifests the anguish of losing the other through the survival of self" (12). The self is indeed nourished and healed, resuscitated through devouring. While the Electra of Attic tragedy does not use metaphors of incorporation to cope with her mourning, her actions are nevertheless motivated by her ancestors' cannibalism.

Unlike the mythological heroine, whose role she poetically enacts, Plath is self-conscious about her own psychological state, immersing

5. Ziarek (1993) questions the ethics of matricide as the condition of subjectivity, concluding that it merely "confirms the primacy of identity and its violence in Western metaphysics" (75). Ziarek wonders if the violence inherent in the neutralization of the other is necessary and if the mother and the subject's identity are mutually exclusive. Perhaps it need not come down to a question of the one or the other if language can be trusted to mediate such negotiations.

herself in Freud's theories and attempting self-diagnosis. She usurps the role of the analyst in much the same way as do H.D., Anna O., and Hofmannsthal's Elektra. Plath writes in her journal for December 27, 1958:

> Read Freud's *Mourning and Melancholia* this morning after Ted left for the library. An almost exact description of my feelings and reasons for suicide: a transferred murderous impulse from my mother onto myself: the "vampire" metaphor Freud uses, "draining the ego": that is exactly the feeling I have getting in the way of my writing. (Plath 1982, 279)

Plath comes to the conclusion that in order to gain power over her mother's image, she must either appease that "vampire" with food, "like the old witches for whom one sets out plates of milk and honey," or she must "write" (279). Paradoxically, however, she feels that her mother stands in the way of her writing, even though writing is the only way she can control her mother. Plath continues to analyze her relationship to her mother in Freudian terms: "How much of life I have known: love, disillusion, madness, hatred, murderous passions. . . . I will write mad stories. But honest. I know the horror of primal feelings, obsessions. A ten-page diatribe against the Dark Mother. The Mummy. Mother of shadows. An analysis of the Electra complex" (316). Plath is already one step ahead of Freud in her perception that the Electra complex has as much to do with unraveling the lost mother in the mummy as it does with the daughter's desire for her father's love.

It is as if the poet anticipates Kristeva's theory of the Semiotic when she suggests writing as an antidote for the incorporation of the lost object, in fact equating the two when she suggests in a diary entry that the remedy for suppressed talent is "feeding food and words to all the world's other. . . . Bites and wry words" (Plath 1982, 187), a metaphor that appears in "The Thin People," where the menace of the famished victims is not so much insatiable craving but "a thin silence" (1981, 64). The remedy for the agonizing hunger of silence is "*a modification in signifying bonds*," says Kristeva (1989), and yet it is the "*signifier's failure*" that distinguishes inconsolable melancholia from normal mourning (10). Thus, language appears to collapse into a fragile and unstable symbolic system unable to compensate for the object loss, and this leads to an attempt at sublimation: "Through melody, rhythm, semantic polyvalency, the so-called poetic form, which decomposes and recomposes signs, is the sole 'container' seemingly able to secure an uncertain but adequate hold over the Thing" (14). Plath's frustration with her writing reflects this ambivalent and even distrustful relationship

with signification—after all, if the melancholic feels betrayed and abandoned by the lost object, how is it possible to put faith in a solid bond
between the signifier and the signified? But rather than thinking about
the signifier's inadequacy to express its lost referent as the impossibility
of representation, Eng and Kazanjian (2003) suggest we couch it in
different terms: "Might we interpret it in terms of an extended flexibil-
ity, an expanded capacity for representation?" (4).

The poet's journals are littered with references to her yearning for
the release of satisfying writing, which functions like nourishment for
the thin and hungry: "I sat paralyzed, feeling no person in the world to
speak to. Cut off totally from humanity in a self-induced vacuum. I felt
sicker and sicker. I couldn't happily be anything but a writer and I
couldn't be a writer" (Plath 1982, 248). Still, this apparent disappoint-
ment with the "signifier's failure," when tackled poetically, results precisely in this "expanded capacity for representation." For example, in
"Words," the speaker berates the lexemes for their infidelity by calling
them "Words dry and riderless" but immediately contradicts this statement by drawing attention to their unstoppable rhythms and movement: "The indefatigable hoof-taps." Indeed the first stanza announces
the very potent force of words:

> Axes
> After whose stroke the wood rings,
> And the echoes!
> Echoes traveling
> Off from the center like horses.
> (1981, 270)

Language here is anything but an empty shell devoid of authenticity or
feeling; Kristeva (1986) calls attention to this phenomenon in Plath and
characterizes her as a "woman disillusioned with meanings and words,
who took refuge in lights, rhythms and sounds" (157). We note the explosive k sounds in "axes" and "echoes" knifing their way to meaning
only to give way suddenly to the softer sibilants and unvoiced f and h in
the last line, mimicking aurally what Plath demonstrates semantically.

The very first poem in Plath's *Collected Poems* introduces the theme
of language and questions its capacity to mend the speaker's fractured
object-relations, here labeled "appalling ruin": "What ceremony of
words can patch the havoc?" (1981, 21). By the end of the volume we are
met with apparent silence: "Voicelessness. The snow has no voice"
(263). And yet as Kristeva suggests, Plath's life-drive is exhibited in the

rhythms and sounds that pervade her work with urgent nonsemantic communication. Precisely in this poem, "The Munich Mannequins," which announces the pristine white silence of snow, wave after wave of sound drives the poem until we have a wall of relentless noise. The quick succession of explosive utterances and front-loaded lines with weak endings forces the reader to move on:

> Perfection is terrible, it cannot have children.
> Cold as snow breath, it tamps the womb
>
> Where the yew trees blow like hydras,
> The tree of life and the tree of life
>
> Unloosing their moons, month after month, to no purpose.
> The blood flood is the flood of love . . .
>
> (1981, 263)

The reader is inundated with images of fertility, maternity, and the fleshy corporeality of the female body. Menstruation is not a burden but a sensuous ritual of love, a generous gift of excess. The explosive sounds of p, c, and t of the first stanza give way to the soft consonants m, f, l of a mother's whisper that dominate the poetic landscape of the third stanza. The long and short o vowels here weave and undulate the lines, in direct contrast to the compelling repetition of life-abundant images. It is the very contradictions of heady sonorous qualities, stylistic devices, and images that make Plath's poetry so full of potential energy and indeed "embryonic."[6]

Melancholia or Reverse Incorporation?

Kristeva observes that the the word *melancholy* comes from the Greek *melanos* and *kole*, meaning "black bile," one of the four humors. According to Aristotle, melancholia is a result of an imbalance in the system, an excess of black bile (Kristeva 1989, 6). This surplus presumably needs to be offset through the consumption of a contrasting element. Plath writes in her journal of the rage she feels at her colleagues at

---

6. Tuhkunen-Couzic (2002, 360) speaks of Plath's poetry as a space of potential creation, with the locus in the female and specifically maternal body. Plath's work manifests the potential energy of future creative bursts and is temporary like ocean waves, the buzz of bees, and even ejaculation.

Smith College, where she taught in 1957–58: "How I am exorcising them from my system. Like bile" (1982, 185). This anecdote mirrors the poet's expulsion of the father figure in her poetry—after consuming his image through metaphors of orality, he is expelled in a reverse incorporation as a "Colossus," a gigantic monster bearing no resemblance to the actual father Plath knew as a child.

Kristeva (1989) reminds us that any loss evokes the memory of the primary loss of the mother and results in an attempt to recuperate her image or to suture over these damaged object-relations through language. However, these efforts to fill the void with words are frustrated, since the depressive subject is "unbelieving in language," a result of the fact that the object is "unnameable, supreme good, or something unrepresentable" (13–14). In Plath's poetry, the father takes on hypertrophic proportions precisely because he is the unsignifiable "Thing." If his image cannot be saturated fully with words, then he is nothing more than a hoax, a poor substitute for reality. As if compensating for the unrepresentability of the object, the father becomes distorted beyond recognition. As Esther Greenwood puts it: "The person you thought all your life was your father is a sham" (Plath 1963, 34). Kristeva (1989) explains this phenomenon in terms of a "denial of negation," whereby, in the manic phase, the depressive elaborates a "false language . . . ersatz, imitation, or carbon copy," which, "if it isn't an antidepressant, is at least a survival, a resurrection" (50–51). Plath demonstrates this willingness to go to extreme lengths to falsify the image of the father, as if it might provide some relief no matter how tentative.

There is no more blatant example of this than the speaker's description of her father's grave in "Electra on Azalea Path," where the paternal image is substituted with kitschy ornamentation in a "cramped necropolis":

> Nobody died or withered on that stage
> . . . .
> The artificial red sage does not stir
> In the basket of plastic evergreens they put
> At the headstone next to yours, nor does it rot,
> Although the rains dissolve a bloody dye:
> The ersatz petals drip, and they drip red
> . . . .
> The stony actors poise and pause for breath.
>   (1981, 116–117)

The physical father who succumbed to "gangrene" is here replaced
with cheap imitation flowers, fading but stubbornly refusing to rot
while their fake color stains the ground as Agamemnon's blood stained
Electra's memory. The imagery of "stage" and "stony actors" evokes
the theatricality of death and its performance as a "*hypersign* around
and with the depressive void" (Kristeva 1989, 99). Kristeva calls this
heightened emphasis upon artifice "*allegory*, as lavishness of that which
no longer is, but which regains for myself a higher meaning because I am
able to remake nothingness" (99). The forced alliteration ("The day
you died I went into the dirt") and assonance ("Small as a doll in my
dress of innocence") heighten the sense of baroque ornamentation and
reinforce the poem's intricate façade.

Plath demonstrates the allegorical tension between hypersign and
the nothingness it recreates in the wordplay on her mother's name
"Aurelia Plath" and "Azalea Path." Not only is the lost maternal body
recuperated as the resting place of the father, but the substitution is
further emphasized in the unreality of the "ersatz petals," which give
away their status as trompe l'oeil. And yet in this phrase, the flower
name functions merely as a modifier for "Path," the dirt walkway trampled underfoot by the mourning speaker. A further association is the
translation of Plath's name, which shares an etymological connection
to the German *platt* meaning flat. Perhaps the mother is turned into
the path to be trampled and flattened, tortured for denying her daughter the love she deserved, and the daughter, who also bears the name
"Plath," is as flat and hungry as the "thin people." Or could it be that
the poet is playing on the same lexical affinity when the speaker invokes Agamemnon's "*flat sea purpled*"? The German *platt* also means
"boring, dull, uninspired," here evident in the tawdry azaleas, but also
in the mundane "stony actors" and the monotone drone of the poetic
voice here:[7]

---

7. While this reading may appear to stretch the limits of authorial intent, it retains
some of its validity as analogy and possible subconscious subtext (after all, Plath does make
constant references in her journal to studying German). Plath's poetry has often been dismissed as "confessional" and "stream of consciousness," though Hugh Kenner was one of
the first critics to praise her craft and rhetorical skill: "Sylvia Plath was counting her lines
and governing her rhetoric. . . . These are shaped poems. . . . The resulting control, sometimes *look* of control, is a rhetoric, as cunning in its power over our nerves as the stream of
repulsions" (quoted in Haberkamp 1997, 12). Plath was carefully negotiating her object-relations in rhetorical terms, skillfully working each line to achieve specific allusions,
rhythm, and tonal quality. She was very much a perfectionist and scrutinized every last
word. Brain (2001, 22) notes that any thought that Plath's poems were quickly scribbled-
down cries of personal pain is quickly shaken by a visit to Smith College's Rare Book
Room, where the drafts of Plath's last poems are housed. Boxes and boxes are filled with

Everything took place in a durable whiteness

. . . .
                             no flower
Breaks the soil. This is Azalea Path

. . . .
It was the gangrene ate you to the bone
My mother said; you died like any man.
How shall I age into that state of mind?
I am the ghost of an infamous suicide,
My own blue razor rusting in my throat.
                         (1981, 117)

The lost mother is made present through the cryptic "Azalea Path" and then negated with the phrase "no flower / Breaks the soil," denying the churchyard its named blossoms. We are reminded of the desertlike "durable whiteness." We can extend the analogy of barrenness further, if we consider the etymology of "azalea" from the Greek *azaleos*, meaning "dry," corresponding to the arid soil that supports only artificial greenery. As rich as the poem's complex imagery and lexical play may be, Plath seems to install rhetorical authority only to negate it with the rot of "gangrene" and the "rust" of the "blue razor" that threatens to gag the speaker's throat and suspend the poem. Plath vows to silence the voice of this poem for good, declaring that she would not publish it because it is "too forced and rhetorical" (1982, 300). Vendler (2003, 119) suggests that Plath rejects not the poem itself but the obvious influence of her teacher, Robert Lowell.

In comparison to "Colossus," the later incarnation of the same Electra material, "Azalea Path" is rooted solidly in the local, with its clinging relationships to the physical geography of the cemetery and the temporality of the visit to the grave. Vendler (2003, 123) points out that "Colossus," written a mere seven months later, explodes the dimensions of the speaker's perspective. Electra is now an ant and her war-hero father arches above like the giant Agamemnon motif that begins Strauss's opera: "A blue sky out of the Oresteia / Arches above us" (Plath 1981, 129). As Vendler observes, the poem hints at the mature poet by introducing many of the themes that will preoccupy Plath throughout the next years: bees, stones, inanimate self, repression (123).

---

dozens of drafts for every poem, lines and stanzas scratched out and rewritten over and over again until they were right. Brain concludes that Plath was calculating in all kinds of ways, right down to the choice of paper itself—the reverse side of Ted Hughes's draft paper.

The repeated negation of life in "Electra on Azalea Path" and the poem's signifying power correspond to Kristeva's "disavowal of negation." Kristeva borrows the term from Freud, who proposes that "negation [*Verneinung*] is a way of taking cognizance of what is repressed," bringing it into consciousness although not necessarily accepting it (Freud 1925a, 235). For Kristeva (1989), language itself performs a negation by providing a substitution for the lost mother, even though depressed persons "*disavow the negation:* they cancel it, they suspend it, and nostalgically fall back on the real object (the Thing) of their loss" (43–44). This double negation or denial of negation is also a manifestation of the death drive in that object relations break down entirely in the failure to recuperate the lost mother in language. Paradoxically, however, this "schizoid fragmentation," although an expression of the death drive, is in fact a "defense against death—against somatization or suicide," which is perceived as a final reunion with the lost paradise of the Thing (Kristeva 1989, 19). Thus, we can see that while Plath's poetic persona mimes the death drive through a "disavowal of negation," illustrated in the failure of language to represent the dead father, this rhetorical denial is nevertheless a defense against death. After all, the last line of "Azalea Path" heralds love as the poem's crucial fuel: "It was my love that did us both to death" (Plath 1981, 117). *Eros* and *thanatos*, libidinal forces and the death drive are bound together in one fiery knot of potential energy.[8] Though the poem ends with the word *death*, it is more a *danse macabre* than a still life. The line also suggests a newfound harmony and union with the father, taken up once again in "Colossus," where the speaker imagines herself not only in symbiosis with the father but actually within him, reversing the scenario of incorporation: "I squat in the cornucopia / Of your left ear" (Plath 1981, 130).

Plath's Electra persona may struggle to keep faith in the signifying bonds of language, but the silence is a very noisy one, embedded in the pounding rhythms, repetitions, assonance, and rhymes of "Daddy." This and other *Ariel* poems have been described as "bad for anyone's soul" (Kenner 1979, 43), and yet the disavowal of negation in the repudiation of language, the retreat into "absurd signs, slackened, scattered, checked

---

8. It should be noted that, as with the distinction between mourning and melancholy, Freud's theory of the death drive is not synonymous with the suicidal impulse. As already mentioned, the death drive Freud introduces in *Beyond the Pleasure Principle* is a regressive tendency. It is the drive to return to primary narcissism, often manifested in a repetition compulsion. It is omnipresent as a part of normal human psychosexual development, whereas the suicidal impulse arises when the death drive is distorted and the subject becomes fixated on primitive object cathexis.

sequences" may be interpreted less as pathology than as *resourcefulness* on the part of the speaker to embrace life in a "poetics of survival" (Kristeva 1989, 73). The collapse of meaning is a bid to take refuge in the unreality of these grotesque images of paternity, in the father's "gobbledygoo." The speaker blames her muteness on the effects of bodily torture:

> I never could talk to you.
> The tongue stuck in my jaw.
>
> It stuck in a barb wire snare.
> Ich, ich, ich, ich,
> I could hardly speak.
> I thought every German was you.
> And the language obscene
> (1981, 223)

The tongue stutters and stammers to spit out the first-person pronoun, displacing and deferring the speaker's positionality through perpetual repetition. The German *Ich* further distances the speaker from her language, absenting her from the mother tongue; conversely, it is also an attempt to get rid of the father by spitting out his language. We might say the poetic persona tries to recuperate her father by speaking his sounds, but on the other hand, we can see it as excising him in a reverse incorporation. It is tempting to read this stammering "Ich" in light of Kristeva's observation (1989) that "the speech of the depressed is to them like an alien skin; melancholy persons are foreigners in their maternal tongue. . . . The dead language they speak, which foreshadows their suicide, conceals a Thing buried alive" (53). In this scenario, the speaker, in a bid for radical self-exile, lays claim to the opposing language of otherness, the speech carrying the memory of genocide: "I began to talk like a Jew / I think I may well be a Jew" (Plath 1981, 223). And yet, as Anthony Easthope (2002) has argued, the speaker exercises remarkable control over the poem, with the insistent presence of the "I" doing the action: "the sustained coherence and stability of its represented speaker, the I which runs across and is confirmed at every instance" (66). Plath's speaker utters the first-person pronoun "I" more than two dozen times in the poem, and even if one agrees with Jacqueline Rose (1992) that the poem speaks to a crisis of language and identity, even if it is true that the "I" is constructed as part of a larger cultural fantasy that includes Nazi Germany as the universal enemy, it can still be argued that the repetition installs rhetorical authority, all the while repositioning it with the repetition of the shifter "I." Rose's points that the poem outlines the conditions of the symbolic function (227) and that the so very problematic identification between Plath and a Jew is "partial, hesitant and speculative" (228) are well taken, but the force behind the "I" within the microcosm of the poem is not mere fantasy.[9]

Plath's speaker seems at first to have a speech impediment, demonstrated in the rhythmic pairing of words bordering on the absurd: "Barely daring to breathe or Achoo. / . . . / I used to pray to recover you. / Ach, du." But the contrast between the nonsemantic onomatopoeia of "Achoo" and the German apostrophic address using the familiar *du* is a striking and sudden shift in tone from playful imitation of a normal bodily function to the seriousness of German as the aggressor's language. The seeming silliness of this coupling also figuratively exorcises the "you/du" in the same way that a sneeze expels germs and disease to restore health. We have here a compelling example of reverse incorporation—instead of being ingested, the lost object is blown clear from the body, exiting through the nasal passages. The aural affinity between the two utterances "Achoo" and "Ach, du" suggests that the speaker, rather than recovering the lost object, can simply sneeze away the dreadful daddy in one violent convulsion.

9. Plath's comparison of her own suffering to that of Holocaust victims has been repudiated as self-aggrandization and criticized for diminishing the real atrocities endured by Jews under Nazi Germany. These invocations have been labeled "monstrous" and "disproportionate" (Calvin Bedient, Irving Howe), or female rage against a "patriarchal and competitive authority structure" (Harold Bloom), but have also been more positively viewed as a model of how "the father-daughter relationship dominates the female psyche in our culture" (Linda Bundtzen) (all quoted in Steinert 1995, 153–155). Perhaps the most sustained commentary on Plath's Holocaust imagery is by James E. Young and Jacqueline Rose. Young (1988) shifts the focus away from the question of whether Plath has the right to invoke the Holocaust to ask "to what extent the writer was traumatized by her literary historical memory of the Holocaust" (127), and suggests that "Daddy" and other poems are symptomatic of a move from public knowledge to public memory. Rose (1992) defends Plath on the grounds that critics of her work mourn the loss of the "objective correlative" and that what is really at stake here is the relationships between metaphor, fantasy and identification. She reads "Daddy" as symptomatic of a larger "crisis of representation" and concludes by asking if women "might not have a special relationship to fantasy" (237). Amy Hungerford (2003) is somewhat skeptical about what she calls Rose's antibiographical stance, the reduction of all Plath's poetry to a problem of representation, and suggests that this type of criticism raises other questions: "What is the relevance of who Plath was to our analysis of the poetry? And what is the relation between Plath and the poetry she wrote?" (31). Hungerford concludes that while Rose claims not to be interested in the person Plath was, she is nevertheless keenly interested in the "kind of psyche" produced by the poems, which turns out to be "both a Jewish survivor and a woman" (45). No doubt there will be further investigations into Plath's use of Holocaust imagery, but for now we must simply conclude that it remains problematic and offensive to many readers. Still, the critical debate on the subject, no matter how serious and interesting, should not overshadow the poetic oeuvre.

The accumulation of words ending in the long *u* vowel creates a semiotic *mise en abyme*, a puzzle within the poem: "black shoe," "Jew," "gobbledygoo," "boot," "brute," "black man who," "stuck me together with glue," "rack and the screw," and so on. This collage of rhyming words is filled with conflicting images of atrocity, but underlying the visual and semantic network is also an aural cue to the universal expression of disgust or repulsion, the "eeew" of a child who has just eaten a revolting morsel. This gagging "eeew" is also found in the ubiquitous "you" designation for "Daddy," signaling yet another opportunity to negate him, this time by metaphorically vomiting his remains, again reversing the cannibalistic tendencies of incorporation. This chorus of nonsense sounds is like the chant of taunting schoolyard children, again signaling the dramatic contrast in tone between the appalling images of Nazi cruelty and the innocent play-words of children. The long *u* sound is repeated an astonishing twenty-two times, multiplying the father figure like the war crimes for which he is blamed. We might read this vowel puzzle as an example of the "repetitive rhythm, monotonous melody," and "recurring, obsessive litanies" that for Kristeva (1989, 33) characterize the speech of the depressed, but while repetitive rhythmic structures crowd the lines of "Daddy," they seem rather to signify a feverish urgency to expel him than depression.

The poem's first line, "You do not do, you do not do," negating the father's actions, is answered near the end with the affirmative: "And I said I do, I do." We are reminded of the cliché expression of matrimonial assent, a match already hinted at in the earlier poem "Colossus," where the speaker echoes Electra's complaint in the Sophoclean tragedy: "My hours are married to shadow" (Plath 1981, 130). This implied nuptial ceremony between the Electra-speaker and the dead Agamemnon is annulled as soon as it is named: "So daddy, I'm finally through." But once is not enough, as the speaker reminds us: "If I've killed one man, I've killed two—." Hence the repetition in the last line of the poem just to make plain: "Daddy, daddy, you bastard, I'm through" (224). The sentence can be interpreted to mean that the poem has come to an end—"through with the poem" or finished with the attempt to suture over the abyss of signification. "Through" also introduces a grammatical ambivalence, and we are reminded of the prohibition (drilled into schoolchildren) against ending a sentence with a preposition—it thus represents a willful defiance of rules.

Moreover "through" signifies a transitional physical state, that of being sandwiched between two objects or even inside the father's body—after all, she says he "Bit my pretty red heart in two" and calls him her "vampire." What began with metaphors of incorporation, mouthing, munching, and ingesting the lost object ends with the opposite, a reversed incorporation. The daughter is now the object being consumed, a repetition of the theme introduced in "Colossus," where the ant-daughter folds herself into the father's ear. We get a similar view from the inside when the miniature speaker exclaims: "For thirty years I have labored / To dredge the silt from your throat" (1981, 129). What are we to make of this shift in focus from the speaker's frantic attempts to stuff her mouth to her looking from the inside out?

So many interpretations of Plath's poems focus on the defeat, helplessness, and desperation of her personas, as if foreshadowing the poet's suicide. It is easy in hindsight to assume that what I am calling "reverse incorporation" foretells her end, the poet eaten by her own poems. Instead, I propose that this is all part of the poetics of survival, the will to take control over the father's image. True, "Colossus" figures Agamemnon as a giant and Electra as a pipsqueak, but it is she who manipulates his image by reversing the perspective—she no longer looks up at the mammoth monster from outside but perches high up, observing great beauty from her ledge: "The sun rises under the pillar of your tongue" (1981, 130). We are invited to imagine not darkness but light, the pink haze of first morning rays, and the tongue is no longer an organ of speech but is silenced and immobilized in the grand architecture of antiquity. The last lines initiate a new calm, a reprieve from the hectic pursuit of father in "Azalea Path":

> No longer do I listen for the scrape of the keel
> On the blank stones of the landing.
>
> (130)

The frenetic pace of the earlier poem gives way to a meandering rhythm. The repetition, alliteration, and assonance that drive "Azalea" forward are replaced with a mixture of vowels and consonants that linger softly on the reader's tongue.

In "Daddy," reverse incorporation functions differently. Again Agamemnon is figured larger than life with "one gray toe / Big as a Frisco seal" (1981, 223), but the Electra speaker does not win power by inhabiting his body per se. Instead, she has colonized his footwear, his "black shoe / In which I have lived like a foot for thirty years" (223). The accusation that he has bitten her and that he, like a vampire, "drank my blood for a year" seems threatening at first, but the satire of the father's power and prestige in the poem turns the horror of being eaten alive into a farce. Even the Luftwaffe is not to be feared, reduced to mere "gobbledygoo"; this may be "a man in black with a Meinkampf look" (224), but his weapons are as harmless as a sneeze.

What, then, are the larger consequences of reversing the scenario of incorporation? For Freud (1917, 250), the regressive "narcissistic oral phase" resulting in the incorporation of the lost object is one of the principal characteristics of melancholia or pathological mourning. Kristeva (1989) is more explicit in her analysis of the relationship between orality and loss:

> My identification with the loved-hated other, through incorporation-introjection-projection, leads me to imbed in myself its sublime component, which becomes my necessary, tyrannical judge, as well as its subject component, which demeans me and of which I desire to rid myself. (11)

Thus if the metaphors of incorporation that inhabit earlier phases of Plath's poetry give way, such that the lost object is no longer devoured but expelled, then we might conclude that her lyric persona manages to break free from the "tyrannical judge" that threatens existence itself.

The Welcoming Belly: Maternal Receptacles

These images of reverse incorporation can be linked to a shift in perspective away from the mourning daughter toward the fertile, creative, and nurturing mother, from Electra to Clytemnestra. As with H.D.'s reorientation from Orestes to Clytemnestra, in many ways Plath's engagement with mothering and the maternal signals the emergence of a new voice with energy and vitality. Tracy Brain notes that many critics have interpreted Plath's experience of mothering as exhausting and draining, sapping her energy and any available time for writing. In contrast, Brain (2001, 12) cites the poet's own account of an outing to a demonstration at Trafalgar Square with her newborn daughter, "an immensely moving experience," to show that motherhood was adventure, challenge, and reward all at the same time.

Maternity sparked Plath's poetic imagination well before she had her own children. "Words for a Nursery" announces in elliptical shorthand the pleasures and pitfalls of mothering, all rooted in the "rosebud" "milk-spout" of the mother's breast. "Parliament Hill Fields" mourns a miscarriage and rejoices in the gift of a healthy growing child. What is remarkable about the conflicting emotions of motherhood here is the way in which the speaker, though regretting the loss of an unborn baby, is nurtured by the physical presence of children and literally enveloped by a throng:

> A crocodile of small girls
> Knotting and stopping, ill-assorted, in blue uniforms,
> Opens to swallow me. I am a stone, a stick,
>
> (1981, 152)

Again, the speaker is not the one consuming but is consumed by the unwitting schoolgirls, who act as a protective gaggle. The last line of the poem bathes the would-be mother in a heartening glow, hearkening back to the age-old connection between home and womb with Hemingway-like simplicity: "I enter the lit house" (153).

Plath's maternal poems abound with images attesting to the healing, nurturing powers of nature. For example in "Parliament Hill Fields," "The wind stops my breath like a bandage" (1981, 152); in "Barren Woman" a celestial lunar body anoints the speaker: "The moon lays a hand on my forehead" (157); and in "Heavy Women," pregnant bodies are blessed and redeemed by the dark blanket of night: "Dusk hoods them in Mary-Blue" (158). The natural world does not just protect and care for mothers but literally midwives them, wrapping them up inside all manner of receptacles. This metaphor is perhaps most cleverly expressed in "Nick and the Candlestick," where the whole microcosm of the poem grows inside the cave, and the mother-speaker reveals herself as a "miner" in "the earthen womb" (240) and is surprised by the wealth of emotion: "O love, how did you get here? / O embryo" (241). Subject and object lose their distinction when the maternal is figured as both having a womb and being encased within the welcoming belly of nature.

Blood colors dominate the palette of the poem: red, ruby, rose, and even "mercuric atoms," which, according to Tuhkunen-Couzic (2002, 262), correspond to the explosive and future-oriented energy of revolt of Plath's later poetry. Together, the red and the embryonic roundness invoke the perfection of a drop of blood, life force and muse, linking the creative power of words and fertility in "Kindness":

> And here you come, with a cup of tea
> Wreathed in steam.
> The blood jet is poetry,
> There is no stopping it.
> You hand me two children, two roses.
>
> (1981, 270)

The steaming tea and the children are united through the act of giving. This generous gesture is both a miracle—birth—and somehow matter-of-fact—the necessity of fluid refreshment. But between these two images is the emergency of a punctured vein and the poems to which it gives birth.

The slick sphere of the blood drop is recuperated in "Balloons"; however, the perspective is the opposite of that of the enclosed cave space in "Nick and the Candlestick." The womblike enclosure buried deep under the heavy earth is replaced with the weightlessness of balloons. Both are receptacles, round and colorful, but one is pulled down by the gravity of new life, while the "globes of thin air" float up, paradoxically buoyed by the same new life :

> Invisible air drifts,
> Giving a shriek and a pop
> When attacked, then scooting to rest, barely trembling.
>
> (1981, 271)

What is embryonic and potential in the earlier poem is revealed as fleeting and vulnerable in the second, but even when an overeager child bites and breaks the balloon, he sits satisfied, round as a balloon in his baby pudge, to admire his achievement:

> He bites,
>
> Then sits
> Back, fat jug
> Contemplating a world clear as water.
> A red
> Shred in his little fist.
>
> (272)

These images of round fullness, of plump nascent energy enact a reverse incorporation, in which the desperation of a hungry daughter is replaced by a mature maternal voice, generous and even overflowing at times with the blood of life. The "red shred" is here figured as a lifeline between mother and child, clutched tight in the small fingers of a chubby hand. It is partial and fragmented—the love between mother and son will mend it.

My analysis of Plath's poetry began by pursuing her own statement that her speaker is a "girl with an Electra complex." Trusting and respecting the intentionality of the writer, I have engaged with her work on these grounds, as have many critics before me. The readings of the poems in question, I believe, are no poorer for their recourse to this much-quoted BBC interview, but the more I read Plath the more I become convinced that her lyric "I" heals herself of any pathological complex through careful attention to the signifying bonds of language, as Kristeva puts it, perhaps through a successful mourning process and a "poetics of survival," but most definitely through the experience of mothering. Maternity in Plath's poetry, paralleled by metaphors of "reverse incorporation," begins to nurture the speaking subject in ways that move her beyond the angry and vengeful daughter that is Electra and toward a new persona. No matter how self-assured and courageously defiant her Electra-voice may have been, I do not think it persists throughout Plath's later corpus. I will not go so far as to say that the beleaguered relationship between Electra and Clytemnestra is healed for good, even if I would want this to be the case. But one thing is sure—this is the voice not of depression and death but of fertility, creativity, and birth. Plath invents and reinvents poetic personas, perhaps to suture over the pain of loss, but with a vibrancy and vitality that gush with life and love, "giving a shriek and a pop."

Conclusion

ELECTRA AND THE NEW MILLENNIUM

I began *Electra after Freud* by asking who dominates the twentieth century, Electra or Oedipus. We might end with the question as to who will dominate the twenty-first century. Only halfway through the first decade of the new millennium, it is too early to predict, but in the post-9/11 age and its culture of revenge, it seems Electra's story is again current—the Atrean princess, fearless and violent in her pursuit of justice. But perhaps there is also room for several other embodiments of Electra, not just the angry young girl but the mature woman with perspective and balance, seeking to understand herself in her relationships to Orestes and even Clytemnestra, to the living and not to the dead or ghosts. No doubt there will be plenty of new adaptations in the years to come as writers turn again to the timelessness and power of this myth to help us answer the complex and often perplexing questions of our age.

I have endeavored to show that Electra is not easily defined but rather plurivocal and multifaceted. The power of mythopoesis lies in the endless deferral of an enduring story. True, there is a permanency in Greek myth, especially in the status we accord it at the very root of Western culture. As such, Electra is forever Agamemnon's daughter and Orestes' sister, their stories stuck together like glue or, as H.D. puts it, Electra and Clytemnestra are "burnt like star-names in the sky" (1983, 383). At the same time, no two renderings of these celestial constellations will ever be the same.

The century started off with Hofmannsthal's defiant femme fatale, an eroticized heroine who single-mindedly plots matricide, throws off the yoke of hysteria, and even triumphs in death itself. A shift occurs with Musil's *The Man without Qualities*, where the pseudo-Electra, Agathe, is focused not on revenge but on her relationship to her figurative Orestes, Ulrich, with questions of subjectivity and sexuality at the fore. Finally, with H.D. and Plath, Electra stands on her own as a poetic trope, achieving autonomy from the myth and the mostly male mythmakers. Orestes is no longer an accomplice and nor is Oedipus a rival. Instead, each of these poets has Electra emerge as a strong and powerful voice in her own right, sexually mature and maternally connoted. Hatred is exchanged for hope, and cruelty for creativity. Death is no longer the sine qua non of Electra's existence, but rather vibrancy and voice. Neither H.D. nor Plath devotes much time to revenge, dwelling instead on the strength of the heroine as an example of fortitude amid difficult circumstances. Matricide simply fades away.

I cannot present a teleological argument that the Electras of the past century started off violent and became progressively thoughtful and introspective. First of all, my sample is far too small and selective. Second, the most recent text considered in this study, Heiner Müller's *Hamletmaschine* written in 1977, contradicts this thesis by dishing up a heroine as cold and cruel as there ever was. As much as I would like it to be the case, it simply is not true that our world is becoming a kinder, gentler place. Indeed, authors have always turned to the Electra myth to tackle troubling and often violent subject matter: Jean-Paul Sartre's *Les Mouches* (1941) is a thinly veiled attack on corruption in the Vichy government during the French Occupation; Eugene O'Neill's *Mourning Becomes Electra* (1931) rejects repressive New England society and depicts families cursed with inherited abuse and addiction; Ezra Pound's *Elektra* (1949) is a diatribe against American involvement in World War II and a defense of his own innocence against allegations of treason.

Still more examples employ the Electra myth as a loose palimpsest to actual events: Athol Fugard's *Orestes* (1971) fuses the Greek tragedy with the terrorist violence of apartheid South Africa. The play tells the story of John Harris, who took a suitcase full of explosives into Johannesburg Railway Station and left it beside a bench, an act that resulted in the death of a young child and his own execution. Barbara Köhler's poem cycle "Elektra. Spiegelungen" (1991) speaks to the immediate post-Wall period in East Germany, when tensions are high and socialist dreams have been shattered. Her Elektra walks wide-eyed to her end and would rather sacrifice herself than compromise her ethical stance. A homage to Heiner Müller's heroine, this Atrean daughter takes on the heavy shame of history: "I WANT TO BE GUILTY . . . I still tolerate (and why) this play of hero and happy end this drama in which all roles are victims / but there is death / and there is a time before it" (Köhler 1991, 23).[1] Orestes is a traitor from the West and comes to kill his mother and forget his sister: "a new play begins and no role proposed for elektra and no language except orest's" (25).[2] Tired of the charade, she leaves the stage, returns to her dressing room, and puts an end to her character: "elektra sits at her makeup table takes off her mask" (25).[3] In the end, Köhler's Elektra chooses death over the sham of a failed socialist revolution: "I don't want to be anymore" (30).[4]

Generally speaking, Electra has gained a more active role in her making throughout time. The character began as nothing more than a name in Homer and progressively gained more status and more lines throughout antiquity, with Euripides and Sophocles each granting her a significant role. In the eighteenth century, she was again present, for example in the dramas of Crébillon and Voltaire, but limited in her freedom to pursue justice and define her own destiny (see introduction). Even so, one cannot say that such trends apply to the twentieth century. While one can cite a proliferation of Electra adaptations, the character has neither gained nor lost status in the past hundred-odd years—she was center stage in Hofmannsthal's *Elektra* and there she has remained.

If chronology has not proven a useful means of categorizing Electra, neither has the gender of the author. Though I have argued in the cases of H.D. and Plath that Electra rejects the violence of matricide and the obsession with revenge, other examples show that women are just as likely to paint a cruel character, hardened and unflinching in her pain. We have already cited Köhler, but Anne Sexton documents Electra's story too without shying away from the reality of death and destruction: "when death comes with its hood / we won't be polite" (1981, 357). Another daringly naked portrayal of Electra's capacity for rage is Marilyn Hacker's "lustful short-haired virgin bitch," although even she contra-

1. "ICH WILL SCHULD SEIN . . . noch (und warum) ertrage ich das spiel von held und happy end das drama in dem alle rollen opfer sind / aber es gibt den tod und / es gibt eine zeit davor."
2. "ein neues stück beginnt und keine rolle vorgesehen für elektra und keine sprache außer der orests"
3. "am schminktisch sitzt elektra legt die maske ab"
4. "nicht länger will ich sein"

dicts her own statements about her "mother monster" when she admits: "I would rather make love and poems than kill / my mother" (1994, 13).

These Electras are not afraid of murder or death. Many women authors invoke the story of the vengeful daughter and demonstrate that violence is part of life, indeed a *way of life* for the Greek heroine. Like her clever manipulation of the pathology of hysteria, cruelty and even her own death are just different means of subverting assumptions and norms, a refusal to play by the rules. Perhaps Marguerite Yourcenar (1954) was right when she had her Pylades announce: "You ought to know that one day or another every man who is a bit clearheaded will end up loving only Electra" (113).[5]

We can find plenty of examples of women writers who use Electra to push the limits of gender norms and social expectations for women with their aggressive heroines, but there are also male writers willing to offer sympathetic portraits of the same character. T.S. Eliot's *The Family Reunion* (1939) delivers a sophisticated and sane, if slightly repressed, leading lady of good breeding. Eliot's Agatha describes herself as an "efficient principal of a women's college" (97), but underneath this façade, she has the wisdom of a sage:

> A curse comes to being,
> As a child is formed.
> In both, the incredible
> Becomes the actual
> Without our intention
> Knowing what is intended.
>
> (106)

In *The Elektra Poems* (1982), Alan Marshfield adds his heroine's name to a long list of "female suicides in mid-career" (56), yet allows for more positive interpretations as well. Marshfield pays tribute to Electra's "aromatic dance, / as sticky as grenadine, as orange" (59), and even admits she is capable of milder moods from time to time: "Although she can rip trees, / drown valleys, she is gentle this evening" (61).

Having ruled out both chronology and gender as means of classifying Electras, we should also consider nationality and cultural difference. Hofmannsthal's Germanic Elektra clearly reflects the cultural psyche of Vienna around 1900 with a dangerous mix of *eros* and

---

5. "Tu devrais savoir que tout homme un peu lucide finit un jour ou l'autre par n'aimer qu'Électre."

thanatos. Heiner Müller follows with an equally frightening heroine, a critique of the Nazi past and East German socialism. H.D.'s Anglo-American Electra is more concerned with regaining voice than with enacting revenge, and Plath's Electra speakers, though troubled, move beyond rage to embrace the maternal. One is tempted to make assumptions. But Musil's *The Man without Qualities,* also rooted in Viennese modernism, portrays an Electra character with none of the bite of her Germanic counterparts. Musil's Agathe is obsessed not with her father's murder or matricide but with sibling symbiosis and the experiment in hermaphroditic subjectivity. Even with this very narrow range of examples, it is not possible to generalize about culturally specific representations of Electra.

Although my observations are by no means scientific, I have come to the conclusion that Electras of the twentieth century cannot easily be classified according to differences of history, culture, or gender. Nor are class, race, and religion likely to prove more solid categories. This is the mystery and magic of myth—its chameleonlike adaptability and amorphous malleability.

Freud for a New Millennium?

This book is called *Electra after Freud,* but can we really imagine a time *after Freud,* a time beyond the influence of his thinking on our social psyche and cultural consciousness? The titles of two related studies have caught my attention because they engage with this question of belatedness—*After Oedipus: Shakespeare in Psychoanalysis* and *After Electra: Rage, Grief, and Hope in Twentieth-Century Fiction* (Lupton and Reinhard 1993; Liddelow 2001). But one has to ask what the word *after* refers to here or even in my own title. Does it imply the time *beyond* Oedipus or Electra or Freud, or does it really imply the *beginning* rather than the end of influence? Should we also consider *after* in the sense of imitating or miming? In the case of *Electra after Freud,* my original intent was to consider the ways in which the myth of Electra has changed as a result of its encounter with psychoanalysis. But should we consider the possibility that more than a hundred years after Freud first coined the term psychoanalysis, its influence may have waned or served its purpose? Is it still relevant?

Certainly, I have not attempted to argue that all adaptations of the Electra myth written since 1900 have engaged actively with the discourse of psychoanalysis. Still, is it possible to erase all knowledge of the questions posed by Freud and brought to the fore by his theories: the development of sexuality and subjectivity, the focus on the individual, the pathologization of the self and society? It is a truism that as a form of medical treatment psychoanalysis is no longer relevant—it has been overshadowed by new methods and by psychopharmacology. It is barely mentioned in introductory courses on psychology, considered rightly both outmoded and unscientific. Feminism, as much as it has appropriated the methods of psychoanalysis to further its cause, has leveled a sharp critique against Freud's assumptions regarding gender and sexual identity. And of course the debates over "recovered memories" have further damaged the reputation of psychoanalysis.

On the one hand inflammatory detractors such as Frederick Crews ask of Freud: "Do you really want him—fanatical, self-inflated, ruthless, myopic, yet intricately devious" (Crews 2000, 22). Crews goes on to attack psychoanalysis as a theory that "derives its conclusions from its postulates" (25) and concludes that the discipline itself is doomed like the *Titanic*: "The iceberg is out there waiting in the dark" (32). On the other hand incorrigible enthusiasts like Paul Robinson speak of Freud with religious fervor: "It's like falling in love all over again. This guy is incredibly powerful. He's not going to go away" (quoted in Brooks 2000, 12). Similarly, Arnold Cooper declares that psychoanalysis is enjoying a renaissance and that "these are the headiest of times since the early days of Freud" (quoted in Brooks 2000, 12). A more measured response comes from Robert Michels (2000, 38), who advocates an attitude of "skepticism, tempered by benevolence" when approaching psychoanalysis.

Freud's early theories of sexual development view Electra only and always through the lens of Oedipus—that which she is not. In Judith Butler's words (2000): "The daughter's incestuous passion is less fully explored in the Freudian corpus, but her renunciation of her desire for her father culminates in an identification with her mother and a turn to the child as a fetish or penis substitute" (40). The problems here are multiple: First of all, if Oedipus is the example of sexual, social, and kinship normalization, then Electra is by default abnormal—her fetish substitute for the penis is pathological. Second, abandoning the desire for the father requires identification with the mother—this can hardly be the case with Electra, who despises Clytemnestra and plots matricide. Third, in the Greek myth, Electra never has a child to whom she can transfer her desire, never has sexual relations with a man, and from this perspective does not fulfill the requirements for psychosexual maturity. Is she then a half-being?

These are the reasons why submitting Electra to a strict Freudian analysis makes absolutely no sense. I have endeavored in *Electra after Freud* to demonstrate more positive ways of reading literary adaptations of the myth in parallel with psychoanalytic thought. Purnima Mehta (2002) criticizes the Electra complex and suggests as I have that it is of little value either for an understanding of female sexuality or for an elucidation of the myth itself. She concludes that "Electra 'waits' around to be rediscovered by contemporary analysts to help throw light on the 'dark continent' that Freud felt women were" (174). Nothing could be further from the truth when it comes to literary adaptations, one of the central points of *Electra after Freud*. While Electra may have been neglected by Freud and Jung, Electra as a character in literature has not had to wait around for anyone.

But there is another reason why we should not compare Electra to Oedipus. Oedipus is an *unconscious* participant in his tragedy, blind and unwitting in his deeds. He is ignorant of his wrongful acts of killing his father and marrying his mother. Electra, on the other hand, is sober and calculating in her preparations for matricide. She is *aware and awake* throughout her drama, the maker of her own destiny. Because of his blindness, Oedipus cannot be held responsible for his actions; he cannot make judgments and participate consciously in the social fabric of the family. In contrast, Electra can be held responsible for her decisions, must indeed be called to account for matricide, which will always be a horrifying atrocity, an incomprehensible crime.

Electra's story is much more troubling than that of Oedipus for this very reason. It shatters us all the more because we know she plotted and premeditated the murder and we cannot fathom a hatred so intense. This, I believe, is what positions her to have ongoing significance for the coming century and indeed millennium. But it is also what has inspired writers throughout time—the fact that Electra makes her decisions with full knowledge of the circumstances and consequences of her actions means that the story has a future, that she is malleable as a character and master of her own destiny. Not only has Electra *not* been subjected to the straitjacket of a psychoanalytic model, but she also has the capacity to be *self-conscious* about her condition and to reflect on her own impossible emotions, to negotiate her relations with others, to contemplate her existence in the world. Unlike Oedipus, she cannot have recourse to self-pity. She must look herself squarely in the face and accept her culpability. It is for all these reasons that Electra has more *ethical potential* than Oedipus. I say potential because it is by no means a foregone conclusion that her actions will produce an ethics. Even Hamlet, whom Freud himself posited as a surrogate for Oedipus, does not have the conviction of an Electra. Though he is conscious of his actions, hesitation is his impediment. I believe her consciousness and her conviction will allow Electra to surpass both Oedipus and Hamlet as a compelling character into the new millennium. After all, even Lacan declared that the Oedipus tragedy was mere "scraps and fragments" (quoted in Lupton and Reinhard 1993, 2).

In many ways, *Electra* is the book Freud did not write. The death of his own father was the crisis in Freud's life that brought about *The Interpretation of Dreams* and the Oedipus complex. Freud could only view this crisis from his perspective, but this was not enough. He was compelled to generate a universal theory out of his own personal experience. Thus we have a model that systematically suppresses the mother. What would have happened if the crisis-cum-complex had arisen out of the death of Freud's mother or sister or child? We will never know the answers to these questions, but I for one am very glad Freud did not shape Electra into the everywoman that Oedipus has become. Indeed, it is perhaps this very oversight that made the present book possible.

Bibliography

Abbate, Carolyn. 1989. "Elektra's Voice: Music and Language in Strauss's Opera." In *Richard Strauss: "Elektra,"* ed. Derrick Puffet. Cambridge: Cambridge University Press. 107–127.

———. 1991. *The Unsung Voices: Opera and Musical Narrative in the Nineteenth Century.* Princeton: Princeton University Press.

Adams, S. M. 1962. *Sophocles, the Playwright.* Toronto: University of Toronto Press.

Adorno, Theodor W. 1966. "Richard Strauss Part II." *Perspectives on New Music* 4 (2): 113–129.

———. 1978. *Musikalische Schriften.* 4 vols. Frankfurt am Main: Suhrkamp.

Adorno, Theodor W., and Max Horkheimer. 1969. *Dialektik der Aufklärung: Philosophische Fragmente.* Frankfurt am Main: S. Fischer.

Aeschylus. 1984. *Oresteia.* Trans. Robert Fagles. Harmondsworth, U.K.: Penguin.

Allison, Alex, ed. 1983. *Norton Anthology of Poetry: Third Shorter Edition.* New York: Norton.

Aristotle. 1982. *Poetics.* Trans. James Hutton. New York: Norton.

Arnold, Herbert A. 1988. "On Myth and Marxism: The Case of Heiner Müller and Christa Wolf." *Germanica* 21: 58–69.

Axelrod, Stephen Gould. 1990. *Sylvia Plath: The Wound and the Cure of Words.* Baltimore: Johns Hopkins University Press.

Bachofen, Johann Jakob. 1967. *Myth, Religion, and Mother Right: Selected Writings of J. J. Bachofen.* Ed. George Boas. Trans. Ralph Mannheim. Princeton: Princeton University Press.

———. 1984. *Mutterrecht und Urreligion.* Ed. Hans G. Kippenberg. Stuttgart: Alfred Kröner.

Bahr, Hermann. 1968. "Das unrettbare Ich." In *Zur Überwindung des Naturalismus: Theoretische Schriften, 1887–1907,* ed. Gotthard Wunberg. Stuttgart: Kohlhammer. 183–192.

Barreca, Regina. 1993. "Writing as Voodoo: Sorcery, Hysteria, and Art." In *Death and Representation,* ed. Sarah Webster Goodwin and Elisabeth Bronfen. Baltimore: Johns Hopkins University Press. 174–191.

Bataille, Georges. 1985. *Visions of Excess: Selected Writings.* Ed. Allan Stoekl. Minneapolis: University of Minnesota Press.

Batchelder, Ann G. 1995. *The Seal of Orestes: Self-Reference and Authority in Sophocles' Electra*. Lanham, Md.: Rowman and Littlefield.

Bauer, Johan. 1993. "Totentanzadaptionen im modernen Drama und Hörspiel: Hofmannsthal, Horvath, Hausmann, Weyrauch und Hochhuth." In *Tanz und Tod in Kunst und Literatur*, ed. Franz Link. Berlin: Duncker und Humblot. 489–530.

Baumann, Gerhart. 1997. *Robert Musil: Ein Entwurf.* Freiburg: Rombach.

Bayerlein, Sonja. 1996. *Musikalische Psychologie der drei Frauengestalten in der Oper Elektra von Richard Strauss.* Tutzing, Germany: Hans Schnieder.

Benjamin, Walter. 1966. *Briefe II.* Ed. Theodor Adorno and Gershom Scholem. Frankfurt am Main: Suhrkamp.

———. 1972a. "Destruktive Charakter." In *Gesammelte Schriften* (*GS*), ed. Rolf Tiedemann and Hermann Schweppenhäuser. Frankfurt am Main: Suhrkamp. Vol. 4, bk. 1, 396–398.

———. 1972b. "Über den Begriff der Geschichte." In *GS*. Vol. 1, bk. 2, 691–702.

———. 1972c. *Der Ursprung des deutschen Trauerspiels.* In *GS*. Vol. 1, bk. 1, 203–409.

———. 1977. *The Origin of German Tragic Drama.* Trans. John Osborne. London: Verso.

Bennett, Benjamin. 2002. "Hofmannsthal's Theater of Adaptation." In *A Companion to the Works of Hugo von Hofmannsthal*, ed. Thomas Kovach. Rochester, N.Y.: Camden House. 97–116.

Berg, Henk de. 2003. *Freud's Theory and Its Use in Literary and Cultural Studies: An Introduction.* Rochester, N.Y.: Camden House.

Bernstein, Michael André. 2000. *Five Portraits: Modernity and the Imagination in Twentieth-Century German Writing.* Evanston, Ill.: Northwestern University Press.

Betz, Werner. 1979. "Vom Götterwort zum Massentraumbild: Zur Wortgeschichte von Mythos." In *Mythos und Mythologie in der Literatur des 19. Jahrhunderts*, ed. Helmut Koopmann. Frankfurt am Main: Klostermann. 11–16.

Beye, Charles Rowan. 1989. "Pound and Sophocles." *Parnassus* 15: 83–98.

Birkin, Kenneth. 2002. "Richard Struass' zweite Gedanken: Ein Kommentar über die Opern-Retouchen der späteren Jahre." *Richard Strauss Blätter* 48: 3–42.

Blumenberg, Hans. 1971. "Wirklichkeitsbegriff und Wirkungspotential des Mythos." In *Terror und Spiel: Probleme der Mythenrezeption*, ed. Manfred Fuhrmann. Munich: Wilhelm Fink. 11–66.

Blundell, Mary Whitlock. 1989. *Helping Friends and Harming Enemies:A Study in Sophocles and Greek Ethics.* Cambridge: Cambridge University Press.

Blundell, Sue. 1995. *Women in Ancient Greece.* London: British Museum Press.

Boas, George. 1967. Preface to *Myth, Religion, and Mother Right: Selected Writings of J. J. Bachofen*, ed. George Boas. Princeton: Princeton University Press. xi–xxiv.

Bohnenkamp, Klaus E. 1976. "Deutsche Antiken-Übertragungen als Grundlage der Griechendramen Hofmannsthals." *Euphorion* 70: 198–202.

Bolz, Norbert, and Willem van Reijen. 1996. *Walter Benjamin.* Trans. Laimdota Mazzarins. Atlantic Highlands, N.J.: Humanities Press.

Bondy, François, Ivo Frenzel, Joachim Kaiser, Lew Kopelew, and Hilde Spiel, eds. 1971. *Lexikon der Weltliteratur.* Ed. Gero von Wilpert. 4 vols. Munich: Deutscher Taschenbuch Verlag.

Borch-Jacobsen, Mikkel. 1996. *Remembering Anna O.: A Century of Mystification.* New York: Routledge.

Böschenstein, Bernhard, and Marie-Louise Roth, eds. 1995. *Hommage à Musil: Genfer Kolloquium zum 50. Todestag von Robert Musil.* Bern: Peter Lang.

Bossinade, Johanne. 1990. *Das Beispiel Antigone: Textsemiotische Untersuchungen zur Präsentation der Frauenfigur: von Sophokles bis Ingeborg Bachman.* Cologne: Böhlau.

Bottenberg, Joanna. 1996. *Shared Creation: Words and Music in the Hofmannsthal-Strauss Operas.* Frankfurt am Main: Peter Lang.

Bowra, C. M. 1944. *Sophoclean Tragedy.* Oxford: Clarendon Press.

Braidotti, Rosi. 1994. *Nomadic Subjects: Sexual Difference in Contemporary Feminist Theory.* New York: Columbia University Press.

Brain, Tracy. 2001. *The Other Sylvia Plath.* Harlow, U.K.: Longman.

Braun, Mattias. 1970. *Elektras Tod.* Frankfurt am Main: S. Fischer.

Bremer, Jan Maarten. 1991a. "Exit Elektra." *Gymnasium* 98: 325–342.

———. 1991b. "Three Approaches to Sylvia Plath's 'Electra on Azalea Path.'" *Neophilologus* 76: 305–316.

Breuer, Robert. 1993. "Elektra in der Bearbeitung von Sophokles und Hofmannsthal-Strauss." *Richard Strauss-Blätter* 30: 22–34.

Bronfen, Elisabeth. 1992. *Over Her Dead Body: Death, Femininity, and the Aesthetic.* New York: Routledge.

———. 1996. "Fatal Conjunctions: Gendering Representations of Death." In *Lacan, Politics, Aesthetics,* ed. Willy Apollon and Richard Feldstein. Albany: State University of New York Press. 237–262.

———. 1998. *The Knotted Subject: Hysteria and Its Discontents.* Princeton: Princeton University Press.

Brooks, Daniel J. 1989. *Musil's Socratic Discourse in Der Mann ohne Eigenschaften: A Comparative Study of Ulrich and Socrates.* New York: Peter Lang.

Brooks, Peter. 2000. Introduction to *Whose Freud? The Place of Psychoanalysis in Contemporary Culture,* ed. Peter Brooks and Alex Woloch. New Haven: Yale University Press. 1–12.

Brunel, Pierre. 1971. *Le Mythe d'Électre.* Paris: Armand Colin.

Buck-Morss, Susan. 1989. *The Dialectics of Seeing: Walter Benjamin and the Arcades Project.* Cambridge: MIT Press.

Bundtzen, Lynda K. 1983. *Plath's Incarnations: Women and the Creative Process.* Ann Arbor: University of Michigan Press.

———. 2001. *The Other Ariel.* Amherst: University of Massachusetts Press.

Burnett, Gary. 1990. *H.D. between Image and Epic: The Mysteries of Her Poetics.* Ann Arbor: UMI Research Press.

Butler, E. M. 1938–1939. "Hoffmannsthal's *Elektra*: A Graeco-Freudian Myth." *Journal of the Warburg Institute* 2: 164–175.

Butler, Judith. 1993. *Bodies That Matter: On the Discursive Limits of "Sex."* New York: Routledge.

———. 1990. *Gender Trouble: Feminism and the Subversion of Identity.* New York: Routledge.

———. 1996. "Gender Trouble: Feminism and the Subversion of Identity." In *Feminist Literary Theory: A Reader.* 2nd ed. Ed. Mary Eagleton. Oxford: Blackwell. 367–373.

———. 2000. "Quandaries of the Incest Taboo." In *Whose Freud? The Place of Psychoanalysis in Contemporary Culture,* ed. Peter Brooks and Alex Woloch. New Haven: Yale University Press. 39–46.

Calderón de la Barca, Pedro. 1993. *La vida es sueño.* Ed. Antonio Asencio Gomez. Malaga, Spain: Editorial Agora.

Campbell, Joseph. 1967. Introduction to *Myth, Religion, and Mother Right: Selected Writings of J. J. Bachofen.* Princeton: Princeton University Press. xxv–lvii.

———. 1972. *The Hero with a Thousand Faces*. Princeton: Princeton University Press.

Cantarella, Eva. 1987. *Pandora's Daughters: The Role and Status of Women in Greek and Roman Antiquity*. Baltimore: Johns Hopkins University Press.

Carner, Mosco. 1971. "Witches' Cauldron: The Harsh, Inexorable Spirit of Ancient Myth Boils Up in Strauss' 'Elektra.'" *Opera News*, 27 February, 24–27.

Carpenter, Tethys. 1989. "The Musical Language of Elektra." In *Richard Strauss: "Elektra,"* ed. Derrick Puffet. Cambridge: Cambridge University Press. 74–94.

Carson, Anne. 2001. Foreword to *Sophocles Electra*. New York: Oxford University Press. 41–49.

Cech, Lois Mary. 1984. "Becoming a Heroine: A Study of the Electra Theme." Ph.D. diss., University of California, Riverside.

Chanter, Tina. 1995. *Ethics of Eros: Irigaray's Rewriting of the Philosophers*. New York: Routledge.

Charcot, Jean-Martin, and Paul Richer. 1972. *Démoniaques dans l'art*. Amsterdam: B. M. Israel.

Cixous, Hélène, and Catherine Clément. 1986. *The Newly Born Woman*. Trans. Betsy Wing. Minneapolis: University of Minnesota Press.

Clark, James M. 1950. *The Dance of Death in the Middle Ages and the Renaissance*. Glasgow: Jackson.

Clément, Catherine. 1988. *Opera or the Undoing of Women*. Trans. Betsy Wing. Minnesota: University of Minnesota Press.

Cone, Edward. 1989. *Music: A View from Delft*. Ed. Robert P. Morgan. Chicago: University of Chicago Press.

Crews, Frederick. 1995. *The Memory Wars: Freud's Legacy in Dispute*. New York: New York Review of Books.

———. 2000. "Unconscious Deeps and Empirical Shadows." In *Whose Freud? The Place of Psychoanalysis in Contemporary Culture*, ed. Peter Brooks and Alex Woloch. New Haven: Yale University Press. 19–32.

———. 2003. "Psychoanalysis and Literary Criticism." *PMLA* 118: 615–616.

Cropp, M. J., trans. and comp. 1988. *Electra: Euripides*. Warminster, U.K.: Aris and Phillips.

Cupitt, Don. 1982. *The World to Come*. London: SCM Press.

Curtius, Ernst Robert. 1950. *Kritische Essays zur europäischen Literatur*. Bern: A. Francke.

Dahlhaus, Carl. 1991. "Die Tragödie als Oper: *Elektra* von Hofmannsthal und Strauss." In *Geschichte und Dramaturgie des Operneinakters*, ed. Winfried Kirsch and Sieghart Döhring. Laaber, Germany: Laaber Press. 277–284.

Davies, Malcolm. 1999. "The Three Electras: Strauss, Hofmannsthal, Sophocles and the Tragic Vision." *Antike und Abendland* 45: 36–65.

Deleuze, Gilles, and Félix Guattari. 1983. *Anti-Oedipus: Capitalism and Schizophrenia*. Trans. Robert Hurley, Mark Seem, and Helen Lane. Minneapolis: University of Minnesota Press.

Denniston, J. D., trans. 1964. Introduction to *Electra: Euripides*. Oxford: Clarendon Press. i–xliv.

Derrida, Jacques. 1981. *Dissemination*. Trans. Barbara Johnson. Chicago: University of Chicago Press.

———. 1994. "Structure, Sign, and Play in the Discourse of the Human Sciences." In *A Postmodern Reader*, ed. Joseph Natoli and Linda Hutcheon. Albany: State University of New York Press. 223–242.

Dieckmann, Liselotte. 1960. "The Dancing Elektra." *Texas Studies in Literature and Language* 2: 3–16.

Doane, Janice, and Devon Hodges. 1992. *From Klein to Kristeva: Psychoanalytic Feminism and the Search for the "Good Enough" Mother*. Ann Arbor: University of Michigan Press.

Duplessis, Rachel Blau. 1986. *H.D.: The Career of That Struggle*. Brighton, U.K.: Harvester Press.

Dupriez, Bernard. 1991. *A Dictionary of Literary Devices*. Trans. Albert W. Halsall. Toronto: University of Toronto Press.

Easthope, Anthony. 2002. *Privileging Difference*. Houndsmill, U.K.: Palgrave.

Edmunds, Susan. 1994. *Out of Line: History, Psychoanalysis, and Montage in H.D.'s Long Poems*. Stanford: Stanford University Press.

Eisele, Ulf. 1984. *Die Struktur des modernen deutschen Romans*. Tübingen: Niemeyer.

Eissen, Ariane. 1993. *Les Mythes grecs*. Paris: Belin.

Eliade, Mircea. 1963. *Myth and Reality*. Trans. Willard R. Trask. New York: Harper and Row.

Eliot, T.S. 1939. *The Family Reunion: A Play*. London: Faber and Faber.

———. 1975. "Ulysses, Order, and Myth." In *Selected Prose of T.S. Eliot*, ed. Frank Kermode. New York: Farrar. 175–178.

Eng, David L., and David Kazanjian. 2003. "Introduction: Mourning Remains." In *Loss: The Politics of Mourning*, ed. David L. Eng and David Kazajian. Berkeley: University of California Press. 1–25.

Esselborn, Karl G. 1969. *Hofmannsthal und der antike Mythos*. Munich: Wilhelm Fink.

Euripides. 1964. *Electra*. Trans. J. D. Denniston. Oxford: Clarendon Press.

Eysoldt, Gertrud. 1996. *Der Sturm Elektra. Gertrud Eysoldt—Hugo von Hofmannsthal: Briefe*. Ed. Leonhard M. Fiedler. Salzburg: Residenz.

Fagles, Robert, and W. B. Stanford. 1977. Introduction to *The Oresteia*. Harmondsworth, U.K.: Penguin.

Fantham, Elaine, Helene Peet Foley, Natalie Boymel Kampen, and H. A. Shapiro. 1994. *Women in the Classical World: Image and Text*. New York: Oxford University Press.

Feldman, Burton, and Robert D. Richardson. 1972. *The Rise of Modern Mythology: 1680–1860*. Bloomington: Indiana University Press.

Felman, Shoshana. 1985. *Writing and Madness*. Trans. Martha Noel Evans, Shoshana Felman, and Brian Massumi. Ithaca: Cornell University Press.

———. 1993. *What Does a Woman Want? Reading and Sexual Difference*. Baltimore: Johns Hopkins University Press.

Fields, Kenneth. 1974. Introduction to *Tribute to Freud*. Boston: David R. Godine. i–xviv.

Fodor, Nandor, and Frank Gaynor, eds. 1958. *Freud: Dictionary of Psychoanalysis*. Greenwich, Conn.: Fawcett.

Forsyth, Karen. 1989. "Hofmannsthal's *Elecktra*: From Sophocles to Strauss." In *Richard Strauss: Elektra*, ed. Derrick Puffet. Cambridge: Cambridge University Press. 17–32.

Frank, Manfred. 1983a. "Auf der Suche nach einem Grund über den Umschlag von Erkenntniskritik in Mythologie bei Musil." In *Mythos und Moderne*, ed. Karl Heinz Bohrer. Frankfurt am Main: Suhrkamp. 318–362.

———. 1983b. "Die Dichtung als 'Neue Mythologie.'" In *Mythos und Moderne*, ed. Karl Heinz Bohrer. Frankfurt am Main: Suhrkamp. 15–40.

Freud, Sigmund. 1895. "The Case of Fräulein Anna O." In *The Standard Edition of the Complete Psychological Works of Sigmund Freud (SE)*. 24 vols. London: Hogarth Press, 1953–1974. 2:21–47.

——. 1896. "The Aetiology of Hysteria." In *SE*, 3:189–221.

——. 1897. "Extracts from the Fliess Papers. Letter 71." In *SE*, 1:263–266.

——. 1900. *The Interpretation of Dreams*. Vols. 4 and 5 of *SE*.

——. 1905. "Three Essays on the Theory of Sexuality." In *SE*, 7:125–246.

——. 1908. "Hysterical Phantasies and Their Relation to Bisexuality." In *SE*, 9:157–166.

——. 1913. "Totem and Taboo." In *SE*, 13:1–161.

——. 1916a. *Introductory Lectures on Psycho-Analysis*. Vols. 15 and 16 of *SE*.

——. 1916b. "Thoughts for the Times on War and Death." In *SE*, 14:273–302.

——. 1917. "Mourning and Melancholia." In *SE*, 14:237–243.

——. 1919. "The Uncanny." In *SE*, 17:217–256.

——. 1920. "Beyond the Pleasure Principle." In *SE*, 18:1–64.

——. 1924. "The Dissolution of the Oedipus Complex." In *SE*, 19:173–178.

——. 1925a. "On Negation." In *SE*, 19:235–240.

——. 1925b. "Some Psychological Consequences of the Anatomical Distinction between the Sexes." In *SE*, 19:241–260.

——. 1931. "Female Sexuality." In *SE*, 21:223–243.

——. 2000a. "Brief an Arthur Schnitzler 8. Mai 1906." In *Die Wiener Moderne: Literatur, Kunst und Musik zwischen 1890 und 1910*, ed. Gotthart Wunberg. Stuttgart: Reclam. 651.

——. 2000b. "Brief an Arthur Schnitzler 14. Mai 1922." In *Die Wiener Moderne: Literatur, Kunst und Musik zwischen 1890 und 1910*, ed. Gotthart Wunberg. Stuttgart: Reclam. 652.

Friedman, Lawrence J. 1968. *psy'cho-a-nal'-y-sis*. New York: Paul S. Eriksson.

Friedman, Susan Stanford. 1981. *Psyche Reborn: The Emergence of H.D.* Bloomington: Indiana University Press.

——. 1990. *Penelope's Web: Gender, Modernity, H.D.'s Fiction*. Cambridge: Cambridge University Press.

——, ed. 2002. *Analyzing Freud: Letters of H.D., Bryher, and Their Circle*. New York: New Directions.

Fuhrmann, Manfred. 1971. "Mythos als Wiederholung in der griechischen Tragödie und im Drama des 20. Jahrhunderts." In *Terror und Spiel: Probleme der Mythenrezeption*, ed. Manfred Fuhrmann. Munich: Wilhelm Fink. 121–143.

Gilbert, Sandra M. 1986. "Introduction: A Tarantella of Theory." In *The Newly Born Woman*, by Hélène Cixous and Catherine Clément. Minneapolis: University of Minnesota Press. ix–xviii.

Gilliam, Bryan. 1991. *Richard Strauss's Elektra*. Oxford: Clarendon Press.

——. 1999. "Elektras Tanz und Auflösung." In *Compositionswissenschaft: Festschrift Reinhold und Roswitha Schlötterer*, ed. Bernd Edelmann and Sabine Kurth. Augsburg: Wissner. 251–260.

Gilman, Sander L. 1985. *Difference and Pathology: Stereotypes of Sexuality, Race, and Madness*. Ithaca: Cornell University Press.

——. 1993. "The Image of the Hysteric." In *Hysteria beyond Freud*, by Sander L. Gilman, Helen King, Roy Porter, G. S. Rousseau, and Elaine Showalter. Berkeley: University of California Press. 345–454.

Girshausen, Theo, Burkhard Schmiester, and Richard Weber. 1978. "Kommunismus oder Barbarei: über Politik in der *Hamletmaschine*: Ein Gespräch." In *Hamletmaschine: Heiner Müllers Endspiel*, ed. Theo Girshausen. Cologne: Promethverlag. 25–33.

Gmeiner, Josef. 1999. "Ideal und bête noire: Richard Strauss—Alban Berg's beschädigtes Leitbild." In *Musica Conservata: Günter Brosche zum 60. Geburtstag*, ed. Josef Gmeiner, Zsigmond Kokits, Thomas Leibnitz, and Inge Pechotsch-Feichtinger. Tutzing: Hans Schneider. 71–92.

Goodwin, Sarah Webster. 1988. *Kitsch and Culture: The Dance of Death in Nineteenth-Century Literature and Graphic Arts.* New York: Garland.

Grant, Michael, and John Hazel. 1993. *Who's Who in Classical Mythology.* London: J. M. Dent.

Graves, Robert. 1955. *The Greek Myths.* London: Penguin.

Gray, Richard T. 1986. "Aphorism and *Sprachkrise* in Turn-of-the-Century Austria." *Orbis Litterarum* 41 (1): 322–354.

Green, London. 1999. "Welitsch's Salome, Lehmann's Marschallin, Pauly's Elektra." *Opera Quarterly* 15: 401–413.

Green, Martin, and John Swan. 1986. *The Triumph of Pierrot: Commedia dell'Arte and the Modern Imagination.* New York: Macmillan.

Greiner, Bernhard. 1996. "Damenopfer für das Theater: Hofmannsthals und Reinhardts Begegnung in der Arbeit an 'Elektra.'" In *Von Franzos zu Canetti: Jüdische Autoren aus Österreich: Neue Studien,* ed. by Mark H. Gelber, Hans Otto Horch, and Sigurd Paul Scheichl. Tübingen: Max Niemeyer. 253–271.

Grene, David, and Richard Lattimore, eds. and trans. 1960a. *Euripides' Electra.* In vol. 4 of *Greek Tragedies.* Chicago: University of Chicago Press. 397–455.

——. 1960b. Introduction to vol. 2 of *Greek Tragedies.* Chicago: University of Chicago Press. 182–183.

Guttmann, Melinda. 2001. *The Enigma of Anna O.: A Biography of Bertha Pappenheim.* Wickford, R.I.: Moyer Bell.

Haas-Heichen, Kristin. 1994. *Die Gestalt der Elektra in der französischen und deutschen Dramatik des 18. Jahrhunderts.* Munich: Tuduv.

Haberkamp, Frederike. 1997. *Sylvia Plath: The Poetics of Beekeeping.* Salzburg, Austria: Institut für Anglistik und Amerikanistik.

Habermas, Jürgen. 1983. "Die Verschlingung von Mythos und Aufklärung: Bemerkungen zur Dialektik der Aufklärung nach einer erneuten Lektüre." In *Mythos und Moderne,* ed. Karl Heinz Bohrer. Frankfurt am Main: Suhrkamp. 405–531.

Hacker, Marilyn. 1994. *Selected Poems, 1965–1990.* New York: Norton.

Hamann, Brigitte. 2001. "Das Frauenbild um die Jahrhundertwende." In *Richard Strauss—Hugo von Hofmannsthal: Frauenbilder,* ed. Ilija Dürhammer and Pia Janke. Vienna: Edition Praesens. 15–22.

Hamburger, Michael. 1961. "Hofmannsthals Bibliothek." *Euphorion* 55 (1): 15–76.

Hanslick, Eduard. 1986. *On the Musically Beautiful: A Contribution towards the Revision of the Aesthetics of Music.* Trans. Geoffrey Payzant. Indianapolis: Hackett.

Hauptmann, Georg. 1956. *Die Atriden-Tetralogie.* Ed. Hubert Razinger. Gütersloh, Germany: Bertelsmann.

Hauschild, Jan-Christoph. 2001. *Heiner Müller; oder, Das Prinzip Zweifel.* Berlin: Aufbau.

H.D. 1961. *Helen in Egypt.* New York: Grove Press.

——. 1974. *Tribute to Freud.* Boston: David R. Godine.

——. 1983. *Collected Poems, 1912–1944.* Ed. Louis L. Martz. New York: New Directions.

Hegel, G. W. F. 1975. *Aesthetics: Lectures on Fine Art.* Trans. T. M. Knox. Oxford: Clarendon Press.

Herbort, Heinz Josef. 2000. "Ein Gemenge aus Nacht und Licht: Form zwischen Gesetz und Intuition in der *Elektra* bei Hofmannsthal und Strauss." In *Inszenierte Antike: Die Antike, Frankreich und wir,* ed. Henry Thorau and Hartmut Köhler. Frankfurt am Main: Peter Lang. 87–112.

Heubach, Helga, ed. 1992. *Die Anna O.: Sisyphus: Gegen den Mädchenhandel,* by Bertha Pappenheim. Freiburg: Kore.

Highwater, Jamake. 1990. *Myth and Sexuality.* New York: New American Library.

Hirsch, Marianne. 1989. *The Mother Daughter Plot: Narrative, Psychoanalysis, Feminism.* Bloomington: Indiana University Press.

Hirsch, Rudolf. 1971. "Zwei Briefe über den *Schwierigen.*" *Hofmannsthal Blätter* 7 (1): 70–75.

Hofmannsthal, Hugo von. 1937. *Briefe II, 1900–1909.* Vienna: Bermann-Fischer.

———. 1946. "Der Tor und der Tod." In *Gedichte und lyrische Dramen. Gesammelte Werke in Einzelausgaben (GW),* ed. Herbert Steiner. Frankfurt am Main: Fischer. 269–292.

———. 1949. "Poesie und Leben." *Prosa 1.* In *GW.* 260–268.

———. 1951a. "Ein Brief." *Prosa 2.* In *GW.* 7–22.

———. 1951b. "Eleonora Duse." *Prosa 2.* In *GW.* 57–63.

———. 1951c. "Szenische Vorschriften zu 'Elektra.'" *Prosa 2.* In *GW.* 68–71.

———. 1952. "Reden in Skandinavien." *Prosa 3.* In *GW.* 350–368.

———. 1954. "Elektra." *Dramen 2.* In *GW.* 7–75.

———. 1955. "An den Verleger Eugen Rutsch." *Prosa 4.* In *GW.* 477–479.

———. 1958. "Der Turm." *Dramen 4.* In *GW.* 7–208.

———. 1959a. "Ad me ipsum." *Aufzeichnungen.* In *GW.* 211–244.

———. 1959b. "Aufzeichnungen und Tagebücher aus dem Nachlass: 1904–1921." *Aufzeichnungen.* In *GW.* 131–195.

———. 1959c. "Max Reinhardt." *Aufzeichnungen.* In *GW.* 325–332.

———. 1994. *Elektra: Libretto.* Frankfurt am Main: Fischer.

Holst-Warhaft, Gail. 1992. *Dangerous Voices: Women's Laments and Greek Literature.* London: Routledge.

Homer. 1990. *The Iliad.* Trans. Robert Fagles. New York: Viking.

———. 1993. *The Odyssey.* Trans. R. D. Dawe. Sussex, U.K.: Book Guild.

Horgan, John. 1996. "Why Freud Isn't Dead." *Scientific American* 275 (6): 106–111.

Hungerford, Amy. 2003. *The Holocaust of Texts: Genocide, Literature, and Personification.* Chicago: University of Chicago Press.

Hunter, Dianne. 1983. "Hysteria, Psychoanalysis, and Feminism: The Case of Anna O." *Feminist Studies* 9 (3): 465–488.

———. 1993. "Representing Mad Contradictoriness in Dr. Charcot's Hysteria Shows." In *Madness in Drama,* ed. James Redmond. Cambridge: Cambridge University Press. 93–118.

Hutcheon, Linda. 1994. "Freud." In *Johns Hopkins Guide to Literary Theory.* Baltimore: Johns Hopkins University Press. 313–315.

———. 1995. *Irony's Edge.* New York: Routledge.

Indorf, Gerd. 2002. "'Nervencontrapunkt': Die Vertonung von Hofmannsthals *Elektra* durch Richard Strauss." In *Fin de Siècle,* ed. Monika Fludernik and Ariane Huml. Trier: Wissenschaftlicher. 229–250.

Irigaray, Luce. 1993a. *An Ethics of Sexual Difference.* Trans. Carolyn Burke and Gillian C. Gill. Ithaca: Cornell University Press.

———. 1993b. *Sexes and Genealogies.* Trans. Gillian C. Gill. New York: Columbia University Press.

———. 1996. "The Powers of Discourse and the Subordination of the Feminine: The Sex Which Is Not One." In *Feminist Literary Theory: A Reader.* 2nd ed. Ed. Mary Eagleton. Oxford: Blackwell. 316–320.

"Is Freud Finished?" 1992. *Time* (6 July): 60.

Jaeger, Dagmar. 2001. "Digging Deep: The Past Revisited in Works of Elfriede Je-
linek and Heiner Müller." *Focus on German Studies* 8: 45–52.
Jäger, Michael. 1991. "Man töte das Weib." In *Schrift der Flammen: Opfermythen und
Weiblichkeitsentwürfe im 20. Jahrhundert*, ed. Gudrun Kohn–Waechter. Berlin:
Orlanda Frauenverlag. 148–172.
Jamme, Christoph. 1991. *Einführung in die Philosophie des Mythos*. Darmstadt: Wis-
senschaftliche Buchgesellschaft.
Jens, Walter. 1955. *Hofmannsthal und die Griechen*. Tübingen: Max Niemeyer.
Jonsson, Stefan. 2000. *Subject without Nation: Robert Musil and the History of Modern
Identity*. Durham, N.C.: Duke University Press.
Jonte-Pace, Diane, ed. 2003. *Teaching Freud*. New York: Oxford University Press.
Jung, C. G., and C. Kerényi. 1961. *Freud and Psychoanalysis*. Vol. 4 of *The Collected
Works of C. G. Jung*, ed. Sir Herbert Read, Michael Fordham, Gerhard Adler,
and William McGuire. Princeton: Princeton University Press.
——. 1963. *Essays on a Science of Mythology: The Myths of the Divine Child and the Di-
vine Maiden*. Trans. R. F. C. Hull. New York: Harper.
Kahane, Claire. 1989. "Hysteria, Feminism, and the Case of *The Bostonians*." In
Feminism and Psychoanalysis, ed. Richard Feldstein and Judith Roof. Ithaca: Cornell University Press. 280–297.
——. 1995. *The Passions of the Voice: Hysteria, Narrative, and the Figure of the Speaking Woman, 1850–1915*. Baltimore: Johns Hopkins University Press.
Kalb, Jonathan. 1998. *The Theater of Heiner Müller*. Cambridge: Cambridge Uni-
versity Press.
Kellein, Thomas. 1995. *Pierrot: Melancholie und Maske*. Munich: Prestel.
Kells, J. H., trans. 1973. *Sophocles' Electra*. London: Cambridge University Press.
Kelvin, Norman. 2000. "H.D. and the Years of World War I." *Victorian Poetry* 38
(1): 170–196.
Kendall, Tim. 2001. *Sylvia Plath: A Critical Study*. London: Faber and Faber.
Kennedy, Michael. 1995. *Richard Strauss*. Oxford: Clarendon Press.
Kenner, Hugh. 1979. "Sincerity Kills." In *Sylvia Plath: New Essays on the Poetry*, ed.
Gary Lane. Baltimore: Johns Hopkins University Press. 33–43.
Kilgour, Maggie. 1990. *From Communion to Cannibalism*. Princeton: Princeton
University Press.
King, Helen. 1993. "Once upon a Text: Hysteria from Hippocrates." In *Hysteria be-
yond Freud*, by Sander L. Gilman, Helen King, Roy Porter, G. S. Rousseau, and
Elaine Showalter. Berkeley: University of California Press. 3–90.
Kingerlee, Roger. 2001. *Psychological Models of Masculinity in Döblin, Musil, and
Jahnn: Männliches, Allzumännliches*. Lewiston, N.Y.: Edwin Mellen.
Kirk, G. S. 1984. "On Defining Myth." In *Sacred Narrative: Readings in the Theory
of Myth*, ed. Alan Dundes. Berkeley: University of California Press. 53–61.
Klein, Melanie. 1975a. "Early Stages of the Oedipus Conflict." In *Love, Guilt, and
Reparation and Other Works, 1921–1945*. London: Hogarth. 186–198.
——. 1975b. "Mourning and Its Relation to Manic-Depressive States." In *Love,
Guilt, and Reparation and Other Works, 1921–1945*. London: Hogarth. 344–369.
——. 1988a. "On the Theory of Anxiety and Guilt." In *Envy and Gratitude and
Other Works, 1946–1963*. London: Virago. 25–42.
——. 1988b. "Some Reflections on 'The Oresteia.'" In *Envy and Gratitude and
Other Works, 1946–1963*. London: Virago. 275–299.
Klimpe, Peter. 1970. *Die Elektra des Sophokles und Euripides' Iphigenie bei den Taur-
ern*. Göppingen, Germany: Kümmerle.

Kluge, Alexander. 1996. "Es ist ein Irrtum, daß die Toten tot sind." In *Ich Wer ist das: Im Regen aus Vogelkot: Im Kalkfell für Heiner Müller: Arbeitsbuch*, ed. Frank Hörnig, Martin Linzer, Frank Raddatz, Wolfgang Storch, and Holger Teschke. Berlin: Theater der Zeit. 145–147.

Kochs, Angela Maria. 1996. *Chaos und Individuum: Robert Musils philosophischer Roman als Vision der Moderne*. Freiburg: Karl Alber.

Kofman, Sarah. 1985. *The Enigma of Woman: Woman in Freud's Writings*. Trans. Catherine Porter. Ithaca: Cornell University Press.

Köhler, Barbara. 1991. *Deutsches Roulette: Gedichte, 1985–1989*. Frankfurt am Main: Suhrkamp.

König, Christoph. 2001. "Aristenphilologie: Hofmannsthals *Elektra* gegen Sophokles." *Euphorion* 95 (1): 423–440.

Korg, Jacob. 2003. *Winter Love: Ezra Pound and H.D.* Madison: University of Wisconsin Press.

Koritz, Amy. 1997. "Dancing the Orient for England: Maud Allan's *Visions of Salome*." In *Meaning in Motion*, ed. Jane C. Desmond. Durham, N.C.: Duke University Press. 133–154.

Kovach, Thomas. 1985. *Hofmannsthal and Symbolism: Art and Life in the Work of a Modern Poet*. New York: Peter Lang.

——. 2002. "Introduction: Hofmannsthal Today." In *A Companion to the Works of Hugo von Hofmannsthal*, ed. Thomas Kovach. Rochester, N.Y.: Camden House. 1–24.

Kraft, Thomas. 2000. *Musils Mann ohne Eigenschaften*. Munich: Piper.

Kramer, Lawrence. 1993. "Fin-de-siècle Fantasies: Elektra, Degeneration, and Sexual Science." *Cambridge Opera Journal* 5 (2): 141–165.

Kristeva, Julia. 1982. *The Powers of Horror: An Essay on Abjection*. Trans. Leon S. Roudiez. New York: Columbia University Press.

——. 1984. *Revolution in Poetic Language*. Trans. Margaret Waller. New York: Columbia University Press.

——. 1986. "About Chinese Women." In *The Kristeva Reader*, ed. Toril Moi. New York: Columbia University Press. 138–159.

——. 1989. *Black Sun: Depression and Melancholia*. Trans. Leon S. Roudiez. New York: Columbia University Press.

——. 2000. *The Sense and Non-Sense of Revolt: The Powers and Limits of Psychoanalysis*. Trans. Jeanine Herman. New York: Columbia University Press.

Kroll, Judith. 1976. *Chapters in a Mythology: The Poetry of Sylvia Plath*. New York: Harper and Row.

Kronberger, Silvia. 2002. *Die unerhörten Töchter: Fräulein Else und Elektra und die gesellschaftliche Funktion der Hysterie*. Innsbruck: Studienverlag.

Kümmel, Albert. 2001. *Das MoE-Programm: Eine Studie über geistige Organisation*. Munich: Wilhelm Fink.

Kunze, Stefan. 1998. "Von der *Elektra* zum Rosenkavalier: Fortschritt oder Umkehr?" In *De musica: Ausgewählte Aufsätze und Vorträge*, ed. Rudolf Bockholdt and Erika Kunze. Tutzing, Germany: H. Schneider. 503–506.

Kurtz, Leonard P. 1975. *The Dance of Death and the Macabre Spirit in European Literature*. Geneva: Skateline Reprints.

Lacan, Jacques. 1977a. *The Four Fundamental Concepts of Psycho-analysis*. Ed. Jacques-Alain Miller. Trans. Alan Sheridan. London: Hogarth.

——. 1977b. "The Mirror Stage as Formative of the Function of the I as Revealed in Psychoanalytic Theory." In *Ecrits: A Selection*, trans. Alan Sheridan. London: Tavistock. 1–7.

Laity, Cassandra. 1996. *H.D. and the Victorian Fin de Siècle: Gender, Modernism, Decadence.* Cambridge: Cambridge University Press.

Laks, Batya Casper. 1995. *Electra: A Gender-Sensitive Study of the Plays Based on the Myth.* Jefferson, N.C.: McFarland.

Lamberechts, Luc. 2000. "Von der Spätmoderne zu einer resistenten Postmoderne: Über die Dynamik eines Literatur- und Kulturwandels." In *Postmoderne Literatur in deutscher Sprache: Eine Ästhetik des Widerstands,* ed. Henk Harbers. Amsterdam: Rodopi. 59–77.

Lamott, Franziska. 2001. *Die vermessene Frau: Hysterien um 1900.* Munich: Wilhelm Fink.

Laplanche, J., and J. B. Pontalis. 1973. *The Language of Psycho-analysis.* Trans. Donald Nicholson-Smith. New York: Norton.

Lauretis, Teresa de. 1996. "Upping the Anti (sic) in Feminist Theory." In *Feminist Literary Theory: A Reader.* 2nd ed. Ed. Mary Eagleton. Oxford: Blackwell. 382–385.

Lembke, Janet, and Kenneth J. Reckford, trans. 1994. *Euripides: Electra.* New York: Oxford University Press.

Le Rider, Jacques. 1990. "Between Modernism and Postmodernism: The Viennese Identity Crisis." Trans. Ralph Mannheim. In *Vienna 1900: From Altenberg to Wittgenstein,* ed. Edward Timms. Edinburgh: Edinburgh University Press. 1–11.

———. 1993. *Modernity and the Crises of Identity: Culture and Society in Fin-de-Siècle Vienna.* Trans. Rosemary Morris. New York: Continuum.

Lévinas, Emmanuel. 1969. *Totality and Infinity: An Essay on Exteriority.* Trans. Alphonso Lingis. Pittsburgh: Duquesne University Press.

Lewis, Hanna B. 1976. "Salome and Elektra: Sisters or Strangers." *Orbis Litterarum* 31: 125–133.

Liddelow, Eden. 2001. *After Electra: Rage, Grief, and Hope in Twentieth-Century Fiction.* Melbourne: Australian Scholarly.

Loftus, Elizabeth. 1995. "Remembering Dangerously." *Skeptical Inquirer* 20: 20–29.

Loquai, Franz. 1993. *Hamlet und Deutschland: Zur literarischen Shakespeare-Rezeption im 20. Jahrhundert.* Stuttgart: Metzler.

Luft, David S. 2003. *Eros and Inwardness in Vienna: Weininger, Musil, Doderer.* Chicago: University of Chicago Press.

Luprecht, Mark. 1991. *"What People Call Pessimism": Sigmund Freud, Arthur Schnitzler, and Nineteenth-Century Controversy at the University of Vienna Medical School.* Riverside, Calif.: Ariadne Press.

Lupton, Julia Reinhard, and Kenneth Reinhard. 1993. *After Oedipus: Shakespeare in Psychoanalysis.* Ithaca: Cornell University Press.

Luserke, Matthias. 1995. *Robert Musil.* Stuttgart: Metzler.

Mach, Ernst. 1911. *Die Analyse der Empfindungen und das Verhältnis des Physischen zum Psychischen.* Jena: n.p.

———. 1976. *Knowledge and Error: Sketches on the Psychology of Enquiry.* Dordrecht: D. Reidel.

Maier-Schaeffer, Francine. 1995. "Utopie und Fragment: Heiner Müller und Walter Benjamin." In *Heiner Müller—Rückblicke, Perspektiven,* ed. Theo Buck and Jean-Marie Valentin. Frankfurt am Main: Peter Lang. 19–38.

Mallarmé, Stéphane. 1994. *Collected Poems.* Ed. and trans. Henry Weinfield. Berkeley: University of California Press.

Marini, Loredana. 2001. *Der Dichter als Fragmentist: Geschichte und Geschichten in Robert Musils Roman "Der Mann ohne Eigenschaften."* Bern: Peter Lang.

Marshfield, Alan. 1982. *The Elektra Poems.* London: Anvil Press.

Martens, Lorna. 1987. "The Theme of Repressed Memory in Hofmannsthal's *Elektra*." *German Quarterly* 60 (1): 38–51.

Masson, Jeffrey Moussaieff. 1984. *The Assault on Truth: Freud's Suppression of the Seduction Theory*. New York: Farrar, Straus, and Giroux.

Mauser, Wolfram. 1977. *Hugo von Hofmannsthal: Konfliktbewältigung und Werkstruktur: Eine psychosoziologische Interpretation*. Munich: Wilhelm Fink.

Mayer, Mathias. 1993. "Der Tanz der Zeichen und des Todes bei Hugo von Hofmannsthal." In *Tanz und Tod in Kunst und Literatur*, ed. Franz Link. Berlin: Duncker und Humblot. 351–368.

McCarren, Felicia. 1995. "The 'Symptomatic Act' circa 1900: Hysteria, Hypnosis, Electricity, Dance." *Critical Inquiry* 21: 748–774.

———. 1998. *Dance Pathologies: Performance, Politics, Medicine*. Stanford: Stanford University Press.

McClary, Susan. 1991. *Feminine Endings: Music, Gender, and Sexuality*. Minneapolis: University of Minnesota Press.

McCole, John. 1993. *Walter Benjamin and the Antinomies of Tradition*. Ithaca: Cornell University Press.

McDonald, Marianne. 1994. "Elektra's *Kleos Aphthiton*: Sophocles into Opera." In *Modern Critical Theory and Classical Literature*, ed. Irene J. F. De Jong and J. P. Sullivan. Leiden: E. J. Brill. 103–126.

McGrath, William J. 1986. *Freud's Discovery of Psychoanalysis: The Politics of Hysteria*. Ithaca: Cornell University Press.

McMullen, Sally. 1985. "From the Armchair to the Stage: Hofmannsthal's *Elektra* in Its Theatrical Context." *Modern Language Review* 80 (3): 637–651.

Mehigan, Tim. 2001. *Robert Musil*. Stuttgart: Reclam.

Mehta, Purnima. 2002. "Electra Complex." In *The Freud Encyclopedia: Theory, Therapy, and Culture*, ed. Edward Erwin. New York: Routledge. 174–175.

Meister, Monika. 2000. "Die Szene der *Elektra* und die Wiener Moderne. Zu Hugo von Hofmannsthals Umdeutung der griechischen Antike." In *Inszenierte Antike—Die Antike, Frankreich und Wir: Neue Beiträge zur Antikenrezeption in der Gegenwart*, ed. Henry Thorau and Hartmut Köhler. Frankfurt am Main: Peter Lang. 59–86.

———. 2001. "Eine neue Schauspielkunst? Gertrud Eysoldts Elektra-Interpretation in der Uraufführung von 1903." In *Richard Strauss—Hugo von Hofmannsthal: Frauenbilder*, ed. Ilija Dürhammer and Pia Janke. Vienna: Edition Praesens. 195–210.

Messmer, Franzpeter. 1989. *Kritiken zu den Aufführungen der Bühnenwerke Richard Strauss*. Pfaffenhofen, Germany: W. Ludwig.

Micale, Mark. 1995. *Approaching Hysteria: Disease and Its Interpretations*. Princeton: Princeton University Press.

Michael, Nancy K. 2001. *Elektra and Her Sisters: Three Female Characters in Schnitzler, Freud, and Hofmannsthal*. New York: Peter Lang.

Michels, Robert. 2000. "Psychoanalysis and Its Discontents." In *Whose Freud? The Place of Psychoanalysis in Contemporary Culture*, ed. Peter Brooks and Alex Woloch. New Haven: Yale University Press. 33–38.

Micklem, Niel. 1996. *The Nature of Hysteria*. New York: Routledge.

Miller, Alice. 1981. *Du sollst nichts merken*. Frankfurt am Main: Suhrkamp.

Mitchell, Juliet. 1992. "From King Lear to Anna O. and Beyond: Some Speculative Theses on Hysteria and the Traditionless Self." *Yale Journal of Criticism* 5 (2): 91–107.

Moore, Burness E., and Bernard D. Fine, eds. 1990. *Psychoanalytic Terms and Con-*

cepts. New Haven: American Psychoanalytic Association and Yale University Press.

Moreau, Alain. 1984. "Naissance d'Électre." *Pallas* 31 (1): 63–82.

Morris, Adalaide. 2003. *How to Live/What to Do: H.D.'s Cultural Poetics.* Urbana: University of Illinois Press.

Morton, Micheal. 1988. "Chandos and His Plans." *Deutsche Vierteljahrschrift* 62 (3): 637–651.

Moser, Walter. 1980. "Diskurs experimente in Romantext: Zu Musils *Der Mann ohne Eigenschaften.*" In *Robert Musil: Untersuchungen,* ed. Uwe Bauder. Königstein: Athenäum. 170–197.

Mueller, Martin. 1986. "Hofmannsthal's Elektra and Its Dramatic Models." *Modern Drama* 29 (1): 71–91.

Müller, Heiner. 1978. *Hamletmaschine.* In *Hamletmaschine: Heiner Müllers Endspiel,* ed. Theo Girshausen. Cologne: Promethverlag. 11–23.

———. 1982. "Schreiben und Schadenfreude." *Theater heute* 23: 1–3.

———. 1984. *Hamletmachine and Other Texts for the Stage.* Ed. and trans. Carl Weber. New York: PAJ.

———. 1989. *Explosion of a Memory.* Ed. Carl Weber. New York: PAJ.

———. 1992. *Krieg ohne Schlacht: Leben in zwei Diktaturen.* Cologne: Kiepenheuer and Witsch.

———. 1996. "Projektion 1975." In *Theater der Zeit.* Berlin: Akademie der Künste. 16.

———. 2001. *A Heiner Müller Reader: Plays, Poetry, Prose.* Ed. and trans. Carl Weber. Baltimore: Johns Hopkins University Press.

Müller, Heiner, and Michael Opitz. 1992. "Jetzt sind eher die infernalischen Aspekte bei Benjamin wichtig. Gespräche mit Heiner Müller." In *Aber ein Sturm weht vom Paradiese her: Texte zu Walter Benjamin.* Leipzig: Reclam. 348–362.

Musil, Robert. 1955a. "Die Frau gestern und morgen." In *Robert Musil: Gesammelte Werke in Einzelausgaben,* ed. Adolf Frisé. Hamburg: Rowohlt. 2:640–646.

———. 1955b. "Isis und Osiris." In *Robert Musil: Gesammelte Werke in Einzelausgaben,* ed. Adolf Frisé. Hamburg: Rowohlt. 3:597.

———. 1955c. "Der Oedipus bedroht." In *Robert Musil: Gesammelte Werke in Einzelausgaben,* ed. Adolf Frisé. Hamburg: Rowohlt. 3:502–504.

———. 1978. *Gesammelte Werke in neun Bänden.* Ed. Adolf Frisé. 9 vols. Hamburg: Rowohlt.

———. 1983. *Tagebücher.* Ed. Adolf Frisé. Hamburg: Rowohlt.

———. 1996. *The Man without Qualities.* Ed. Burton Pike. Trans. Sophie Wilkins. 2 vols. New York: Vintage International.

———. 1998. *Robert Musil: Selected Writings.* Trans. Burton Pike. New York: Continuum.

Nancy, Jean-Luc. 1991. *The Inoperative Community.* Ed. Peter Connor. Trans. Peter Connor, Lisa Garbus, Michael Holland, and Simona Sawhney. Minneapolis: University of Minnesota Press.

Nasio, Juan-David. 1998. *Hysteria from Freud to Lacan: The Splendid Child of Psychoanalysis.* Trans. Susan Fairfield. New York: Other Press.

Nehrung, Wolfram. 1966. *Die Tat bei Hofmannsthal: Eine Untersuchung zu Hofmannsthals grossen Dramen.* Stuttgart: Metzler.

Neubauer, John. 1986. *The Emancipation of Music from Language: Departure from Mimesis in Eighteenth-Century Aesthetics.* New Haven: Yale University Press.

Nieden, Birgit zur. 1993. *Mythos und Literaturkritik: Zur literaturwissenschaftlichen Mythendeutung der Moderne.* Münster: Waxmann.

Nietzsche, Friedrich. 1969. *Die Geburt der Tragödie aus dem Geiste der Musik*. In vol. 1 of *Werke*, ed. Karl Schlechta. Frankfurt am Main: Ullstein. 21–134.

———. 1976. *The Portable Nietzsche*. Trans. Walter Kaufmann. New York: Penguin.

———. 1995. *Thus Spoke Zarathustra*. Trans. Walter Kaufmann. New York: Modern Library.

Novalis [Georg Friedrich Phillip von Hardenberg]. 1978. *Hymnen an die Nacht*. In *Werke in einem Band*, ed. Hans-Joachim Mähl and Richard Samuel. Munich: Carl Hanser. 147–178.

Ostriker, Alice. 1985. "The Thieves of Language: Women Poets and Revisionist Mythmaking." In *The New Feminist Criticism: Essays on Women, Literature, and Theory*, ed. Elaine Showalter. New York: Pantheon. 314–338.

Oxford Classical Dictionary. 1970. Ed. N. G. S. Hammond and H. H. Scullard. 2nd ed. Oxford: Clarendon Press.

Oxford Encyclopedic English Dictionary. 1970. Ed. Joyce Hawkins and Robert Allen. Oxford: Clarendon Press.

Peel, Robin. 2002. *Writing Back: Sylvia Plath and Cold War Politics*. Madison, N.J.: Fairleigh Dickinson University Press.

Pérez Galdós, Benito. 1998. *Electra*. Madrid: Biblioteca Nueva.

Pettazzoni, Raffaele. 1984. "The Truth of Myth." In *Sacred Narrative: Readings in the Theory of Myth*, ed. Alan Dundes. Berkeley: University of California Press. 98–109.

Pettipiece, Deirdre Anne. 2002. *Sex Theories and the Shaping of Two Moderns: Hemingway and H.D.* New York: Routledge.

Pike, Burton. 1996. "Preface to the Posthumous Papers." In vol. 2 of *The Man without Qualities*. New York: Vintage International. x–xvi.

Plath, Sylvia. 1963. *The Bell Jar*. London: Faber and Faber.

———. 1981. *Collected Poems*. Ed. Ted Hughes. London: Faber and Faber.

———. 1982. *The Journals of Sylvia Plath*. Ed. Ted Hughes and Frances McCullough. New York: Dial Press.

Plato. 1993. *Republic*. Trans. Robin Waterfield. Oxford: Oxford University Press.

Politzer, Heinz. 1973. "Hugo von Hofmannsthals Elektra: Geburt der Tragödie aus dem Geiste der Psychopathologie." *Deutsche Vierteljahrschrift* 47 (1): 95–119.

Potter, John, and Suzanne Potter. 1980. "Prophetic Avenger: The Heroine of Strauss' *Elektra* Foresees Her Destiny, and Fulfills It." *Opera News*, 9 February, 17–36.

Puhvel, Jaan. 1987. *Comparative Mythology*. Baltimore: Johns Hopkins University Press.

Pynsent, Robert B. 1989. "Decadence, Decay, and Innovation." In *Decadence and Innovation: Austro-Hungarian Life and Art at the Turn of the Century*, ed. Robert B. Pynsent. London: Weidenfeld and Nicolson. 211–248.

Raddatz, Frank-Michael. 1991. *Dämonen unterm Roten Stern: Zu Geschichtsphilosophie und Ästhetik Heiner Müllers*. Stuttgart: Metzler.

Rado, Lisa. 2000. *The Modern Androgyne Imagination: A Failed Sublime*. Charlottesville: University of Virginia Press.

Ramazani, Jahan. 1993. " 'Daddy, I have had to kill you': Plath, Rage and the Modern Elegy." *PMLA* 108 (5): 1142–1156.

Ravit, David. 1999/2000. "The Loss of *Hamlet*'s Aura in the Age of the *Machine*: Reflections of the *Passagenwerk* in Heiner Müller's Work." *Journal of Theatre and Drama* 5/6: 171–184.

Rey, William H. 1962. *Weltentzweiung und Weltversöhnung in Hofmannsthals griechischen Dramen*. Philadelphia: University of Pennsylvania Press.

Rich, Adrienne. 1979. *On Lies, Secrets, and Silence: Selected Prose, 1966–1978*. New York: Norton.

———. 1981. *Diving into a Wreck: Poems, 1971–1972*. New York: Norton.

Ricoeur, Paul. 1991. *A Ricoeur Reader: Reflection and Imagination*. Ed. M. J. Valdes. New York: Harvester Wheatsheaf.

Rieckmann, Jens. 1993. "Schools of Inauthenticity: The Role of the *Akademisches Gymnasium* and the *Bürgtheater* in Hofmannsthal's Formative Years." In *Turn of the Century Vienna and Its Legacy: Essays in Honor of Donald G. Daviau*, ed. Jeffrey B. Berlin, Jorun B. Johns, and Richard H. Lawson. Riverside, Calif.: Ariadne. 67–78.

Robertson, Ritchie. 1986. " 'Ich habe ihm das Beil nicht geben können': The Heroine's Failure in Hofmannsthal's *Elektra*." *Orbis Litterarum* 41 (1): 312–331.

Rochlitz, Rainer. 1996. *The Disenchantment of Art: The Philosophy of Walter Benjamin*. Trans. Jane Marie Todd. New York: Guilford.

Rohde, Erwin. 1921. *Psyche: Seelenkult und Unsterblichkeitsglaube der Griechen*. Tübingen: Mohr.

Rose, Jacqueline. 1992. *The Haunting of Sylvia Plath*. Cambridge: Harvard University Press.

Rosenkranz-Kaiser, Jutta. 1995. *Feminismus und Mythos: Tendenzen in Literatur und Theorie der achtziger Jahre*. Münster: Waxmann.

Rousseau, G. S. 1993. "A Strange Pathology: Hysteria in the Early Modern World, 1500–1800." In *Hysteria beyond Freud*, by Sander L. Gilman, Helen King, Roy Porter, G. S. Rousseau, and Elaine Showalter. Berkeley: University of California Press. 2–221.

Rutschky, Michael. 1983. "Freud und die Mythen." In *Mythos und Moderne*, ed. Karl Heinz Bohrer. Frankfurt am Main: Suhrkamp. 217–241.

Ryan, Judith. 1991. *The Vanishing Subject: Early Psychology and Literary Modernism*. Chicago: University of Chicago Press.

Rzehak, Wolfgang. 1993. *Musil und Nietzsche: Beziehungen der Erkenntnisperspektiven*. Frankfurt am Main: Peter Lang.

Sale, William, trans. 1973. *Electra by Sophocles*. Englewood Cliffs, N.J.: Prentice Hall.

Schadewaldt, Wolfgang. 1960. *Hellas und Hesperien: Gesammelte Schriften zur Antike und zur neueren Literatur*. Zurich: Artemis.

Schaps, Regina. 1992. *Hysterie und Weiblichkeit: Wissenschaftsmythen über die Frau*. Frankfurt am Main: Campus.

Schärer, Hans-Rudolf. 1990. *Narzißmus und Utopismus: Eine Literaturpsychologische Untersuchung zu Robert Musils Roman Der Mann ohne Eigenschaften*. Munich: Fink.

Schläder, Jürgen. 1999. "Moderne Musikdramaturgie—konservative Bühnenästhetik, oder: Die theatralische Bedeutung von Richard Strauss' Opern-Orchester." In *Wer war Richard Strauss? Neunzehn Antworten*, ed. Hanspeter Krellmann. Frankfurt am Main: Insel. 73–91.

Schleifer, Ronald. 1993. "Walter Benjamin and the Crisis of Representation: Multiplicity, Meaning, and Athematic Death." In *Death and Representation*, ed. Sarah Webster Goodwin and Elisabeth Bronfen. Baltimore: Johns Hopkins University Press. 313–333.

Schlesier, Renate. 1984. "Können Mythen lügen? Freud, Ödipus und die anstiftenden Mütter." In *Mythos Frau: Projektionen und Inszenierungen im Patriarchat*, ed. Barbara Schaeffer-Hegel and Brigitte Wartmann. Berlin: Publica. 334–348.

Schlötterer, Reinhold. 1987. "Elektras Tanz in der Tragödie Hugo von Hofmannsthals." *Hofmannsthal Blätter* 33 (1): 47–58.

Schneider, Manfred. 1983. "Über den Grund des Vergnügens an neurotischen
Gegenständen: Freud, C. G. Jung und die Mythologie des Unbewußten." In
Mythos und Moderne, ed. Karl Heinz Bohrer. Frankfurt am Main: Suhrkamp.
197–216.

——. 1985. "Hysterie als Gesamtkunstwerk: Aufstieg und Verfall einer Semiotic
der Weiblichkeit." *Merkur* 39 (1): 879–895.

Schopenhauer, Arthur. 1964. *The World as Will and Representation.* Trans. R. B.
Haldane and J. Kemp. 3 vols. London: Routledge and Kegan Paul.

Schorske, Carl E. 1980. *Fin de Siècle Vienna: Politics and Culture.* New York: Knopf.

Schweighofer, Fritz. 1987. *Das Privattheater der Anna O.: Ein psychoanalytisches
Lehrstück. Ein Emanzipationsdrama.* Munich: Ernst Reinhardt.

Seeba, Heinrich. 2002. "Hofmannsthal and *Wiener Moderne.*" In *A Companion to the
Works of Hugo von Hofmannsthal,* ed. Thomas Kovach. Rochester, N.Y.: Camden
House. 25–46.

Seidel, Sebastian. 2001. *Dichtung gibt Sinnbilder: Die Sehnsucht nach Einheit. Das
Lebensbaum-Mythologem und das Isis-Osiris-Mythologem in Robert Musils Roman
"Der Mann ohne Eigenschaften."* Frankfurt am Main: Peter Lang.

Sexton, Anne. 1981. *Complete Poems.* Boston: Houghton Mifflin.

Shaw, Michael. 2001. Introduction to *Sophocles Electra.* New York: Oxford University Press. 3–40.

Showalter, Elaine. 1985. *The Female Malady: Women, Madness, and English Culture,
1830–1880.* New York: Pantheon.

——. 1993. "Hysteria, Feminism, and Gender." In *Hysteria beyond Freud,* by Sander
L. Gilman, Helen King, Roy Porter, G. S. Rousseau, and Elaine Showalter.
Berkeley: University of California Press. 286–344.

——. 1997. *Hystories: Hysterical Epidemics and Modern Culture.* New York: Columbia
University Press.

Silverman, Kaja. 2000. "The Language of Care." In *Whose Freud? The Place of Psychoanalysis in Contemporary Culture,* ed. Peter Brooks and Alex Woloch. New
Haven: Yale University Press. 150–153.

Simon, Bennett. 1978. *Mind and Madness in Ancient Greece:The Classical Roots of
Modern Psychiatry.* Ithaca: Cornell University Press.

Simon, John. 1992. "Daughter of Death: The 'Pathological Case' of Strauss' *Elektra*—and Her Enduring Appeal." *Opera News,* 11 April, 15–18.

Sissa, Giulia. 1990. *Greek Virginity.* Trans. Arthur Goldhammer. Cambridge: Harvard University Press.

Slochower, Harry. 1970. *Mythopoesis: Mythic Patterns in the Literary Classics.* Detroit:
Wayne State University Press.

Sophocles. 1990. *Electra.* Trans. Kenneth McLeish. London: Methuen.

——. 2001. *Electra.* Trans. Anne Carson, with introduction and notes by Michael
Shaw. New York: Oxford University Press.

Sparshott, Francis. 1995. *A Measured Pace: Toward a Philosophical Understanding of
the Arts of Dance.* Toronto: University of Toronto Press.

Specht, Richard. 1921. *Richard Strauss und sein Werk: Der Vokalcomponist, der Dra-
matiker.* Leipzig: E. P. Tal.

Starobinski, Jean. 1989. *The Living Eye.* Trans. Arthur Goldhammer. Cambridge:
Harvard University Press.

Steiner, George. 1969. *Language and Silence: Essays, 1958–1966.* Harmondsworth:
Penguin.

———. 1984. *Antigones*. Oxford: Clarendon Press.

———. 1992. *After Babel: Aspects of Language and Translation*. Oxford: Oxford University Press.

Steinert, Monika. 1995. *Mythos in den Gedichten Sylvia Plaths*. Frankfurt am Main: Peter Lang.

Steinmann, Anne. 1984. "Anna O.: Female, 1880–1882. Bertha Pappenheim: Female, 1980–1982." In *Anna O.: Fourteen Contemporary Reinterpretations*, ed. Max Rosenbaum and Melvin Muroff. New York: Free Press. 118–131.

Stephan, Inge. 1997. *Musen und Medusen: Mythos und Geschlecht in der Literatur des 20. Jahrhundert*. Cologne: Böhlau.

Stern, J. P. 1992. *The Heart of Europe: Essay on Literature and Ideology*. Oxford: Blackwell.

Strauss, Richard. 1953. *Recollections and Reflections*. Ed. Willi Schuh. Trans. L. J. Lawrence. London: Boosey and Hawkes.

———. 1990. *Elektra in Full Score*. New York: Dover.

Strauss, Richard, and Hugo von Hofmannsthal. 1952. *Briefwechsel: Richard Strauss—Hugo von Hofmannsthal*. Ed. Franz Strauss and Alice Strauss with Willi Schuh. Zurich: Atlantis.

Sullivan, Ellie Ragland. 1989. "Seeking the Third Term: Desire, the Phallus, and the Materiality of Language." In *Feminism and Psychoanalysis*, ed. Richard Feldstein and Judith Roof. Ithaca: Cornell University Press. 40–64.

Taylor, Georgina. 2001. *H.D. and the Public Sphere of Modernist Writers, 1913–1946: Talking Women*. Oxford: Clarendon Press.

Teraoka, Arlene Akiko. 1985. *The Silence of Entropy or Universal Discourse: The Postmodern Poetics of Heiner Müller*. New York: Peter Lang.

Thibeault-Schaefer, Jacqueline. 1994. "Récit mythique et transtextualité." In *Mythe et création*, ed. Pierre Cazier. Lille: Lille University Press. 53–66.

Timms, Edward, and Ritchie Robertson, eds. 1992. *Psychoanalysis in Its Cultural Context*. Edinburgh: Edinburgh University Press.

Tuhkunen-Couzic, Taïna. 2002. *Sylvia Plath: Une écriture embryonnaire*. Paris: L'Harmattan.

Turner, Victor. 1979. *Process, Performance, and Pilgrimage: A Study in Comparative Symbology*. New Delhi: Concept.

Urban, Bernd. 1978. *Hofmannsthal, Freud und die Psychoanalyse: Quellenkundliche Untersuchungen*. Frankfurt am Main: Peter Lang.

Vendler, Helen Hennessy. 2003. *Coming of Age as a Poet: Milton, Keats, Eliot, Plath*. Cambridge: Harvard University Press.

Vernant, Jean-Pierre. 1983. *Myth and Thought among the Greeks*. London: Routledge and Kegan Paul.

———. 1994. "Der reflektierte Mythos." In *Mythe et création*, ed. Pierre Cazier. Lille: Lille University Press. 7–11.

Von Nau, Günther. 1971. "Das Leitmotiv bei Richard Strauss dargestellt am Beispiel der *Elektra*." *Neue Zeitschrift für Musik* 130 (8): 418–422.

Wagner, Richard. 1968. *Tristan und Isolde: Opera in Three Acts*. Ed. and trans. William Mann. London: Friends of Covent Garden Royal Opera House.

Wagner-Egelhaaf, Martina. 1989. *Mystik der Moderne: Die visionäre Ästhetik der deutschen Literatur im 20. Jahrhundert*. Stuttgart: Metzler.

Walker, Barbara. 1988. *The Women's Dictionary of Symbols and Sacred Objects*. San Francisco: Harper and Row.

Walsh, Brian. 2001. "The Rest Is Violence: Müller contra Shakespeare." *Journal of Performance and Art* 23: 24–35.

Ward, Philip. 2002. *Hofmannsthal and Greek Myth: Expression and Performance.* Oxford: Peter Lang.

Weber, Carl. 1980. "Heiner Müller: Hope and Despair." *Performing Arts Journal* 12 (1): 135–140.

Weininger, Otto. 1906. *Sex and Character.* London: W. Heinemann.

———. 1980. *Geschlecht und Charakter.* Munich: Matthes and Seitz.

Whitford, Margaret. 1994. "Irigaray, Utopia, and the Death Drive." In *Engaging with Irigaray: Feminist Philosophy and Modern European Thought,* ed. Carolyn Burke, Naomi Schor, and Margaret Whitford. New York: Columbia University Press. 379–400.

Whyte, Lancelot. 1960. *The Unconscious before Freud.* New York: Basic Books.

Wieghaus, Georg. 1984. *Zwischen Auftrag und Verrat: Werk und Ästhetik Heiner Müllers.* Frankfurt am Main: Peter Lang.

Wilcocks, Robert. 1997. "The Way It Was: The Story of Anna O. and Early Psychoanalysis." *Canadian Review of Comparative Literature* 24 (2): 338–351.

Winnington-Ingram, R. P. 1980. *Sophocles: An Interpretation.* Cambridge: Cambridge University Press.

Wintle, Christopher. 1988. "Elektra and the 'Electra-complex.'" In *English National Opera Guide: Salome/Elektra,* ed. Paul Banks. London: Calder. 63–80.

Wirth, Andrzej. 1995. "Heiner Müller and Robert Wilson: An Unlikely Convergence." In *Heiner Müller: Contexts and History,* ed. Gerhard Fischer. Tübingen: Stauffenburg. 213–219.

Wittig, Monique. 1996. "The Straight Mind." In *Feminist Literary Theory: A Reader.* Ed. Mary Eagleton. 2nd ed. Oxford: Blackwell. 408–411.

Woitas, Monika. 2001. "Richard Strauss und das Tanztheater seiner Zeit." In *Richard Strauss und die Moderne: Bericht über das Internationale Symposium München, 21. bis 23. Juli 1999,* ed. Bernd Edelmann, Birgit Lodes, and Reinhold Schlötterer. Berlin: Henschel. 411–421.

Woolf, Virginia. 1992. "On Not Knowing Greek." In *A Woman's Essays,* ed. Rachel Bowlby. London: Penguin. 93–106.

Worbs, Michael. 1983. *Nervenkunst: Literatur und Psychoanalyse im Wien der Jahrhundertwende.* Frankfurt am Main: Europäische.

———. 1999. "Mythos und Psychoanalyse in Hugo von Hofmannsthals *Elektra.*" In *Psychoanalyse in der modernen Literatur: Kooperation und Konkurrenz,* ed. Thomas Anz. Würzburg: Königshausen and Neumann. 3–16.

Wunenberger, Jean-Jacques. 1994. "Principes d'une imagination mytho-poétique." In *Mythe et création,* ed. Pierre Cazier. Lille: Lille University Press. 33–52.

Young, James E. 1988. *Writing and Rewriting the Holocaust: Narrative and the Consequences of Interpretation.* Bloomington: Indiana University Press.

Yourcenar, Marguerite. 1954. *Électre ou La chute des masques.* Paris: Plon.

Zaslavsky, Robert. 1981. *Platonic Myth and Platonic Writing.* Washington, D.C. : University Press of America.

Ziarek, Ewa. 1993. "Kristeva and Levinas: Mourning, Ethics, and the Feminine." In *Ethics, Politics, and Difference in Julia Kristeva's Writing,* ed. Kelly Oliver. New York: Routledge. 62–78.

Zinser, Hartmut. 1991. "Das Problem der psychoanalytischen Mytheninterpretation." In *Faszination des Mythos: Studien zu antiken und modernen Interpretationen,* ed. Renate Schlesier. Basel: Stroemfeld/Roter Stern. 113–124.

Index

Cornell Studies in the History of Psychiatry

A series edited by
Sander L. Gilman
George J. Makari

Compulsion for Antiquity: Freud and the Ancient World
RICHARD H. ARMSTRONG

*Keeping America Sane: Psychiatry and Eugenics in the United States
and Canada, 1880–1940*
IAN ROBERT DOWBIGGIN

Clinical Psychiatry in Imperial Germany: A History of Psychiatric Practice
ERIC J. ENGSTROM

Dreams 1900–2000: Science, Art, and the Unconscious Mind
LYNN GAMWELL, EDITOR

Madness in America: Cultural and Medical Perceptions of Mental Illness before 1914
LYNN GAMWELL AND NANCY TOMES

Freud and His Aphasia Book: Language and the Sources of Psychoanalysis
VALERIE D. GREENBERG

*"Surfacing Up": Madness, Institutionalization, and Social Order in Colonial
Zimbabwe, 1908–1968*
LYNETTE JACKSON

Hysterical Men: War, Psychiatry, and the Politics of Trauma in Germany, 1890–1930
PAUL LERNER

The Mastery of Submission: Inventions of Masochism
JOHN K. NOYES

Reading Psychoanalysis: Freud, Rank, Ferenczi, Groddeck
PETER L. RUDNYTSKY

Electra after Freud: Myth and Culture
JILL SCOTT

Adolf Wölfli: Draftsman, Writer, Poet, Composer
ELKA SPOERRI EDITOR

Sublime Surrender: Male Masochism at the Fin-de-Siècle
SUZANNE R. STEWART